ARON WARNER'S

PARIAH™

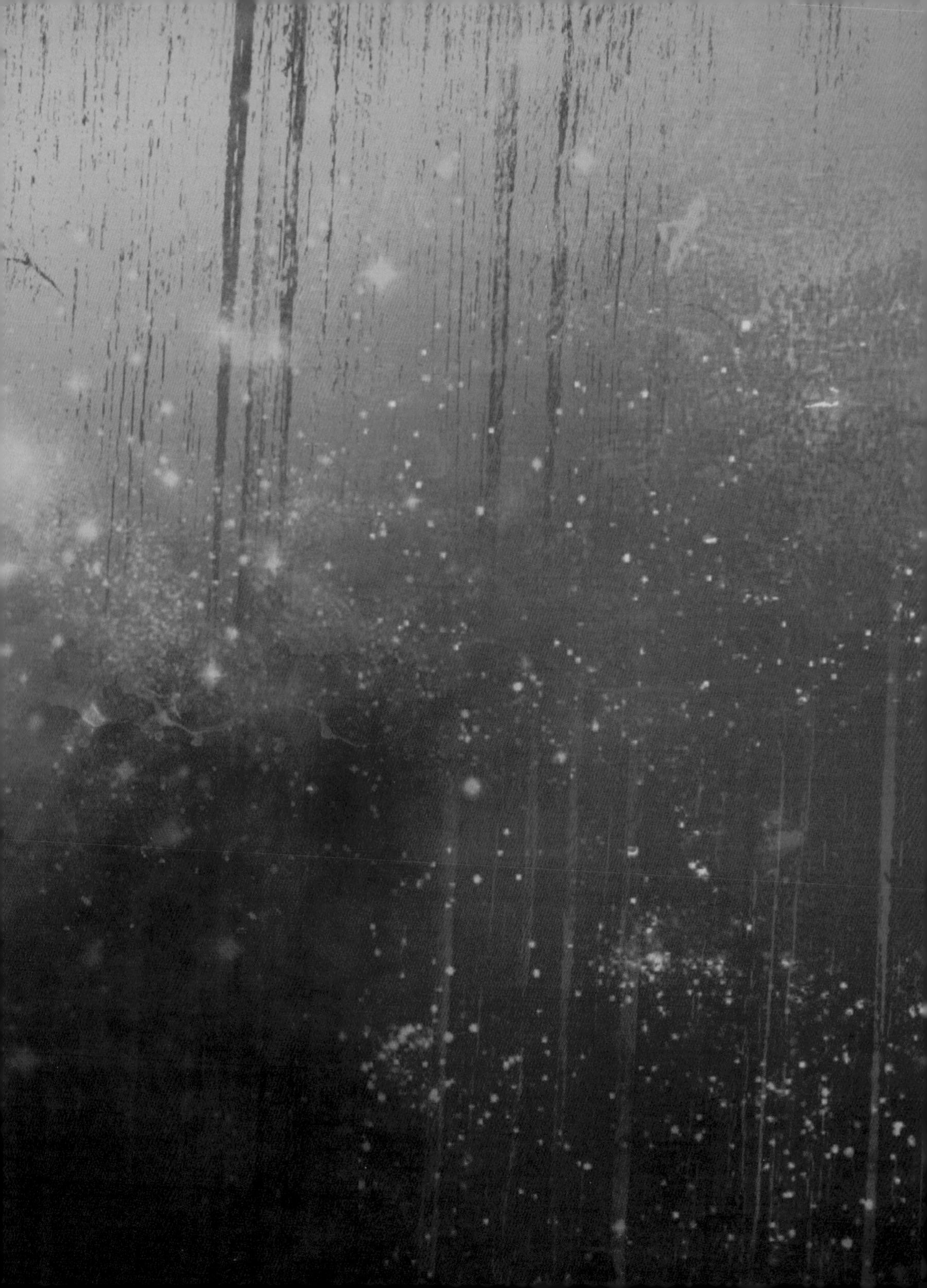

ARON WARNER'S

PARIAH

VOLUME 1

STORY BY
ARON WARNER AND **PHILIP GELATT**

ART AND LETTERING BY
BRETT WELDELE

COVERS BY
PAT LEE AND **BRETT WELDELE**

DARK HORSE BOOKS

EDITOR
DANIEL CHABON

DESIGNER
KAT LARSON

PRESIDENT AND PUBLISHER
MIKE RICHARDSON

SPECIAL THANKS TO HANNAH CHECKLEY

PRESIDENT AND PUBLISHER **MIKE RICHARDSON** EXECUTIVE VICE PRESIDENT **NEIL HANKERSON** CHIEF FINANCIAL OFFICER **TOM WEDDLE** VICE PRESIDENT OF PUBLISHING **RANDY STRADLEY** VICE PRESIDENT OF BOOK TRADE SALES **MICHAEL MARTENS** VICE PRESIDENT OF BUSINESS AFFAIRS **ANITA NELSON** EDITOR IN CHIEF **SCOTT ALLIE** VICE PRESIDENT OF MARKETING **MATT PARKINSON** VICE PRESIDENT OF PRODUCT DEVELOPMENT **DAVID SCROGGY** VICE PRESIDENT OF INFORMATION TECHNOLOGY **DALE LaFOUNTAIN** SENIOR DIRECTOR OF PRINT, DESIGN, AND PRODUCTION **DARLENE VOGEL** GENERAL COUNSEL **KEN LIZZI** EDITORIAL DIRECTOR **DAVEY ESTRADA** SENIOR BOOKS EDITOR **CHRIS WARNER** EXECUTIVE EDITOR **DIANA SCHUTZ** DIRECTOR OF PRINT AND DEVELOPMENT **CARY GRAZZINI** ART DIRECTOR **LIA RIBACCHI** DIRECTOR OF SCHEDULING **CARA NIECE** DIRECTOR OF INTERNATIONAL LICENSING **TIM WIESCH** DIRECTOR OF DIGITAL PUBLISHING **MARK BERNARDI**

PUBLISHED BY DARK HORSE BOOKS
A DIVISION OF DARK HORSE COMICS, INC.
10956 SE MAIN STREET
MILWAUKIE, OR 97222

FIRST EDITION: JANUARY 2014
ISBN 978-1-61655-274-9

1 3 5 7 9 10 8 6 4 2
PRINTED IN CHINA

INTERNATIONAL LICENSING: (503) 905-2377
COMIC SHOP LOCATOR SERVICE: (888) 266-4226

THIS VOLUME COLLECTS *PARIAH* ISSUES #1–#4,
ORIGINALLY PUBLISHED BY SEA LION BOOKS.

PARIAH VOLUME 1

CHAPTER ONE

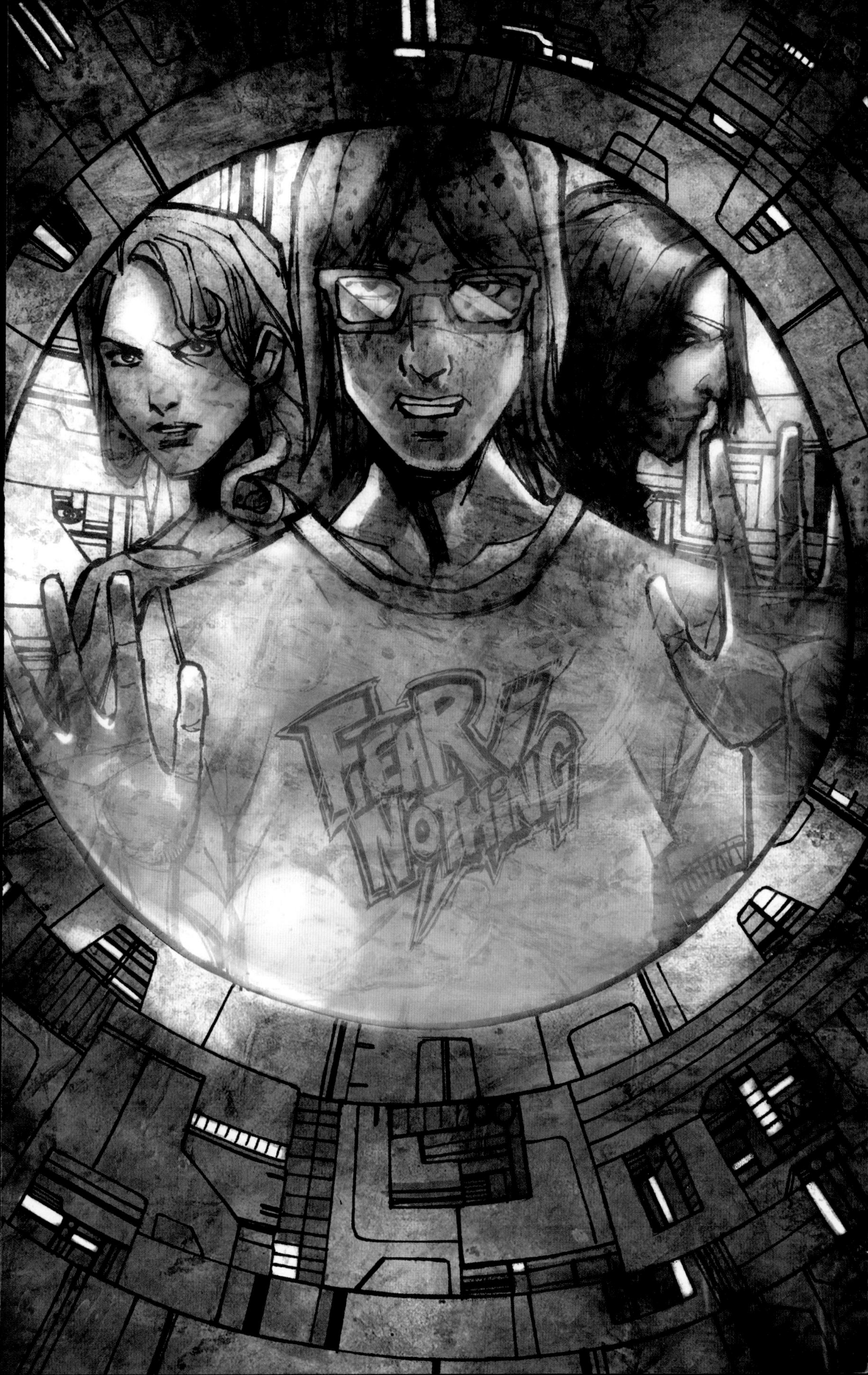
FEAR NOTHING

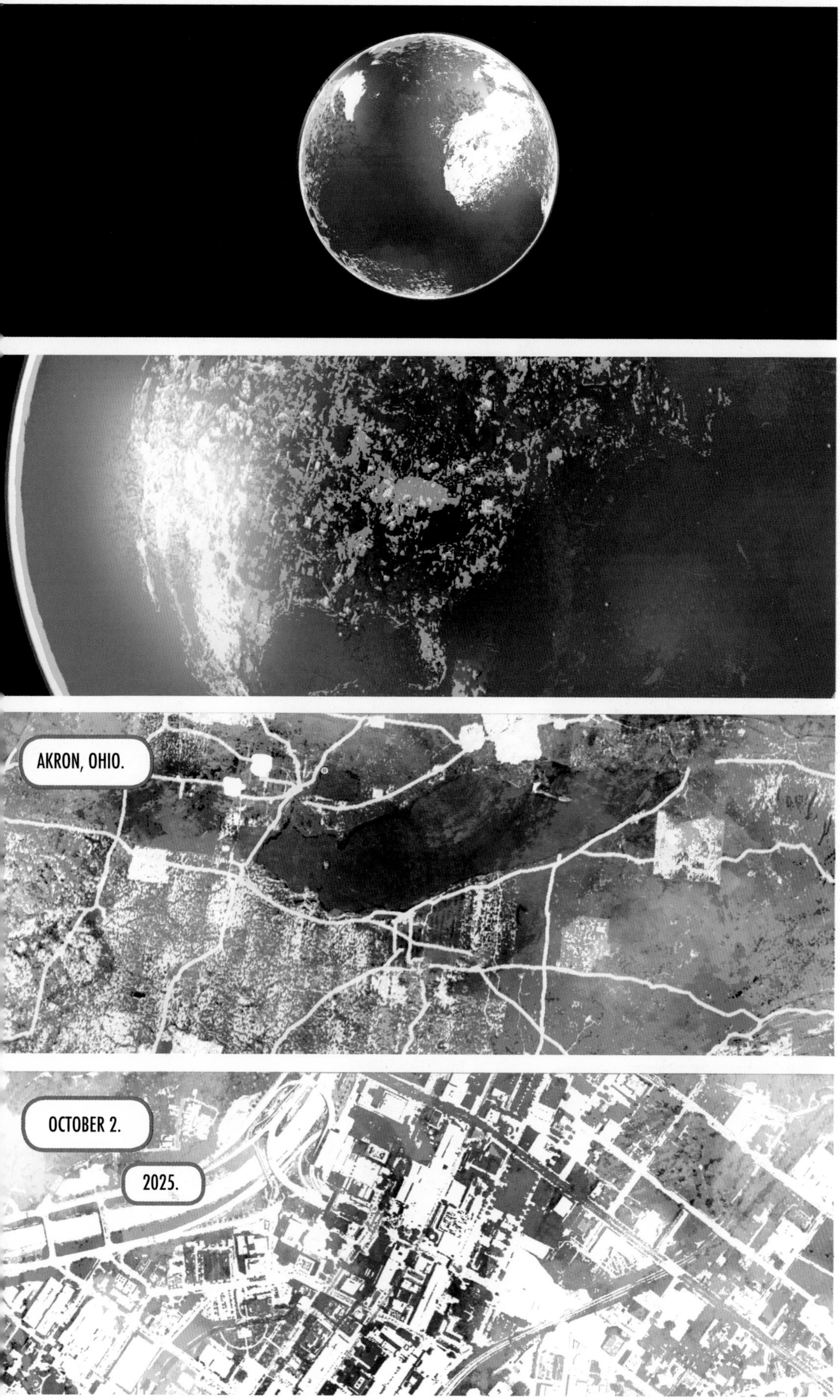
AKRON, OHIO.
OCTOBER 2.
2025.

MY NAME IS BRENT MARKS.

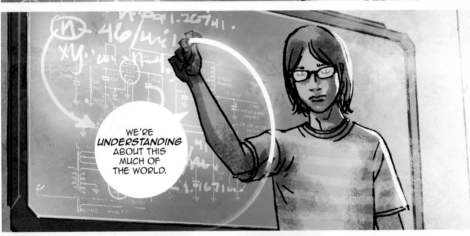

AND I AM NOT A FREAK.

RIGHT NOW, IN THIS ROOM, RIGHT? WE'RE SEEING, LIKE, THIS MUCH OF THE WORLD.

WE'RE **UNDERSTANDING** ABOUT THIS MUCH OF THE WORLD.

ON THE DAY THE WORLD CHANGED FOR ALL OF US VITROS, MY WORLD WAS LARGELY THE SAME.

AND ABOUT THIS MUCH OF THE GALAXY.

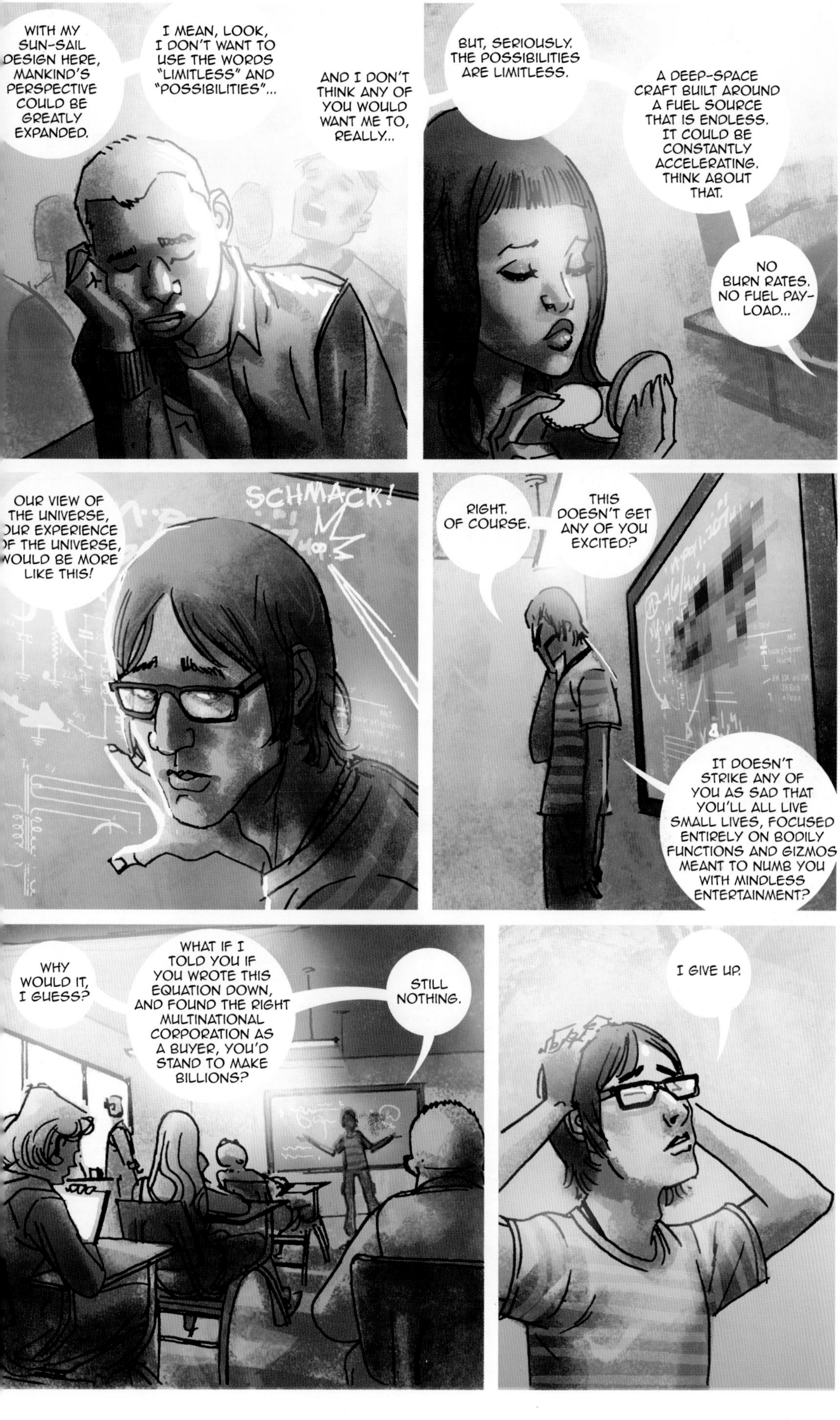
WITH MY SUN-SAIL DESIGN HERE, MANKIND'S PERSPECTIVE COULD BE GREATLY EXPANDED.
I MEAN, LOOK, I DON'T WANT TO USE THE WORDS "LIMITLESS" AND "POSSIBILITIES"...
AND I DON'T THINK ANY OF YOU WOULD WANT ME TO, REALLY...
BUT, SERIOUSLY. THE POSSIBILITIES ARE LIMITLESS.
A DEEP-SPACE CRAFT BUILT AROUND A FUEL SOURCE THAT IS ENDLESS. IT COULD BE CONSTANTLY ACCELERATING. THINK ABOUT THAT.
NO BURN RATES. NO FUEL PAY-LOAD...
OUR VIEW OF THE UNIVERSE, OUR EXPERIENCE OF THE UNIVERSE, WOULD BE MORE LIKE THIS!
SCHMACK!
THIS DOESN'T GET ANY OF YOU EXCITED?
RIGHT. OF COURSE.
IT DOESN'T STRIKE ANY OF YOU AS SAD THAT YOU'LL ALL LIVE SMALL LIVES, FOCUSED ENTIRELY ON BODILY FUNCTIONS AND GIZMOS MEANT TO NUMB YOU WITH MINDLESS ENTERTAINMENT?
WHY WOULD IT, I GUESS?
WHAT IF I TOLD YOU IF YOU WROTE THIS EQUATION DOWN, AND FOUND THE RIGHT MULTINATIONAL CORPORATION AS A BUYER, YOU'D STAND TO MAKE BILLIONS?
STILL NOTHING.
I GIVE UP.

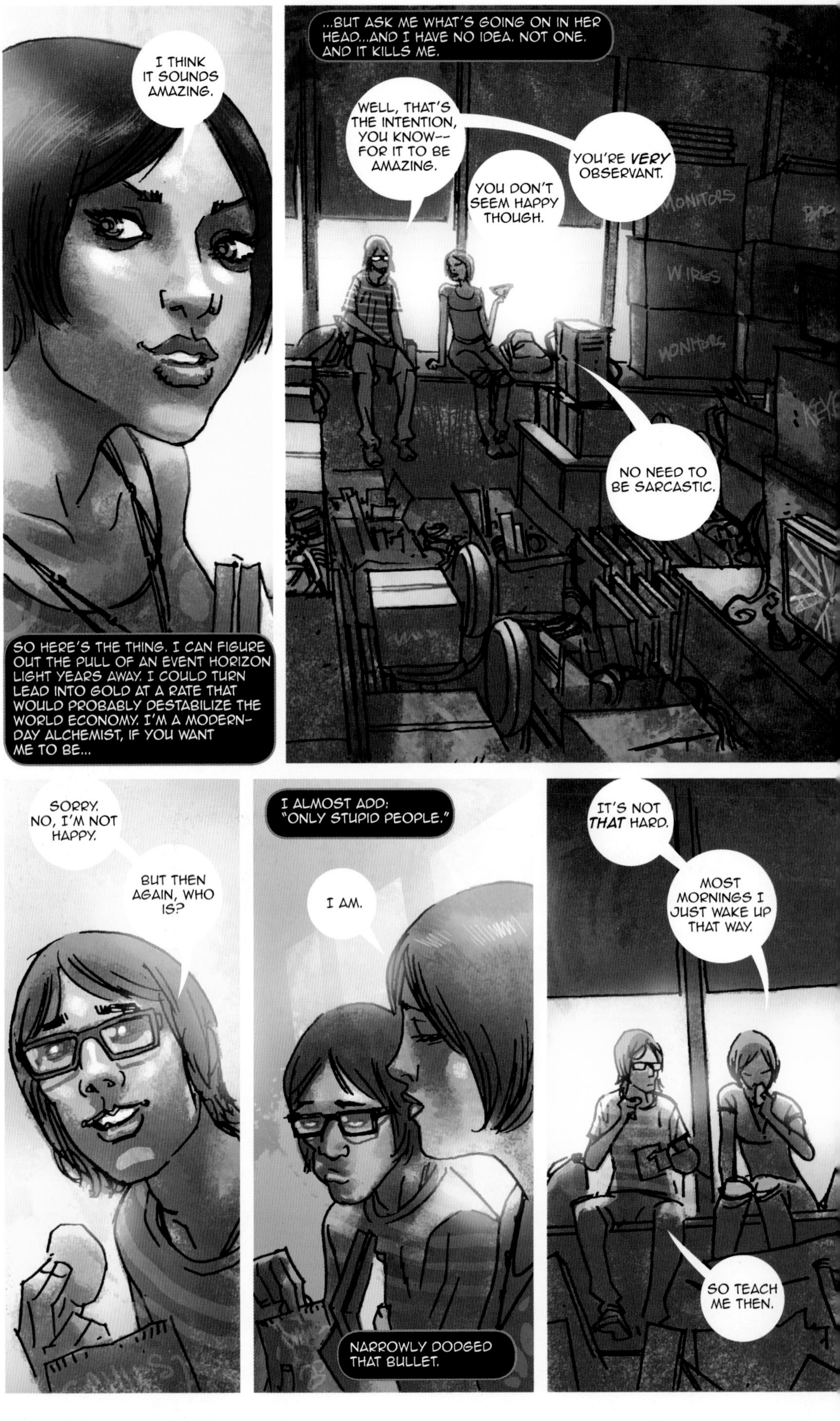
I THINK IT SOUNDS AMAZING.
SO HERE'S THE THING. I CAN FIGURE OUT THE PULL OF AN EVENT HORIZON LIGHT YEARS AWAY. I COULD TURN LEAD INTO GOLD AT A RATE THAT WOULD PROBABLY DESTABILIZE THE WORLD ECONOMY. I'M A MODERN-DAY ALCHEMIST, IF YOU WANT ME TO BE...
...BUT ASK ME WHAT'S GOING ON IN HER HEAD...AND I HAVE NO IDEA. NOT ONE. AND IT KILLS ME.
WELL, THAT'S THE INTENTION, YOU KNOW-- FOR IT TO BE AMAZING.
YOU DON'T SEEM HAPPY THOUGH.
YOU'RE *VERY* OBSERVANT.
NO NEED TO BE SARCASTIC.
MONITORS
WIRES
MONITORS
SORRY. NO, I'M NOT HAPPY.
BUT THEN AGAIN, WHO IS?
I ALMOST ADD: "ONLY STUPID PEOPLE."
I AM.
NARROWLY DODGED THAT BULLET.
IT'S NOT **THAT** HARD.
MOST MORNINGS I JUST WAKE UP THAT WAY.
SO TEACH ME THEN.

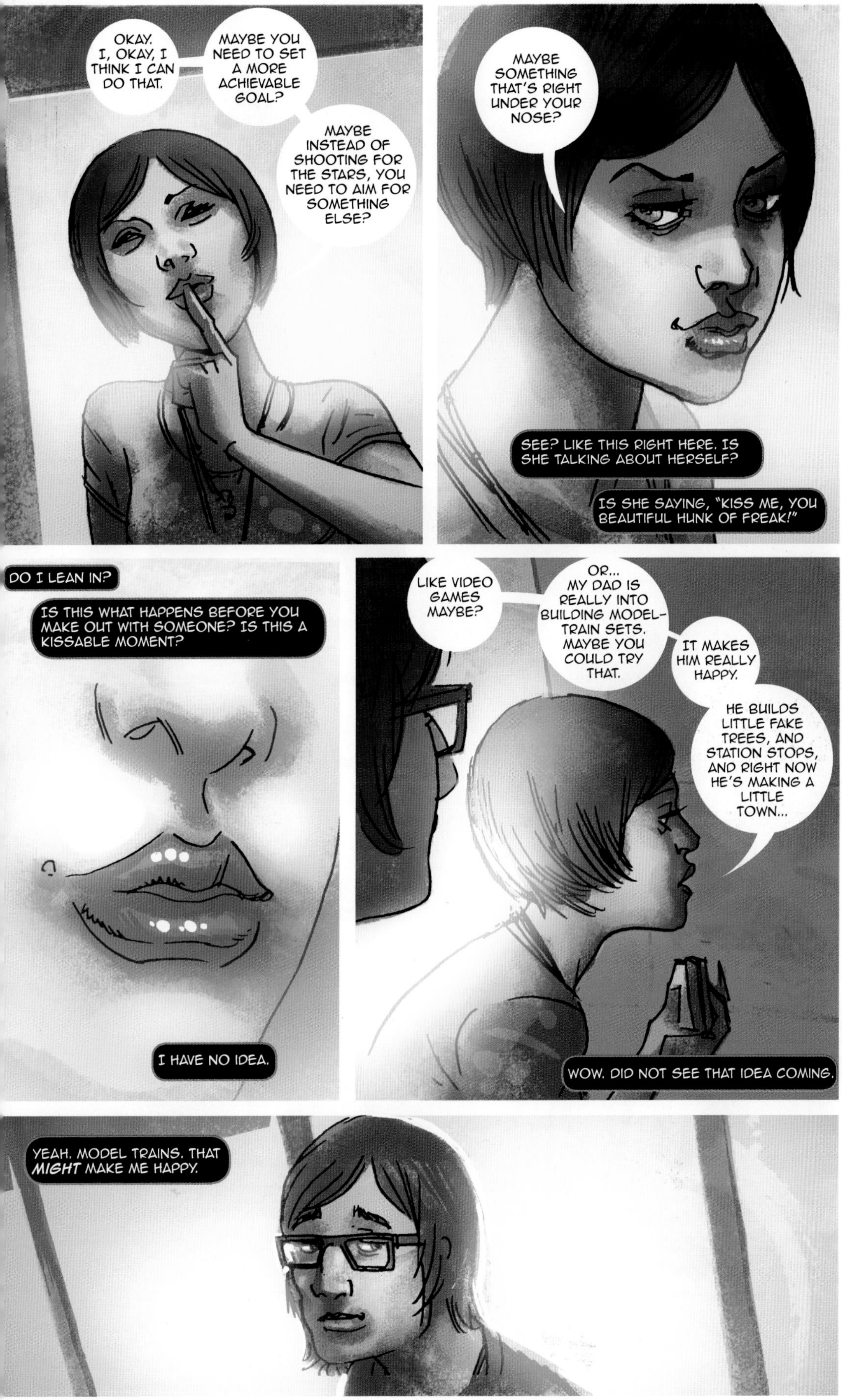
MAYBE YOU NEED TO SET A MORE ACHIEVABLE GOAL?
OKAY. I, OKAY, I THINK I CAN DO THAT.
MAYBE INSTEAD OF SHOOTING FOR THE STARS, YOU NEED TO AIM FOR SOMETHING ELSE?
MAYBE SOMETHING THAT'S RIGHT UNDER YOUR NOSE?
SEE? LIKE THIS RIGHT HERE. IS SHE TALKING ABOUT HERSELF?
IS SHE SAYING, "KISS ME, YOU BEAUTIFUL HUNK OF FREAK!"
DO I LEAN IN?
IS THIS WHAT HAPPENS BEFORE YOU MAKE OUT WITH SOMEONE? IS THIS A KISSABLE MOMENT?
I HAVE NO IDEA.
LIKE VIDEO GAMES MAYBE?
OR... MY DAD IS REALLY INTO BUILDING MODEL-TRAIN SETS. MAYBE YOU COULD TRY THAT.
IT MAKES HIM REALLY HAPPY.
HE BUILDS LITTLE FAKE TREES, AND STATION STOPS, AND RIGHT NOW HE'S MAKING A LITTLE TOWN...
WOW. DID NOT SEE THAT IDEA COMING.
YEAH. MODEL TRAINS. THAT *MIGHT* MAKE ME HAPPY.

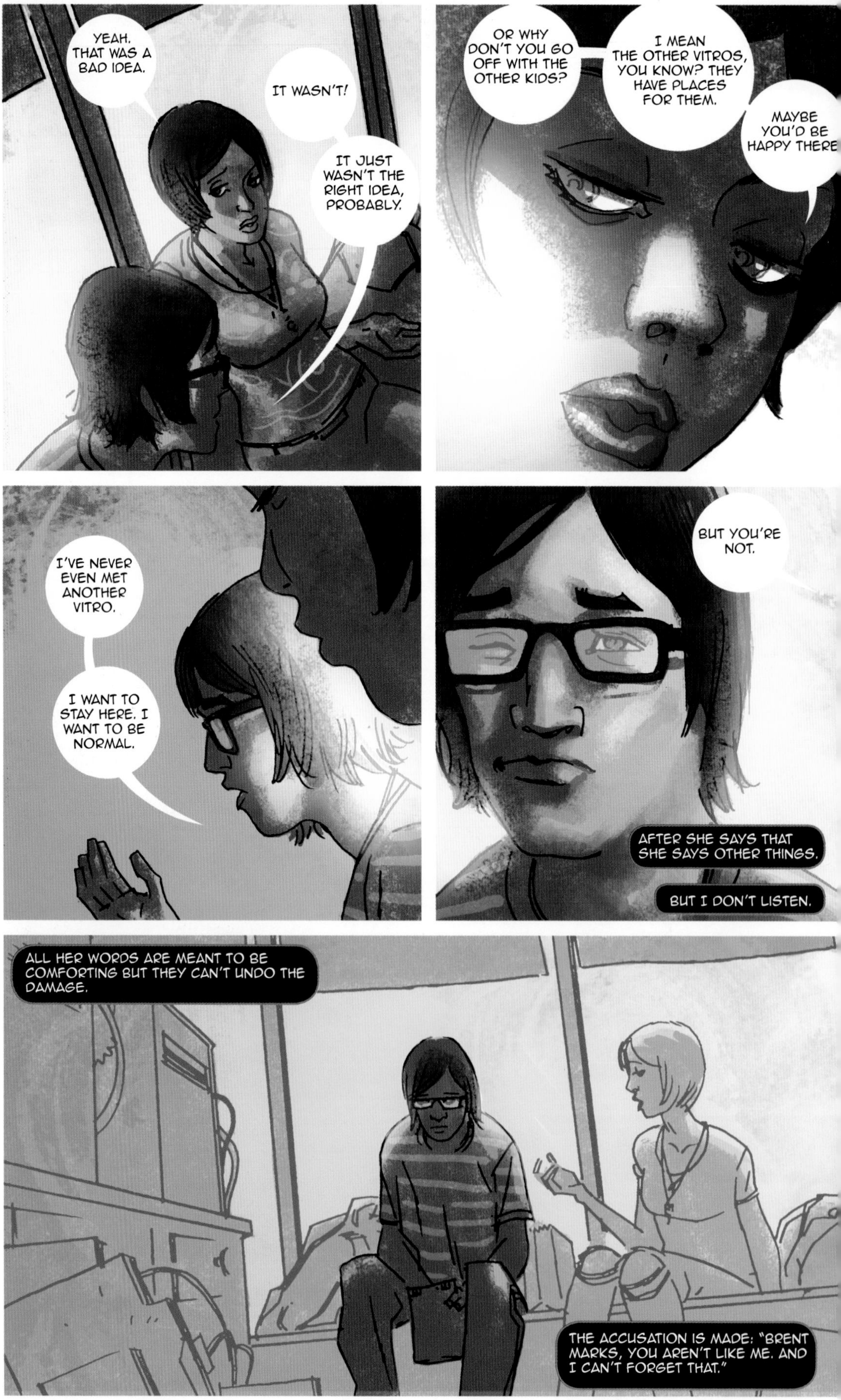
YEAH. THAT WAS A BAD IDEA.
IT WASN'T!
IT JUST WASN'T THE RIGHT IDEA, PROBABLY.
OR WHY DON'T YOU GO OFF WITH THE OTHER KIDS?
I MEAN THE OTHER VITROS, YOU KNOW? THEY HAVE PLACES FOR THEM.
MAYBE YOU'D BE HAPPY THERE
I'VE NEVER EVEN MET ANOTHER VITRO.
I WANT TO STAY HERE. I WANT TO BE NORMAL.
BUT YOU'RE NOT.
AFTER SHE SAYS THAT SHE SAYS OTHER THINGS.
BUT I DON'T LISTEN.
ALL HER WORDS ARE MEANT TO BE COMFORTING BUT THEY CAN'T UNDO THE DAMAGE.
THE ACCUSATION IS MADE: "BRENT MARKS, YOU AREN'T LIKE ME. AND I CAN'T FORGET THAT."

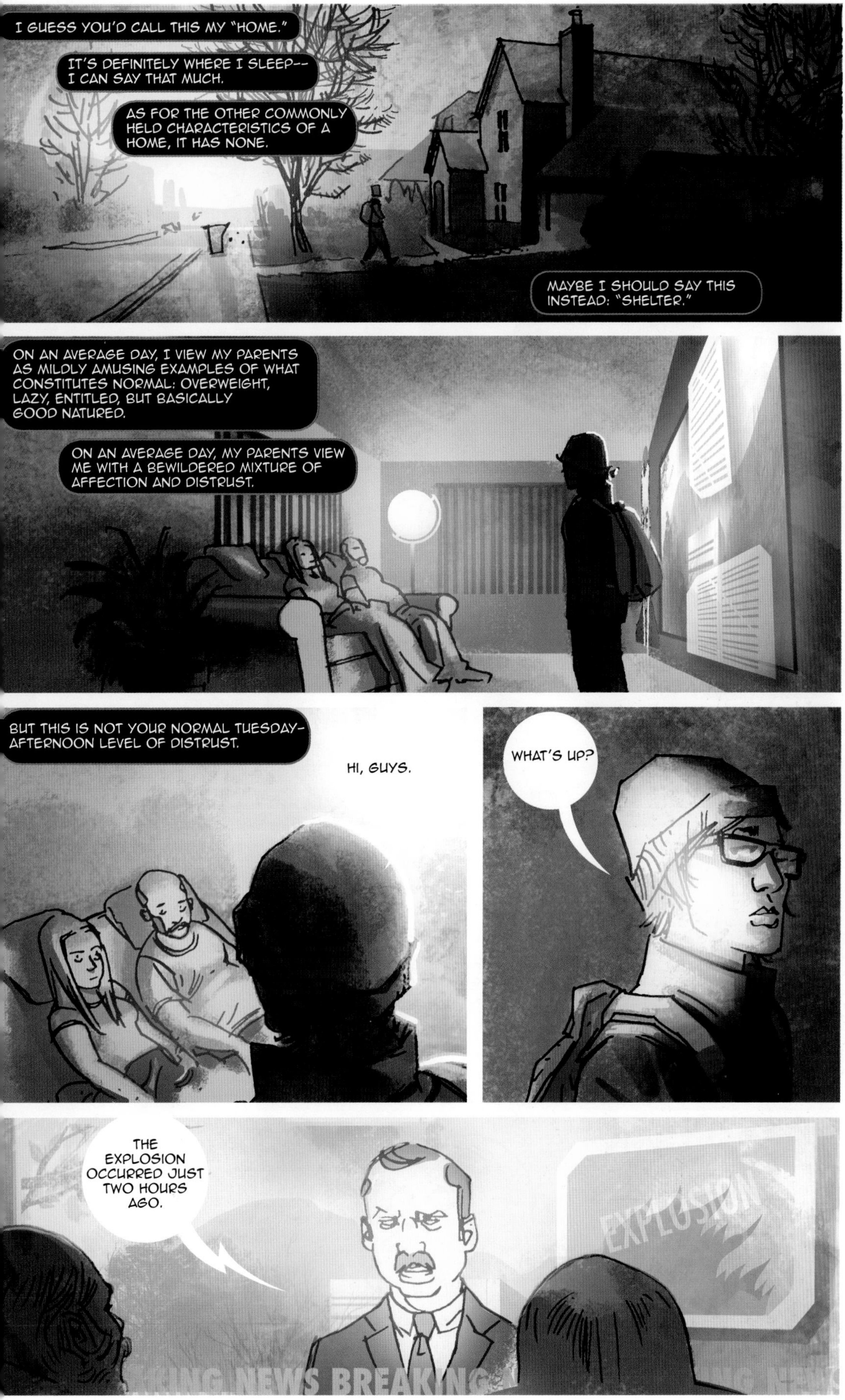
I GUESS YOU'D CALL THIS MY "HOME."
IT'S DEFINITELY WHERE I SLEEP-- I CAN SAY THAT MUCH.
AS FOR THE OTHER COMMONLY HELD CHARACTERISTICS OF A HOME, IT HAS NONE.
MAYBE I SHOULD SAY THIS INSTEAD: "SHELTER."
ON AN AVERAGE DAY, I VIEW MY PARENTS AS MILDLY AMUSING EXAMPLES OF WHAT CONSTITUTES NORMAL: OVERWEIGHT, LAZY, ENTITLED, BUT BASICALLY GOOD NATURED.
ON AN AVERAGE DAY, MY PARENTS VIEW ME WITH A BEWILDERED MIXTURE OF AFFECTION AND DISTRUST.
BUT THIS IS NOT YOUR NORMAL TUESDAY-AFTERNOON LEVEL OF DISTRUST.
HI, GUYS.
WHAT'S UP?
THE EXPLOSION OCCURRED JUST TWO HOURS AGO.
EXPLOSION
KING NEWS BREAKING

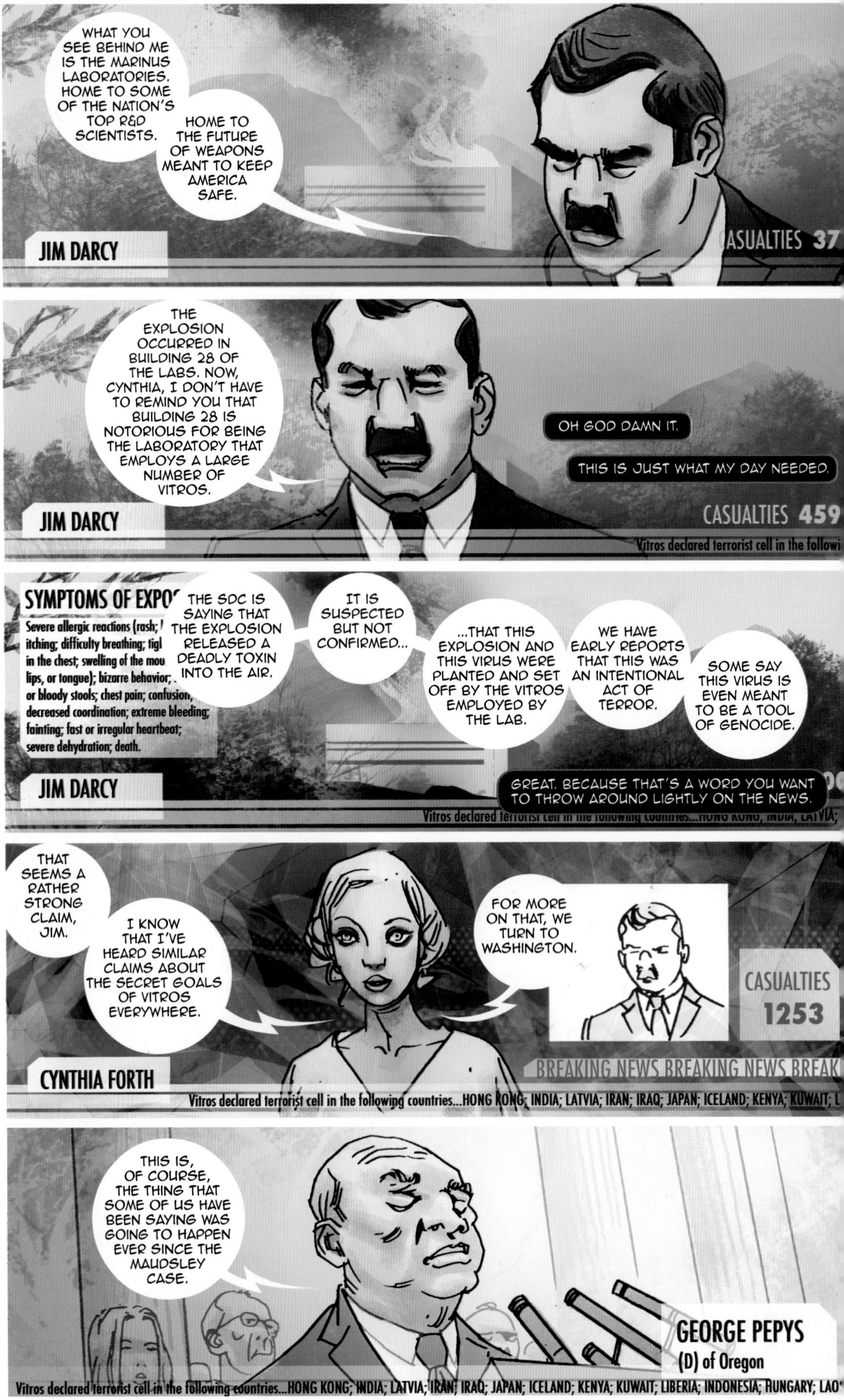
WHAT YOU SEE BEHIND ME IS THE MARINUS LABORATORIES. HOME TO SOME OF THE NATION'S TOP R&D SCIENTISTS.
HOME TO THE FUTURE OF WEAPONS MEANT TO KEEP AMERICA SAFE.
JIM DARCY
CASUALTIES 37
THE EXPLOSION OCCURRED IN BUILDING 28 OF THE LABS. NOW, CYNTHIA, I DON'T HAVE TO REMIND YOU THAT BUILDING 28 IS NOTORIOUS FOR BEING THE LABORATORY THAT EMPLOYS A LARGE NUMBER OF VITROS.
OH GOD DAMN IT.
THIS IS JUST WHAT MY DAY NEEDED.
JIM DARCY
CASUALTIES 459
Vitros declared terrorist cell in the followi
SYMPTOMS OF EXPO
Severe allergic reactions (rash;
itching; difficulty breathing; tig
in the chest; swelling of the mou
lips, or tongue); bizarre behavior;
or bloody stools; chest pain; confusion;
decreased coordination; extreme bleeding;
fainting; fast or irregular heartbeat;
severe dehydration; death.
THE SDC IS SAYING THAT THE EXPLOSION RELEASED A DEADLY TOXIN INTO THE AIR.
IT IS SUSPECTED BUT NOT CONFIRMED...
...THAT THIS EXPLOSION AND THIS VIRUS WERE PLANTED AND SET OFF BY THE VITROS EMPLOYED BY THE LAB.
WE HAVE EARLY REPORTS THAT THIS WAS AN INTENTIONAL ACT OF TERROR.
SOME SAY THIS VIRUS IS EVEN MEANT TO BE A TOOL OF GENOCIDE.
GREAT. BECAUSE THAT'S A WORD YOU WANT TO THROW AROUND LIGHTLY ON THE NEWS.
JIM DARCY
THAT SEEMS A RATHER STRONG CLAIM, JIM.
I KNOW THAT I'VE HEARD SIMILAR CLAIMS ABOUT THE SECRET GOALS OF VITROS EVERYWHERE.
FOR MORE ON THAT, WE TURN TO WASHINGTON.
CASUALTIES 1253
BREAKING NEWS BREAKING NEWS BREAK
CYNTHIA FORTH
Vitros declared terrorist cell in the following countries...HONG KONG; INDIA; LATVIA; IRAN; IRAQ; JAPAN; ICELAND; KENYA; KUWAIT; L
THIS IS, OF COURSE, THE THING THAT SOME OF US HAVE BEEN SAYING WAS GOING TO HAPPEN EVER SINCE THE MAUDSLEY CASE.
GEORGE PEPYS
(D) of Oregon
Vitros declared terrorist cell in the following countries...HONG KONG; INDIA; LATVIA; IRAN; IRAQ; JAPAN; ICELAND; KENYA; KUWAIT; LIBERIA; INDONESIA; HUNGARY; LAO

AS LONG AS THE VITROS ARE FREE AND OUT IN THE WORLD, THIS WILL HAPPEN AGAIN. AND AGAIN. AND AGAIN.

IT IS BECAUSE OF THIS THAT THE HOUSE HAS INTRODUCED AND FAST TRACKED LEGISLATION DECLARING THE VITROS A TERRORIST CELL.

BREAKING NEWS
Special session of Congress has been called to order.

I SUSPECT THINGS WILL CALM DOWN.

I DON'T THINK ANYONE REALLY WANTS A DAY OF RECKONING FOR THE VITROS.

WE'RE JUST KIDS, AFTER ALL.

GUYS...

YOU KNOW THIS HAS NOTHING TO DO WITH ME, RIGHT?

GEORGE PEPYS
MP of Oregon

I'M JUST YOUR SON.

I'M PERFECTLY NORMAL.

OF COURSE, SON.

YES DEAR, WE KNOW.

MY PARENTS, LADIES AND GENTLEMEN: THE WORST LIARS IN THE BUCKEYE STATE.

IF YOU NEED ME I'LL BE UP IN MY ROOM.

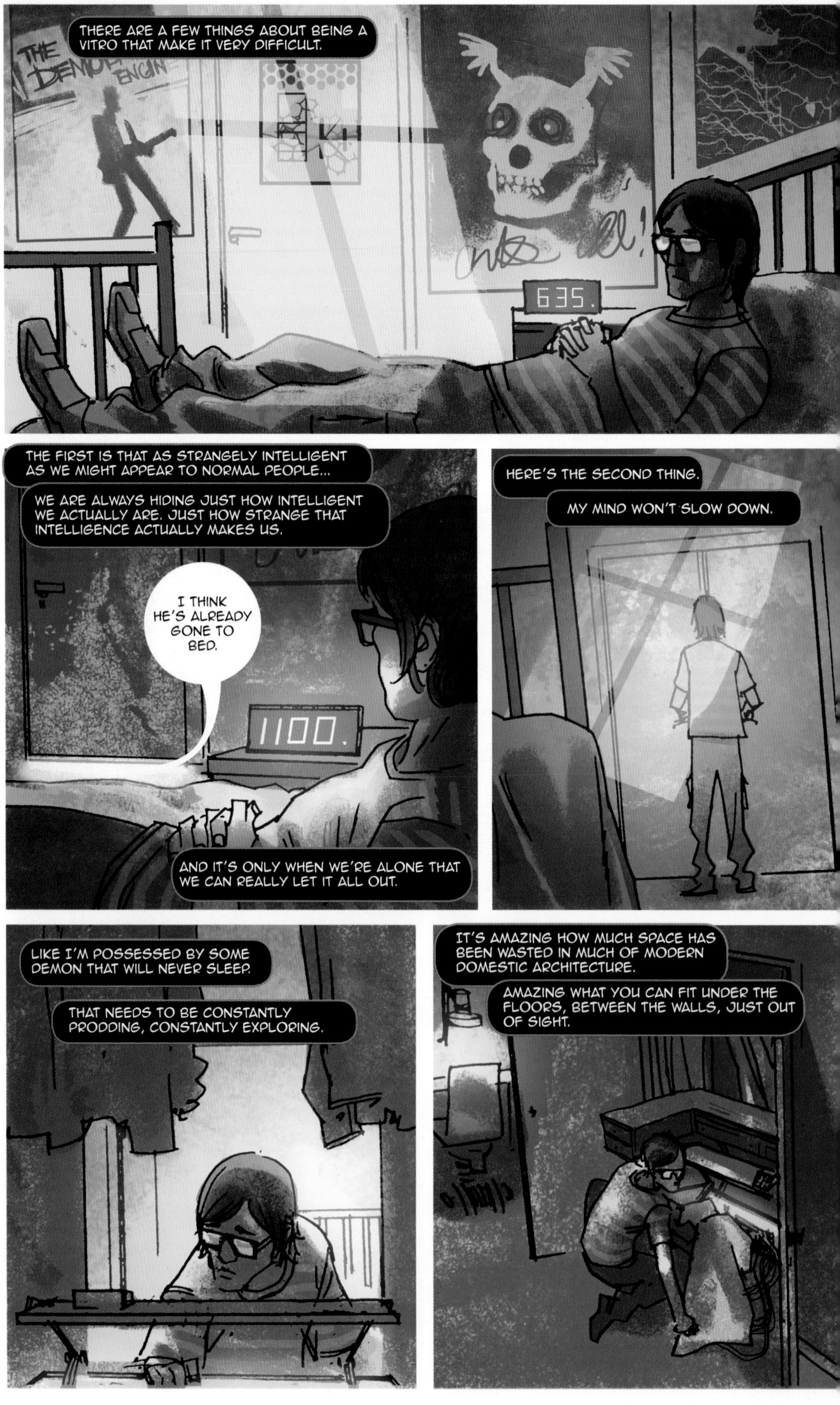

THERE ARE A FEW THINGS ABOUT BEING A VITRO THAT MAKE IT VERY DIFFICULT.
THE DEMON ENGIN
635.
THE FIRST IS THAT AS STRANGELY INTELLIGENT AS WE MIGHT APPEAR TO NORMAL PEOPLE...
WE ARE ALWAYS HIDING JUST HOW INTELLIGENT WE ACTUALLY ARE. JUST HOW STRANGE THAT INTELLIGENCE ACTUALLY MAKES US.
I THINK HE'S ALREADY GONE TO BED.
1100.
AND IT'S ONLY WHEN WE'RE ALONE THAT WE CAN REALLY LET IT ALL OUT.
HERE'S THE SECOND THING.
MY MIND WON'T SLOW DOWN.
LIKE I'M POSSESSED BY SOME DEMON THAT WILL NEVER SLEEP.
THAT NEEDS TO BE CONSTANTLY PRODDING, CONSTANTLY EXPLORING.
IT'S AMAZING HOW MUCH SPACE HAS BEEN WASTED IN MUCH OF MODERN DOMESTIC ARCHITECTURE.
AMAZING WHAT YOU CAN FIT UNDER THE FLOORS, BETWEEN THE WALLS, JUST OUT OF SIGHT.

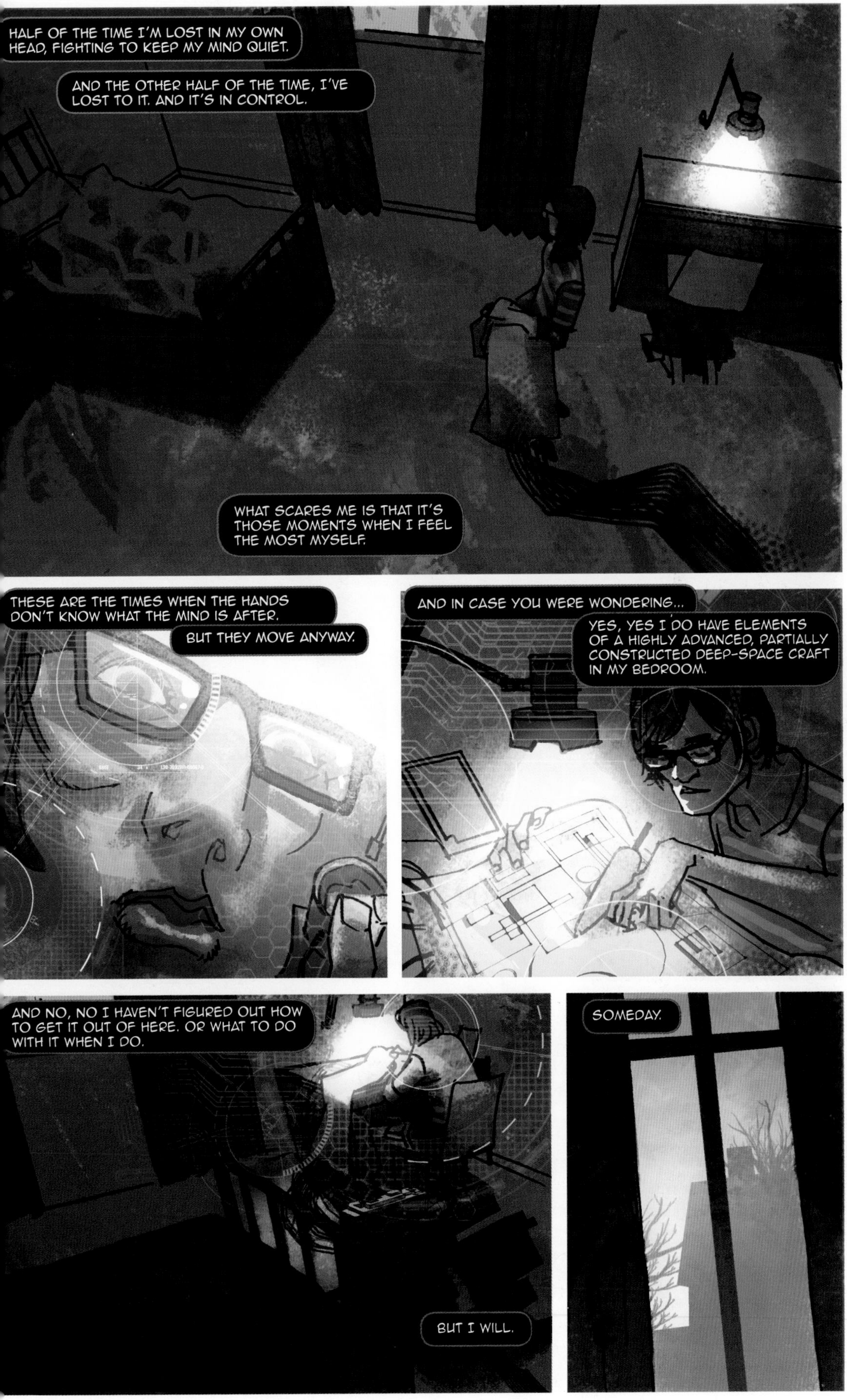
HALF OF THE TIME I'M LOST IN MY OWN HEAD, FIGHTING TO KEEP MY MIND QUIET.
AND THE OTHER HALF OF THE TIME, I'VE LOST TO IT. AND IT'S IN CONTROL.
WHAT SCARES ME IS THAT IT'S THOSE MOMENTS WHEN I FEEL THE MOST MYSELF.
THESE ARE THE TIMES WHEN THE HANDS DON'T KNOW WHAT THE MIND IS AFTER.
BUT THEY MOVE ANYWAY.
AND IN CASE YOU WERE WONDERING...
YES, YES I DO HAVE ELEMENTS OF A HIGHLY ADVANCED, PARTIALLY CONSTRUCTED DEEP-SPACE CRAFT IN MY BEDROOM.
AND NO, NO I HAVEN'T FIGURED OUT HOW TO GET IT OUT OF HERE. OR WHAT TO DO WITH IT WHEN I DO.
BUT I WILL.
SOMEDAY.

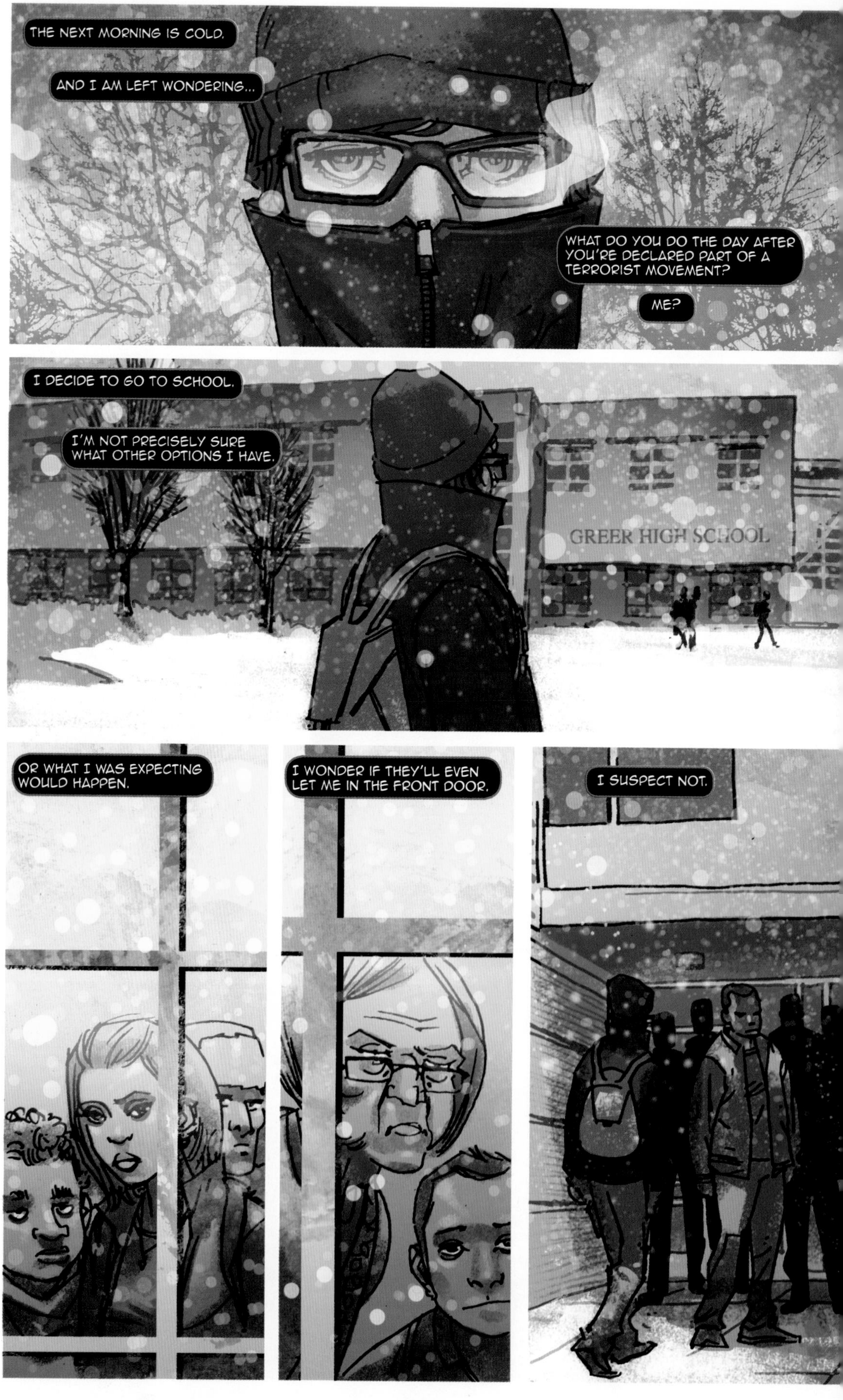
THE NEXT MORNING IS COLD.
AND I AM LEFT WONDERING...
WHAT DO YOU DO THE DAY AFTER YOU'RE DECLARED PART OF A TERRORIST MOVEMENT?
ME?
I DECIDE TO GO TO SCHOOL.
I'M NOT PRECISELY SURE WHAT OTHER OPTIONS I HAVE.
GREER HIGH SCHOOL
OR WHAT I WAS EXPECTING WOULD HAPPEN.
I WONDER IF THEY'LL EVEN LET ME IN THE FRONT DOOR.
I SUSPECT NOT.

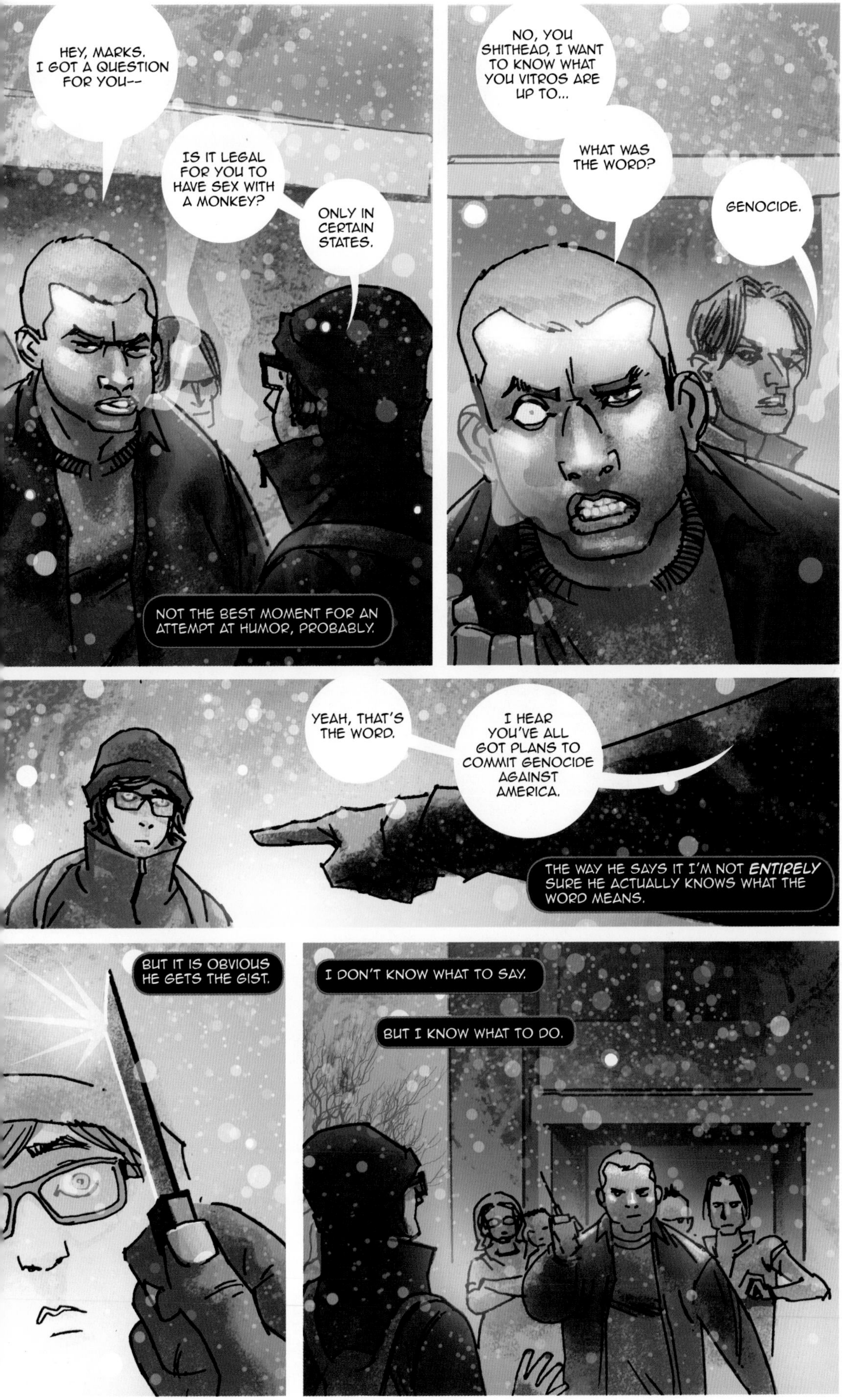

HEY, MARKS. I GOT A QUESTION FOR YOU--
IS IT LEGAL FOR YOU TO HAVE SEX WITH A MONKEY?
ONLY IN CERTAIN STATES.
NOT THE BEST MOMENT FOR AN ATTEMPT AT HUMOR, PROBABLY.
NO, YOU SHITHEAD, I WANT TO KNOW WHAT YOU VITROS ARE UP TO...
WHAT WAS THE WORD?
GENOCIDE.
YEAH, THAT'S THE WORD.
I HEAR YOU'VE ALL GOT PLANS TO COMMIT GENOCIDE AGAINST AMERICA.
THE WAY HE SAYS IT I'M NOT *ENTIRELY* SURE HE ACTUALLY KNOWS WHAT THE WORD MEANS.
BUT IT IS OBVIOUS HE GETS THE GIST.
I DON'T KNOW WHAT TO SAY.
BUT I KNOW WHAT TO DO.

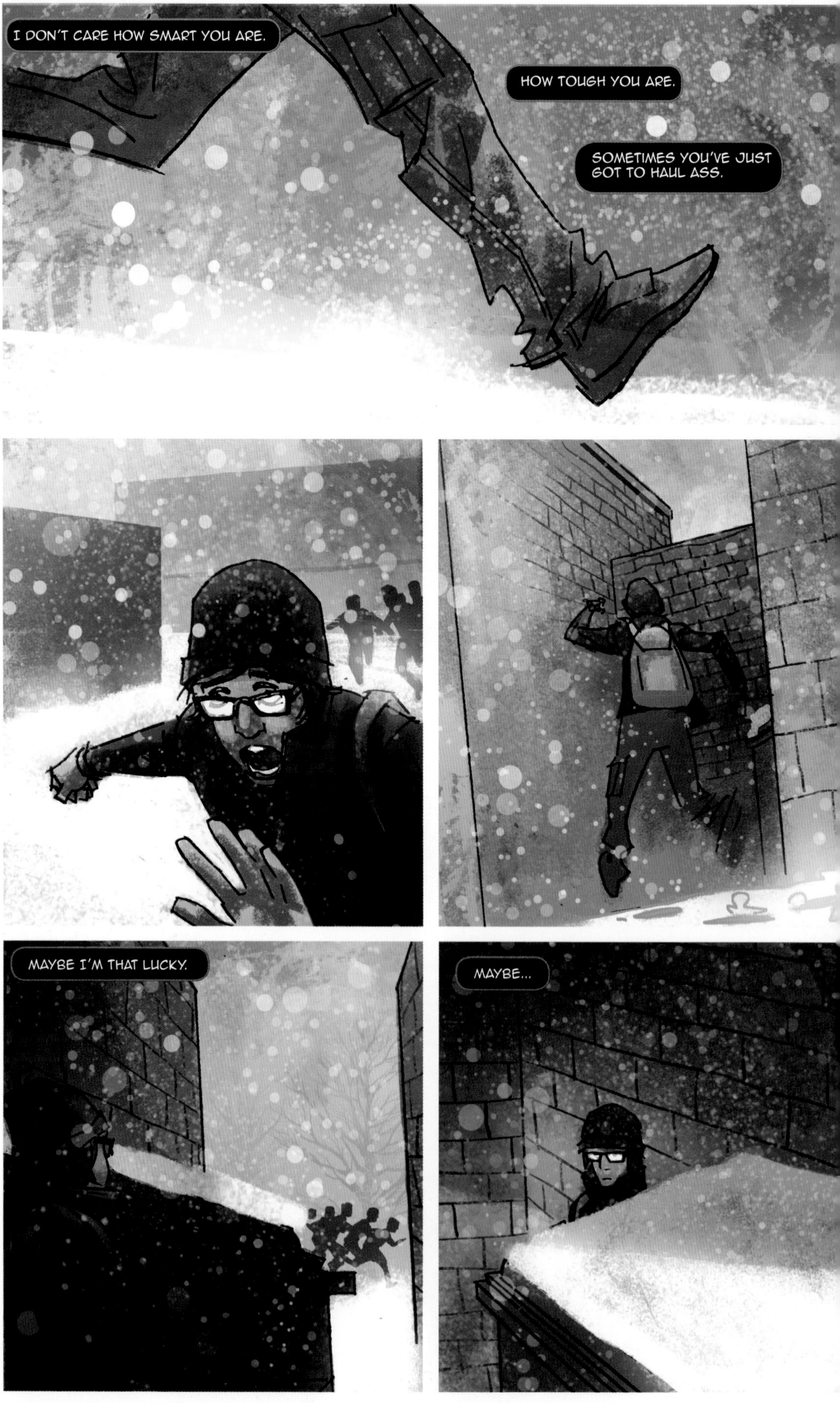
I DON'T CARE HOW SMART YOU ARE.
HOW TOUGH YOU ARE.
SOMETIMES YOU'VE JUST GOT TO HAUL ASS.
MAYBE I'M THAT LUCKY.
MAYBE...

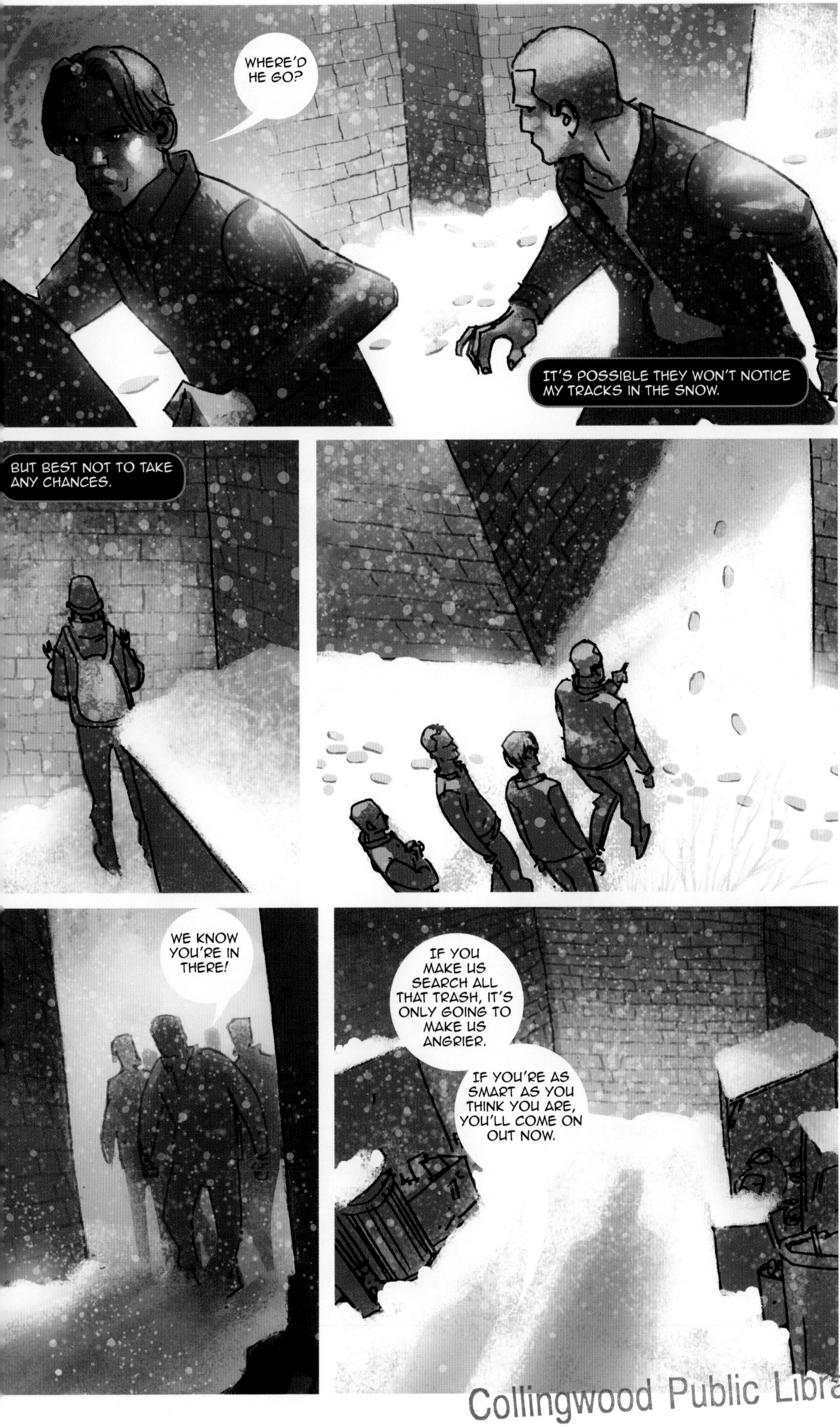
WHERE'D HE GO?
IT'S POSSIBLE THEY WON'T NOTICE MY TRACKS IN THE SNOW.
BUT BEST NOT TO TAKE ANY CHANCES.
WE KNOW YOU'RE IN THERE!
IF YOU MAKE US SEARCH ALL THAT TRASH, IT'S ONLY GOING TO MAKE US ANGRIER.
IF YOU'RE AS SMART AS YOU THINK YOU ARE, YOU'LL COME ON OUT NOW.

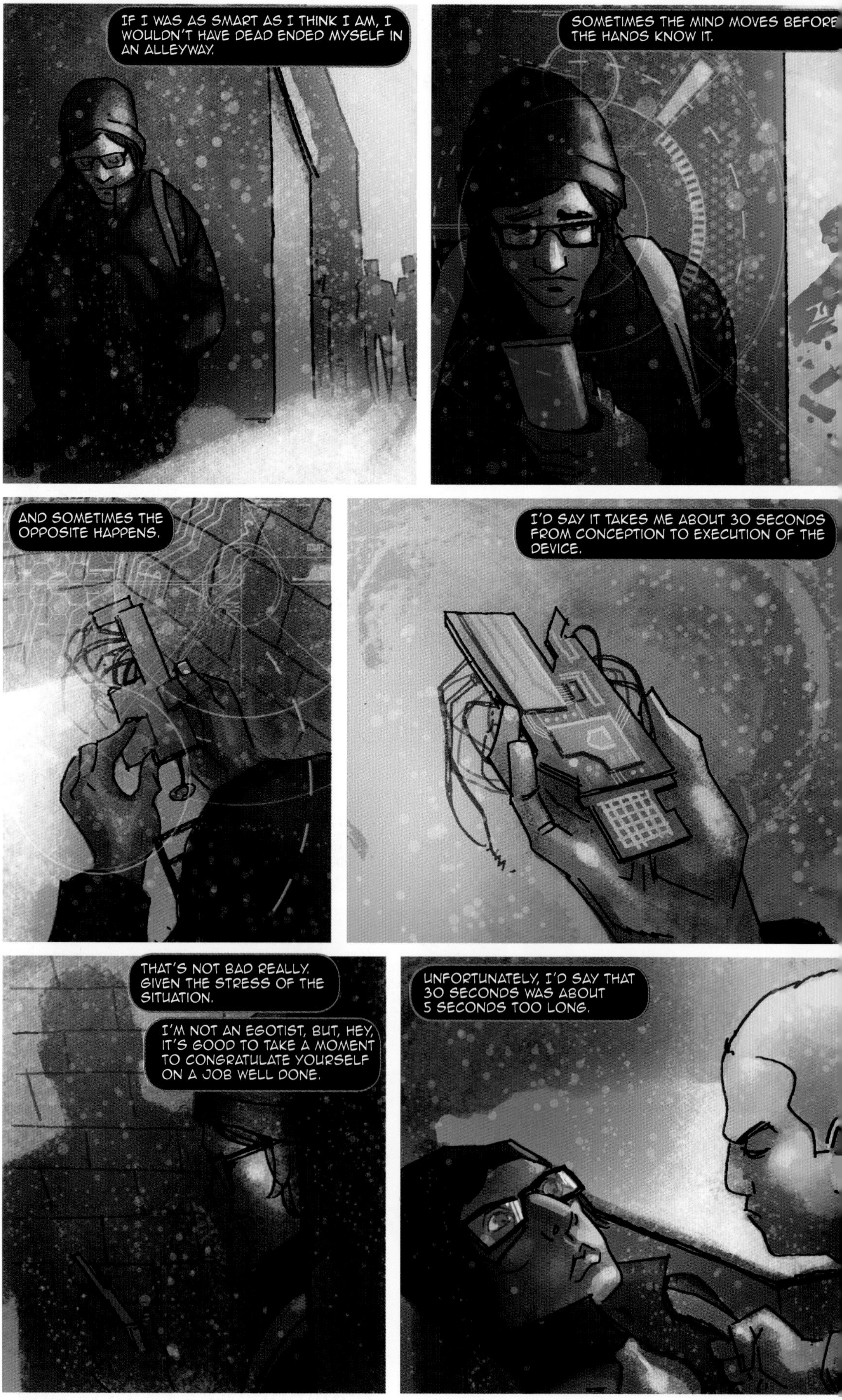
IF I WAS AS SMART AS I THINK I AM, I WOULDN'T HAVE DEAD ENDED MYSELF IN AN ALLEYWAY.
SOMETIMES THE MIND MOVES BEFORE THE HANDS KNOW IT.
AND SOMETIMES THE OPPOSITE HAPPENS.
I'D SAY IT TAKES ME ABOUT 30 SECONDS FROM CONCEPTION TO EXECUTION OF THE DEVICE.
THAT'S NOT BAD REALLY. GIVEN THE STRESS OF THE SITUATION.
I'M NOT AN EGOTIST, BUT, HEY, IT'S GOOD TO TAKE A MOMENT TO CONGRATULATE YOURSELF ON A JOB WELL DONE.
UNFORTUNATELY, I'D SAY THAT 30 SECONDS WAS ABOUT 5 SECONDS TOO LONG.

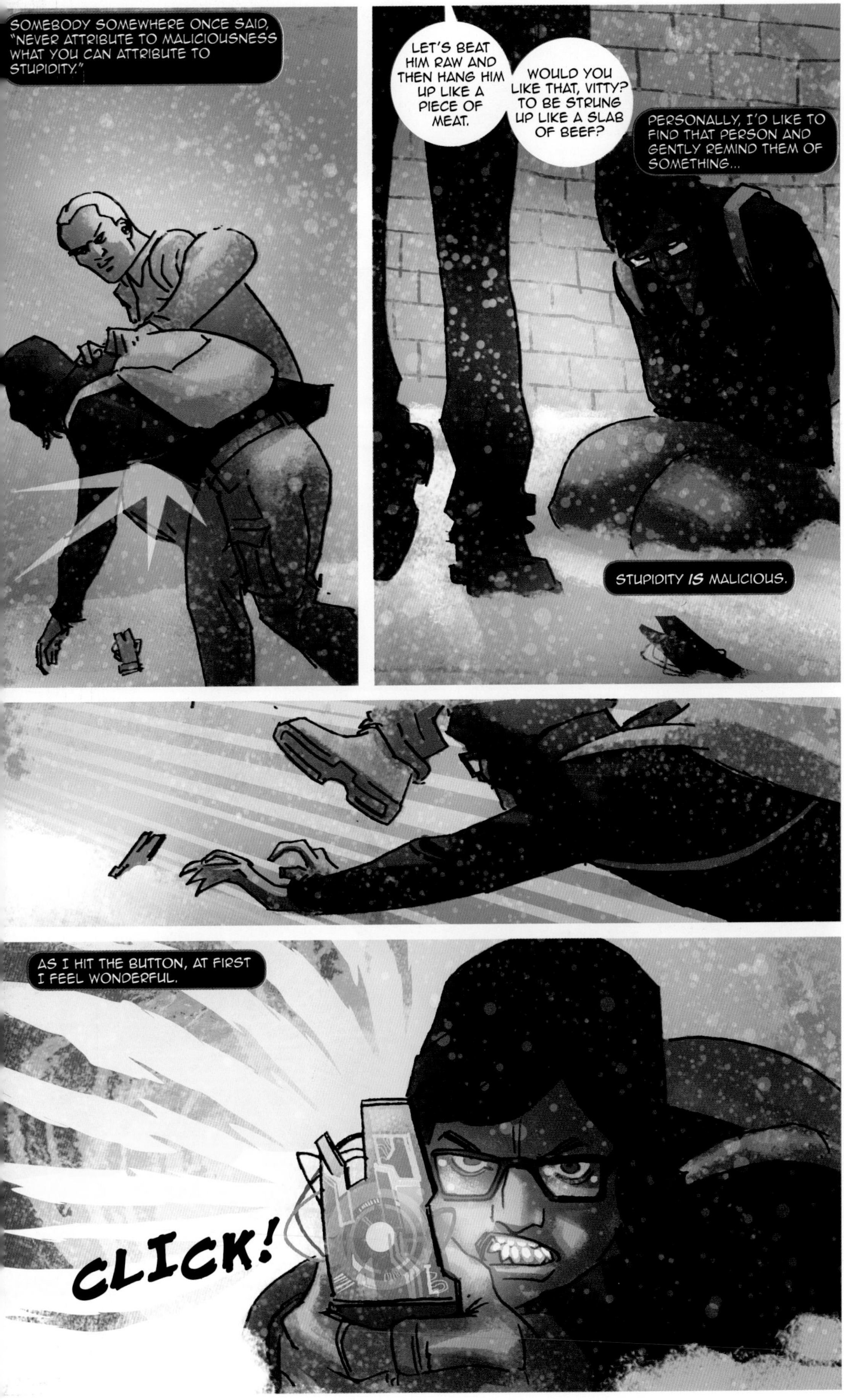

SOMEBODY SOMEWHERE ONCE SAID, "NEVER ATTRIBUTE TO MALICIOUSNESS WHAT YOU CAN ATTRIBUTE TO STUPIDITY."
LET'S BEAT HIM RAW AND THEN HANG HIM UP LIKE A PIECE OF MEAT.
WOULD YOU LIKE THAT, VITTY? TO BE STRUNG UP LIKE A SLAB OF BEEF?
PERSONALLY, I'D LIKE TO FIND THAT PERSON AND GENTLY REMIND THEM OF SOMETHING...
STUPIDITY *IS* MALICIOUS.
AS I HIT THE BUTTON, AT FIRST I FEEL WONDERFUL.
CLICK!

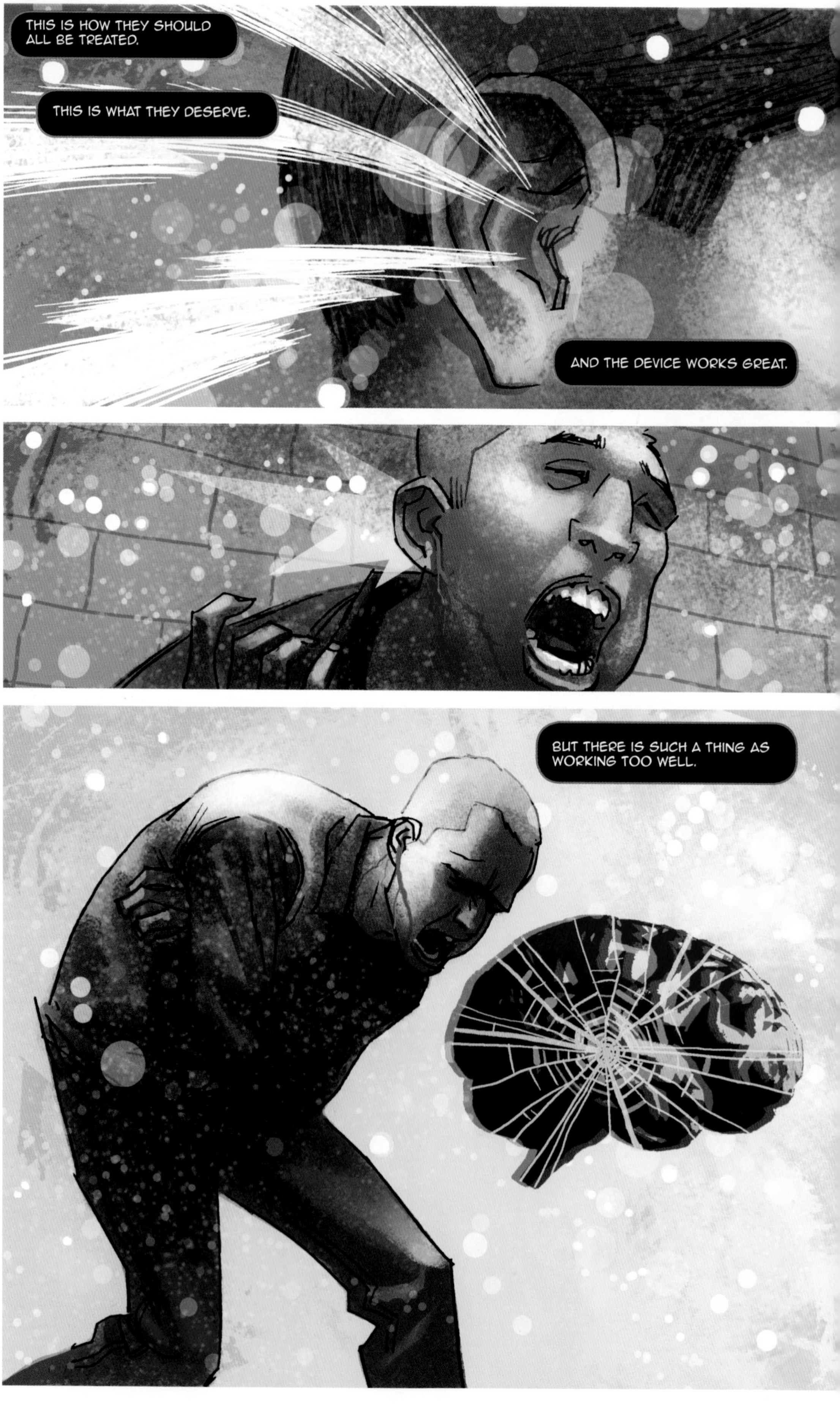
THIS IS HOW THEY SHOULD ALL BE TREATED.
THIS IS WHAT THEY DESERVE.
AND THE DEVICE WORKS GREAT.
BUT THERE IS SUCH A THING AS WORKING TOO WELL.

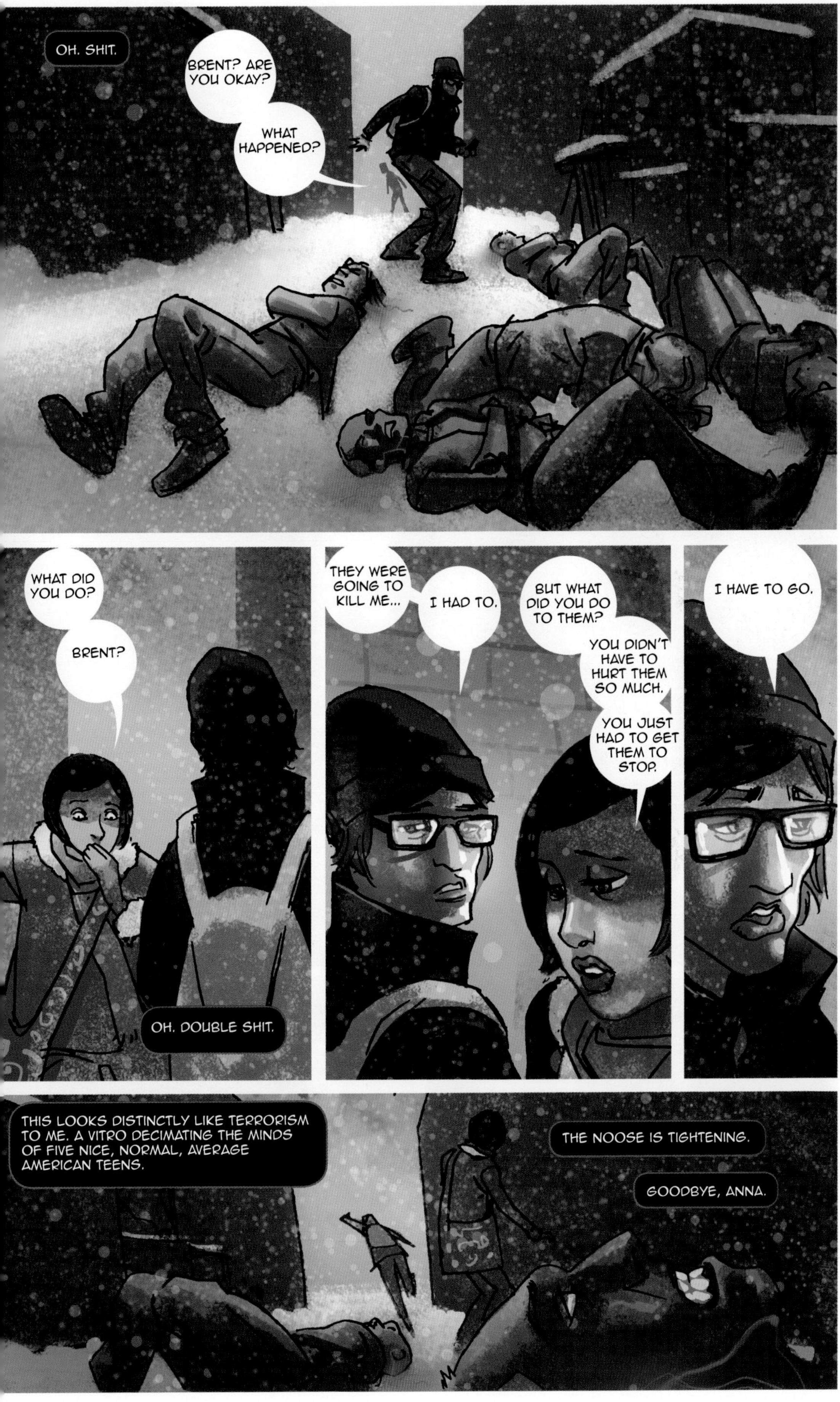
OH. SHIT.
BRENT? ARE YOU OKAY?
WHAT HAPPENED?
WHAT DID YOU DO?
BRENT?
OH. DOUBLE SHIT.
THEY WERE GOING TO KILL ME...
I HAD TO.
BUT WHAT DID YOU DO TO THEM?
YOU DIDN'T HAVE TO HURT THEM SO MUCH.
YOU JUST HAD TO GET THEM TO STOP.
I HAVE TO GO.
THIS LOOKS DISTINCTLY LIKE TERRORISM TO ME. A VITRO DECIMATING THE MINDS OF FIVE NICE, NORMAL, AVERAGE AMERICAN TEENS.
THE NOOSE IS TIGHTENING.
GOODBYE, ANNA.

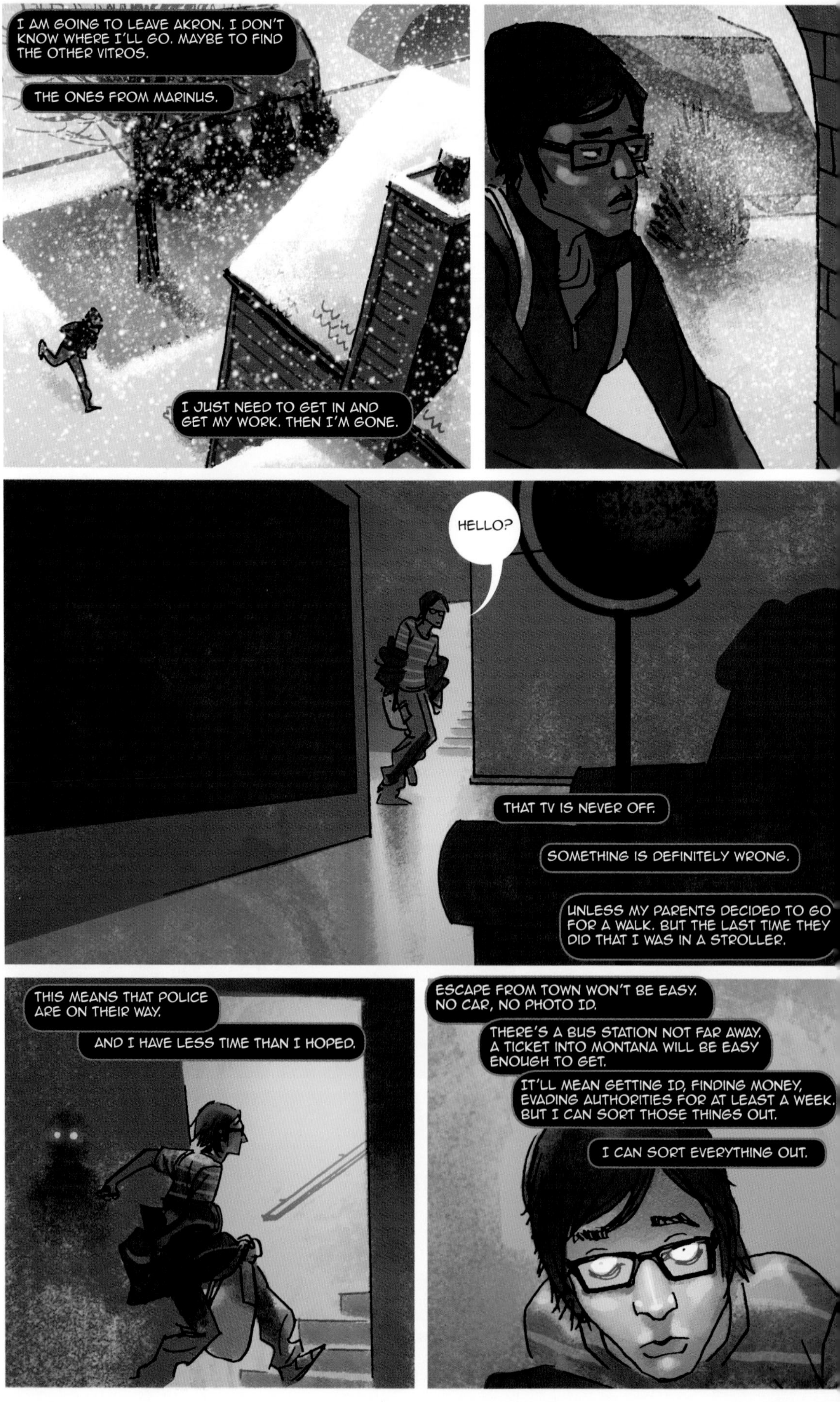

I AM GOING TO LEAVE AKRON. I DON'T KNOW WHERE I'LL GO. MAYBE TO FIND THE OTHER VITROS.
THE ONES FROM MARINUS.
I JUST NEED TO GET IN AND GET MY WORK. THEN I'M GONE.
HELLO?
THAT TV IS NEVER OFF.
SOMETHING IS DEFINITELY WRONG.
UNLESS MY PARENTS DECIDED TO GO FOR A WALK. BUT THE LAST TIME THEY DID THAT I WAS IN A STROLLER.
THIS MEANS THAT POLICE ARE ON THEIR WAY.
AND I HAVE LESS TIME THAN I HOPED.
ESCAPE FROM TOWN WON'T BE EASY. NO CAR, NO PHOTO ID.
THERE'S A BUS STATION NOT FAR AWAY. A TICKET INTO MONTANA WILL BE EASY ENOUGH TO GET.
IT'LL MEAN GETTING ID, FINDING MONEY, EVADING AUTHORITIES FOR AT LEAST A WEEK. BUT I CAN SORT THOSE THINGS OUT.
I CAN SORT EVERYTHING OUT.

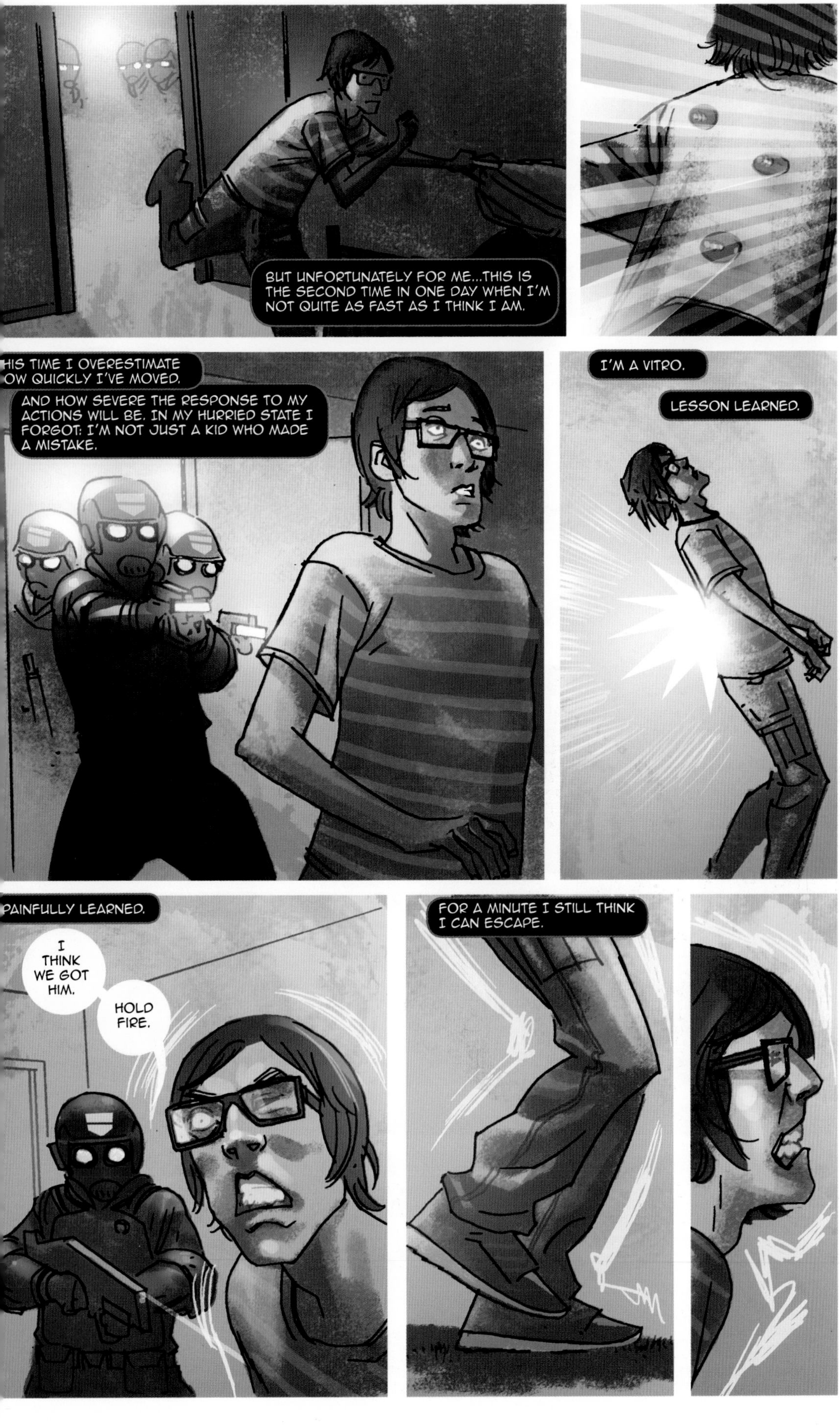
BUT UNFORTUNATELY FOR ME...THIS IS THE SECOND TIME IN ONE DAY WHEN I'M NOT QUITE AS FAST AS I THINK I AM.
HIS TIME I OVERESTIMATE OW QUICKLY I'VE MOVED.
AND HOW SEVERE THE RESPONSE TO MY ACTIONS WILL BE. IN MY HURRIED STATE I FORGOT: I'M NOT JUST A KID WHO MADE A MISTAKE.
I'M A VITRO.
LESSON LEARNED.
PAINFULLY LEARNED.
I THINK WE GOT HIM.
HOLD FIRE.
FOR A MINUTE I STILL THINK I CAN ESCAPE.

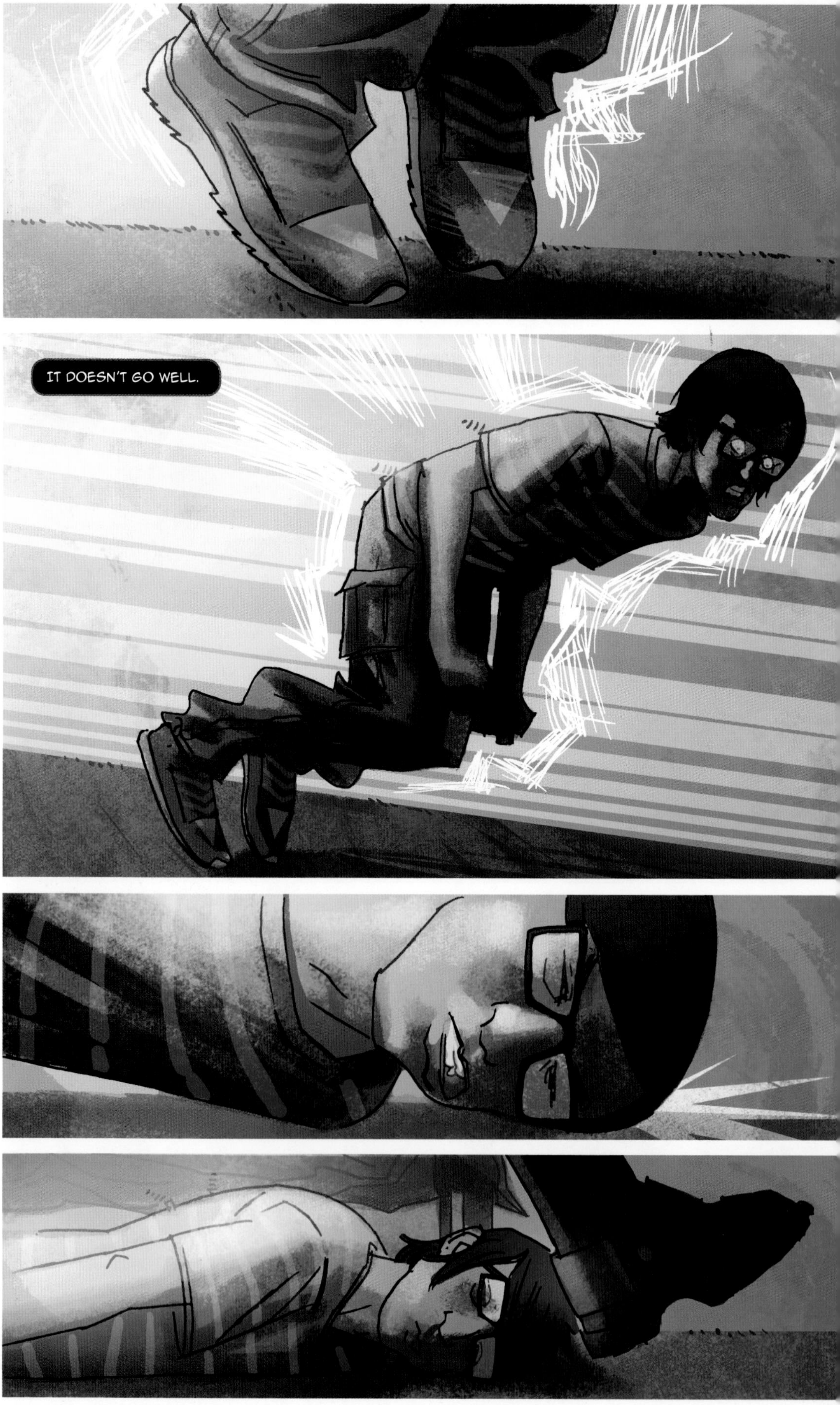
IT DOESN'T GO WELL.

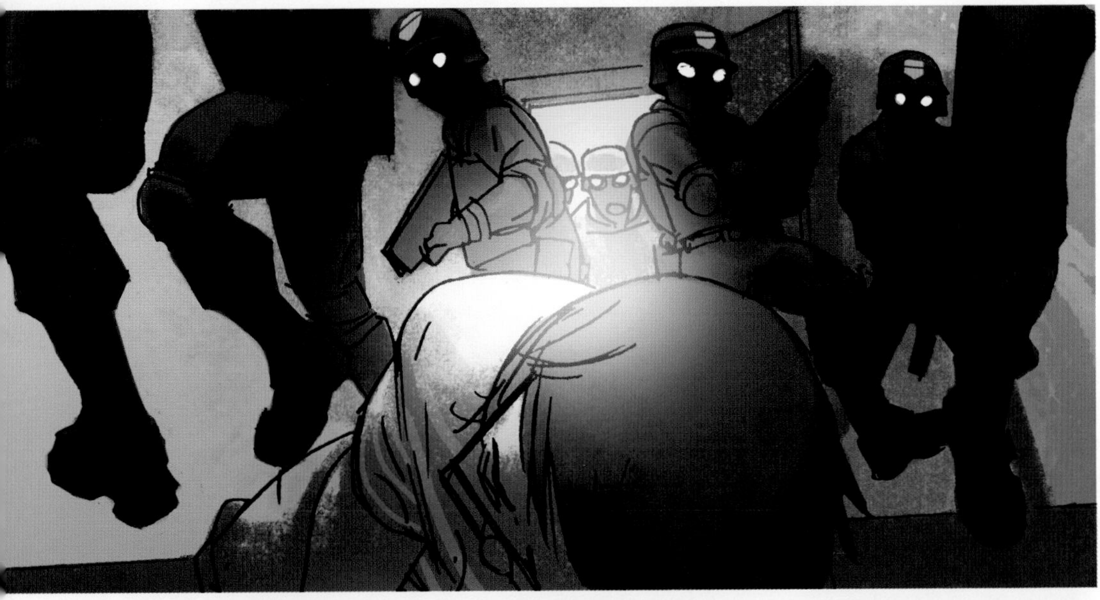

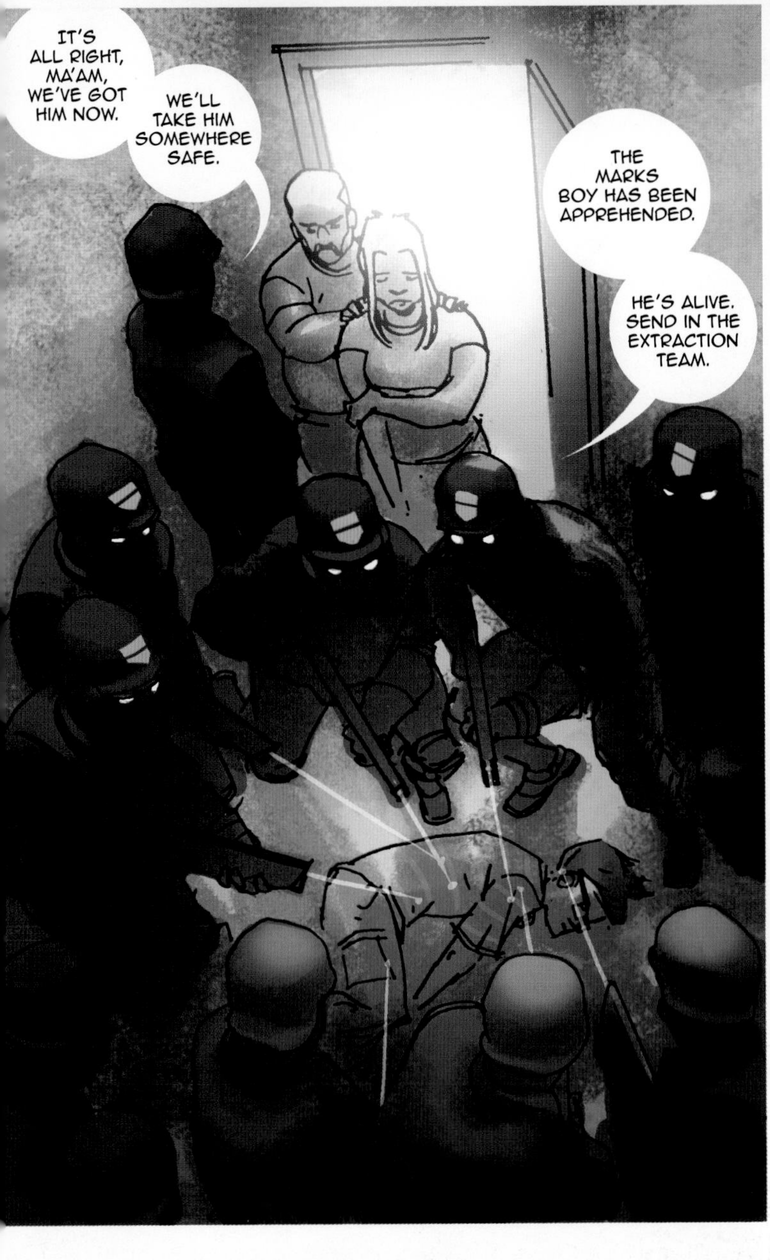

IT'S ALL RIGHT, MA'AM, WE'VE GOT HIM NOW.
WE'LL TAKE HIM SOMEWHERE SAFE.
THE MARKS BOY HAS BEEN APPREHENDED.
HE'S ALIVE. SEND IN THE EXTRACTION TEAM.

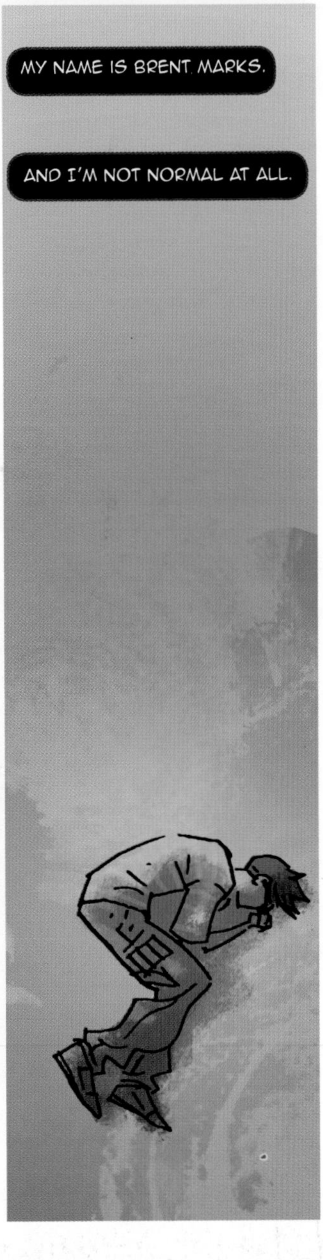

MY NAME IS BRENT MARKS.
AND I'M NOT NORMAL AT ALL.

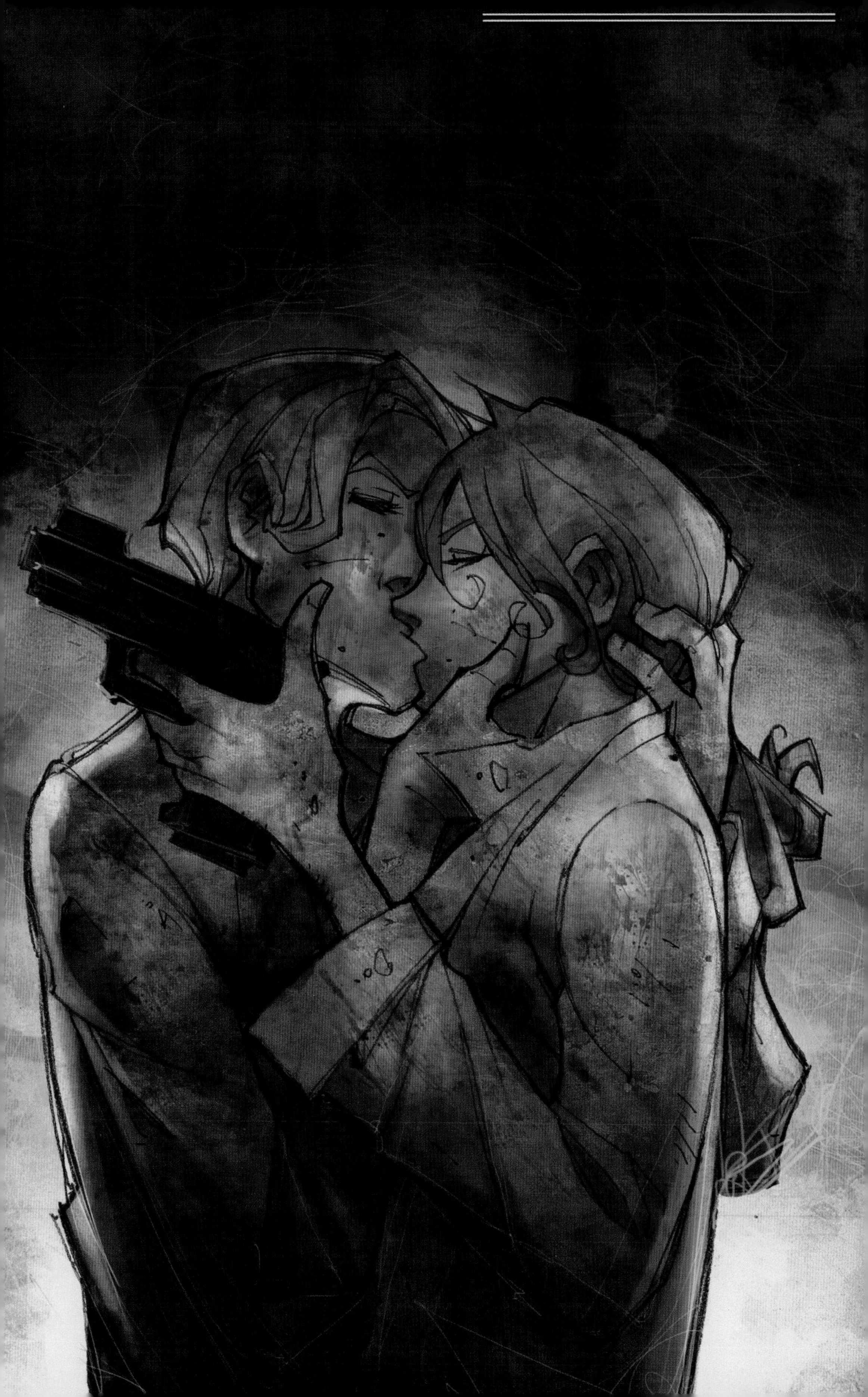

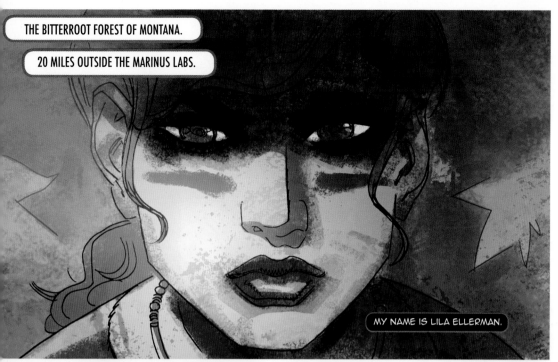

THE BITTERROOT FOREST OF MONTANA.

20 MILES OUTSIDE THE MARINUS LABS.

MY NAME IS LILA ELLERMAN.

OCTOBER 9.

2025.

AND I'M NOT SURE I EVEN KNOW WHAT NORMAL IS.

NONE OF US DO.

WHY SHOULD WE? WE'RE VITROS. AND WE'RE PROUD OF IT.

BUT NOW WE'RE BEING HUNTED FOR SOMETHING WE DID NOT DO.

SHIT!

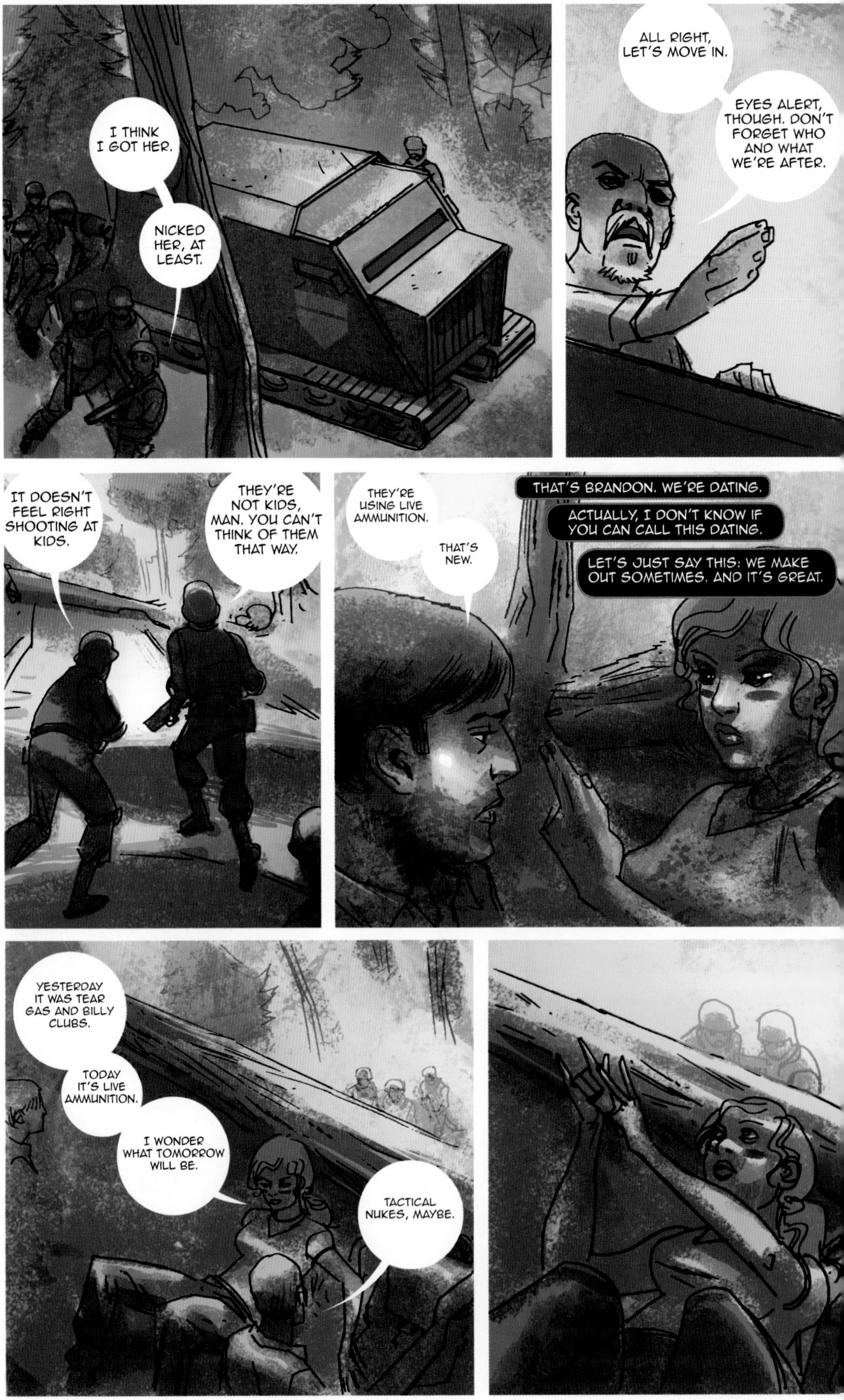
I THINK I GOT HER.
NICKED HER, AT LEAST.
ALL RIGHT, LET'S MOVE IN.
EYES ALERT, THOUGH. DON'T FORGET WHO AND WHAT WE'RE AFTER.
IT DOESN'T FEEL RIGHT SHOOTING AT KIDS.
THEY'RE NOT KIDS, MAN. YOU CAN'T THINK OF THEM THAT WAY.
THEY'RE USING LIVE AMMUNITION.
THAT'S NEW.
THAT'S BRANDON. WE'RE DATING.
ACTUALLY, I DON'T KNOW IF YOU CAN CALL THIS DATING.
LET'S JUST SAY THIS: WE MAKE OUT SOMETIMES. AND IT'S GREAT.
YESTERDAY IT WAS TEAR GAS AND BILLY CLUBS.
TODAY IT'S LIVE AMMUNITION.
I WONDER WHAT TOMORROW WILL BE.
TACTICAL NUKES, MAYBE.

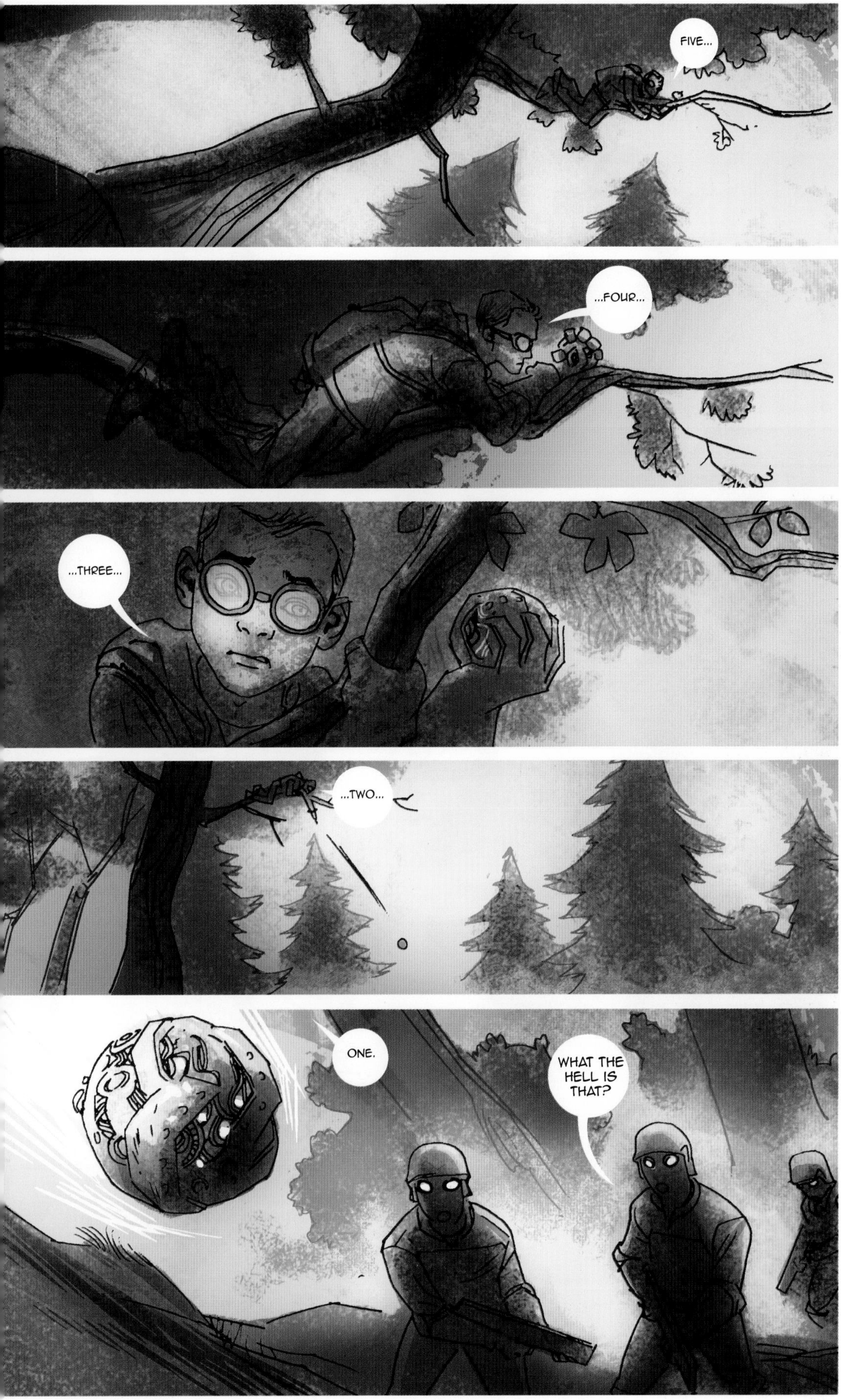
FIVE...
...FOUR...
...THREE...
...TWO...
ONE.
WHAT THE HELL IS THAT?

BASE CAMP, BASE CAMP, COME IN! WE HAVE MULTIPLE TARGETS, REQUIRE BACKUP.

WE'RE IN QUADRANT 67, JUST WEST OF--

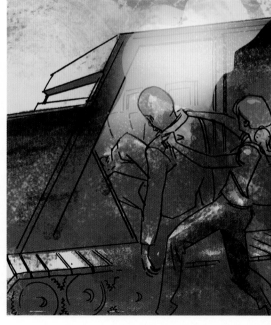

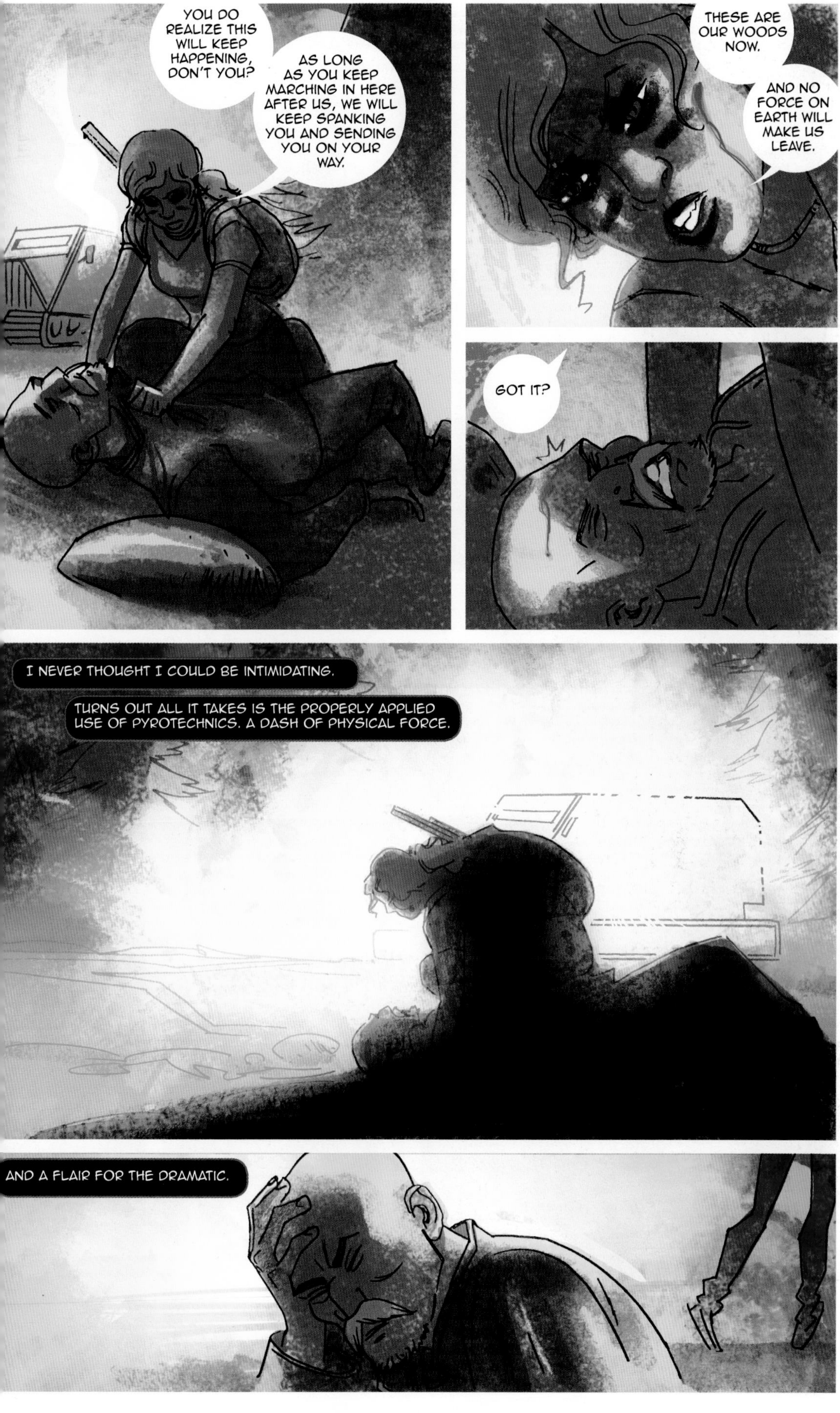
YOU DO REALIZE THIS WILL KEEP HAPPENING, DON'T YOU?
AS LONG AS YOU KEEP MARCHING IN HERE AFTER US, WE WILL KEEP SPANKING YOU AND SENDING YOU ON YOUR WAY.
THESE ARE OUR WOODS NOW.
AND NO FORCE ON EARTH WILL MAKE US LEAVE.
GOT IT?
I NEVER THOUGHT I COULD BE INTIMIDATING.
TURNS OUT ALL IT TAKES IS THE PROPERLY APPLIED USE OF PYROTECHNICS. A DASH OF PHYSICAL FORCE.
AND A FLAIR FOR THE DRAMATIC.

A WEEK AGO, I'D NEVER GIVEN A SINGLE THOUGHT TO HOW I MIGHT BE ABLE TO MAKE A GROWN MAN SHIT HIMSELF.

A WEEK AGO, IN BUILDING 28 OF THE MARINUS LABS, I REALLY ONLY HAD TWO CONCERNS.

ONE: WHAT USE, ULTIMATELY, IS DARK MATTER?

FUEL? WEAPON?

THERE MUST BE SOME OTHER WAY TO USE IT...

TIMES HAVE CERTAINLY CHANGED.

TWO: AM I BRANDON'S GIRLFRIEND? OR ARE WE JUST "HAVING FUN"?

INTERNAL PRESSURE IS 30 KPA... I'M GONNA DROP IT RAPIDLY TO SIMULATE A TYPICAL NON-ATMOSPHERIC SET OF CONDITIONS.

I LOVE IT WHEN HE TALKS THAT WAY.

WE'D ALL BEEN HIRED BY MARINUS CORPORATION ABOUT A YEAR PRIOR. IT WAS A BRILLIANT MOVE ON THEIR PART, IF I DO SAY SO MYSELF, HIRING UP A GENERATION OF BURGEONING GENIUSES AND PUTTING THEM TO WORK ON THEIR MOST RADICAL PROJECTS.

AND THE LABS WERE LIKE A HIGH SCHOOL MADE JUST FOR US.

NOT *EVERY* VITRO TOOK THE OFFER. BUT AS FAR AS I'M CONCERNED, ALL OF THEM WITH ANY SENSE DID.

BUT OF COURSE, ALL SYSTEMS TREND TOWARDS CHAOS.

SADLY THAT'S NOT JUST A CLICHÉ. I CAN SHOW YOU THE MATH IF YOU WANT.

DROPPING PRESSURE NOW--

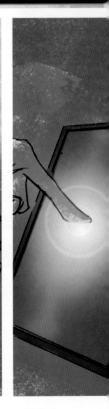

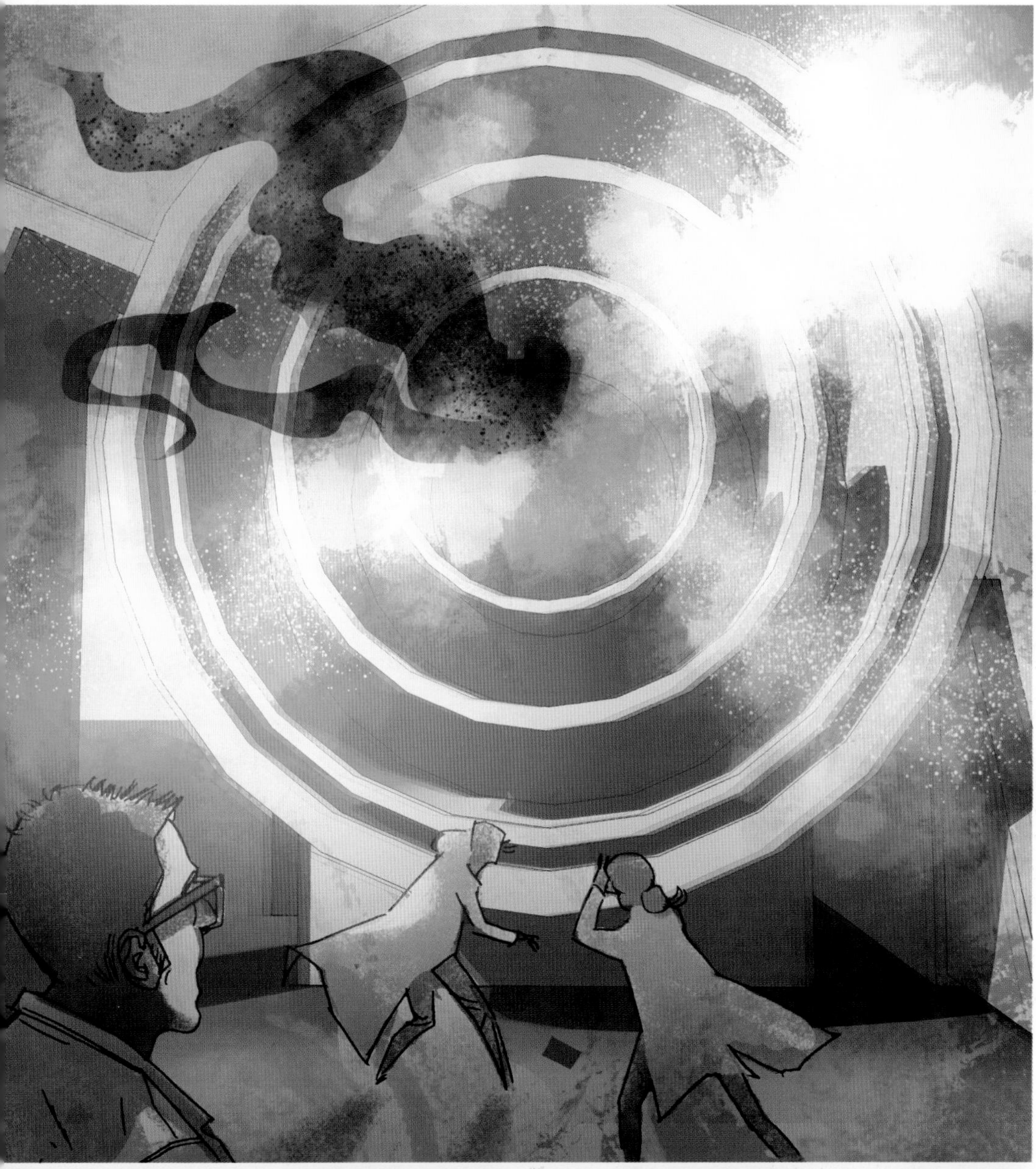

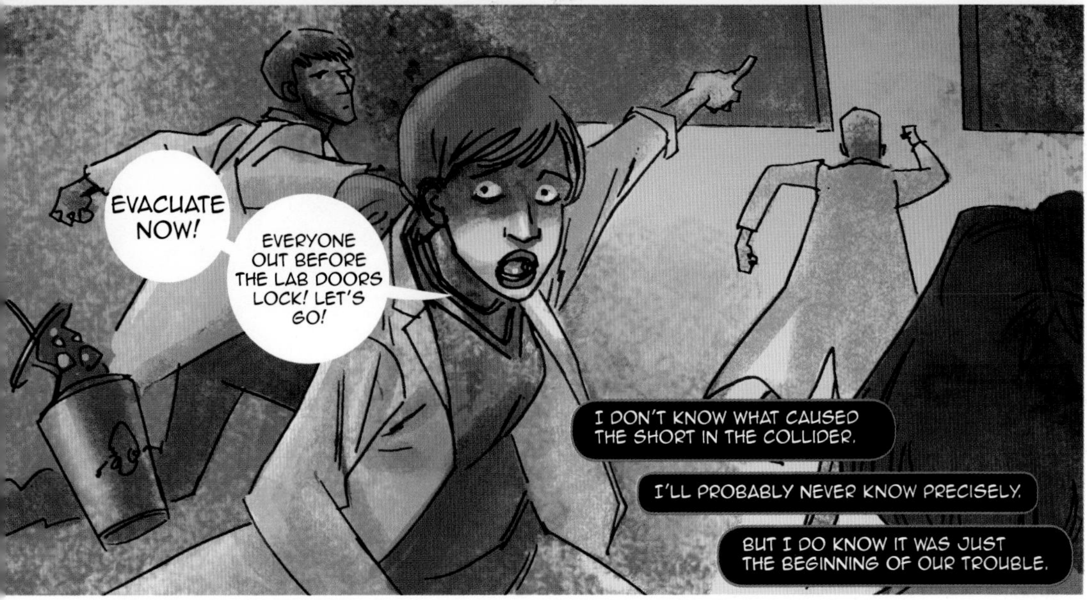
EVACUATE NOW!
EVERYONE OUT BEFORE THE LAB DOORS LOCK! LET'S GO!
I DON'T KNOW WHAT CAUSED THE SHORT IN THE COLLIDER.
I'LL PROBABLY NEVER KNOW PRECISELY.
BUT I DO KNOW IT WAS JUST THE BEGINNING OF OUR TROUBLE.

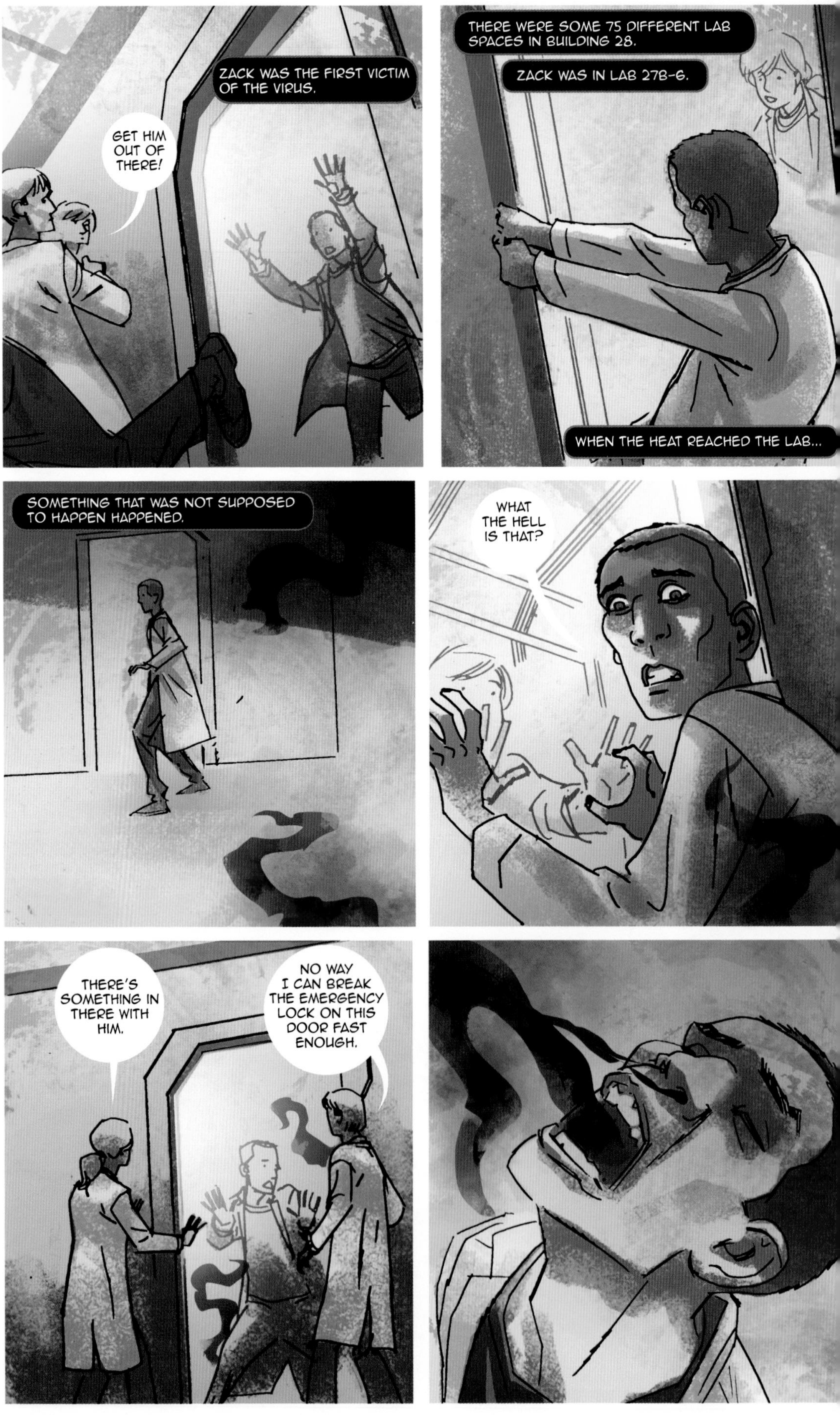
ZACK WAS THE FIRST VICTIM OF THE VIRUS.
GET HIM OUT OF THERE!
THERE WERE SOME 75 DIFFERENT LAB SPACES IN BUILDING 28.
ZACK WAS IN LAB 27B-6.
WHEN THE HEAT REACHED THE LAB...
SOMETHING THAT WAS NOT SUPPOSED TO HAPPEN HAPPENED.
WHAT THE HELL IS THAT?
THERE'S SOMETHING IN THERE WITH HIM.
NO WAY I CAN BREAK THE EMERGENCY LOCK ON THIS DOOR FAST ENOUGH.

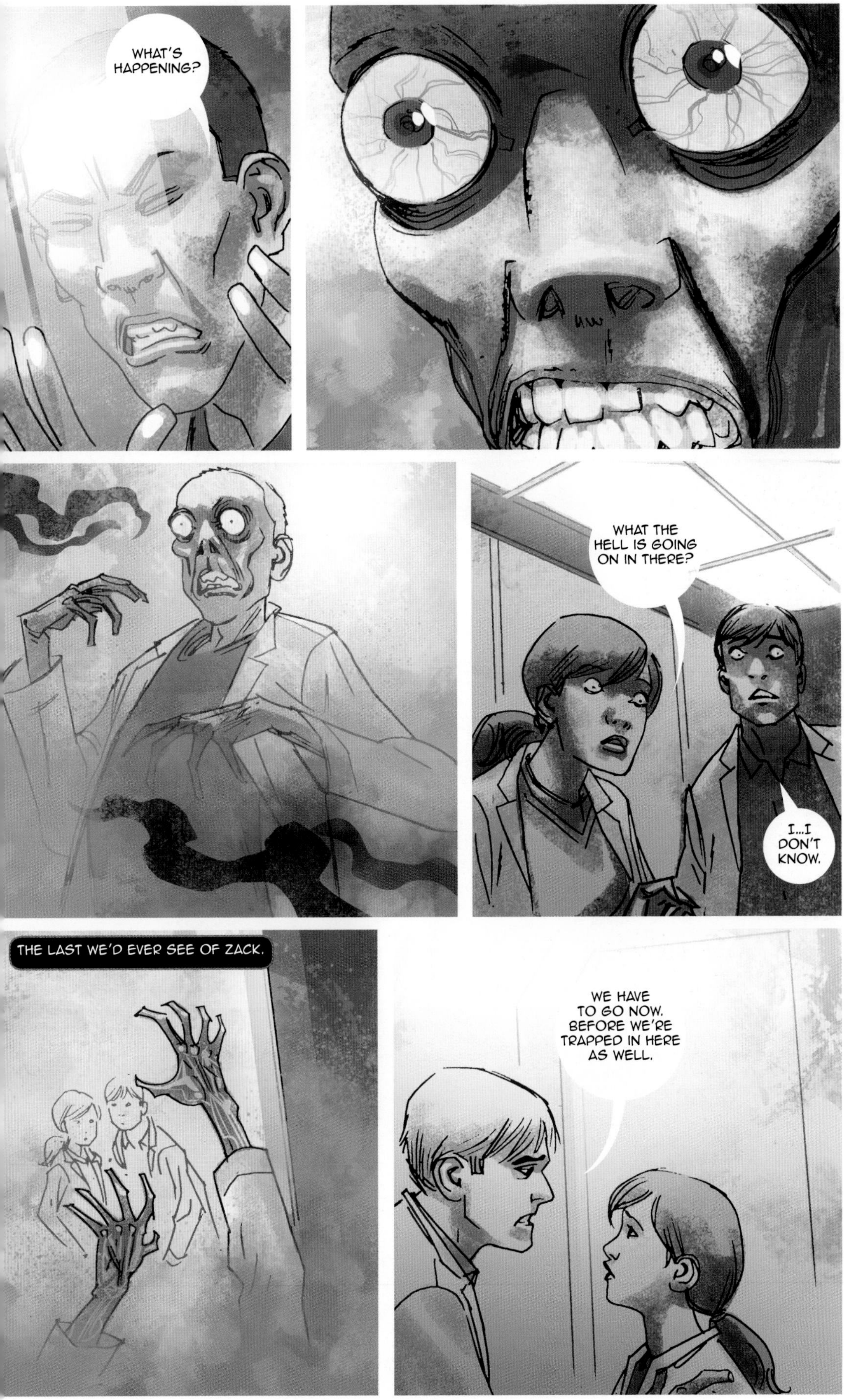
WHAT'S HAPPENING?
WHAT THE HELL IS GOING ON IN THERE?
I...I DON'T KNOW.
THE LAST WE'D EVER SEE OF ZACK.
WE HAVE TO GO NOW. BEFORE WE'RE TRAPPED IN HERE AS WELL.

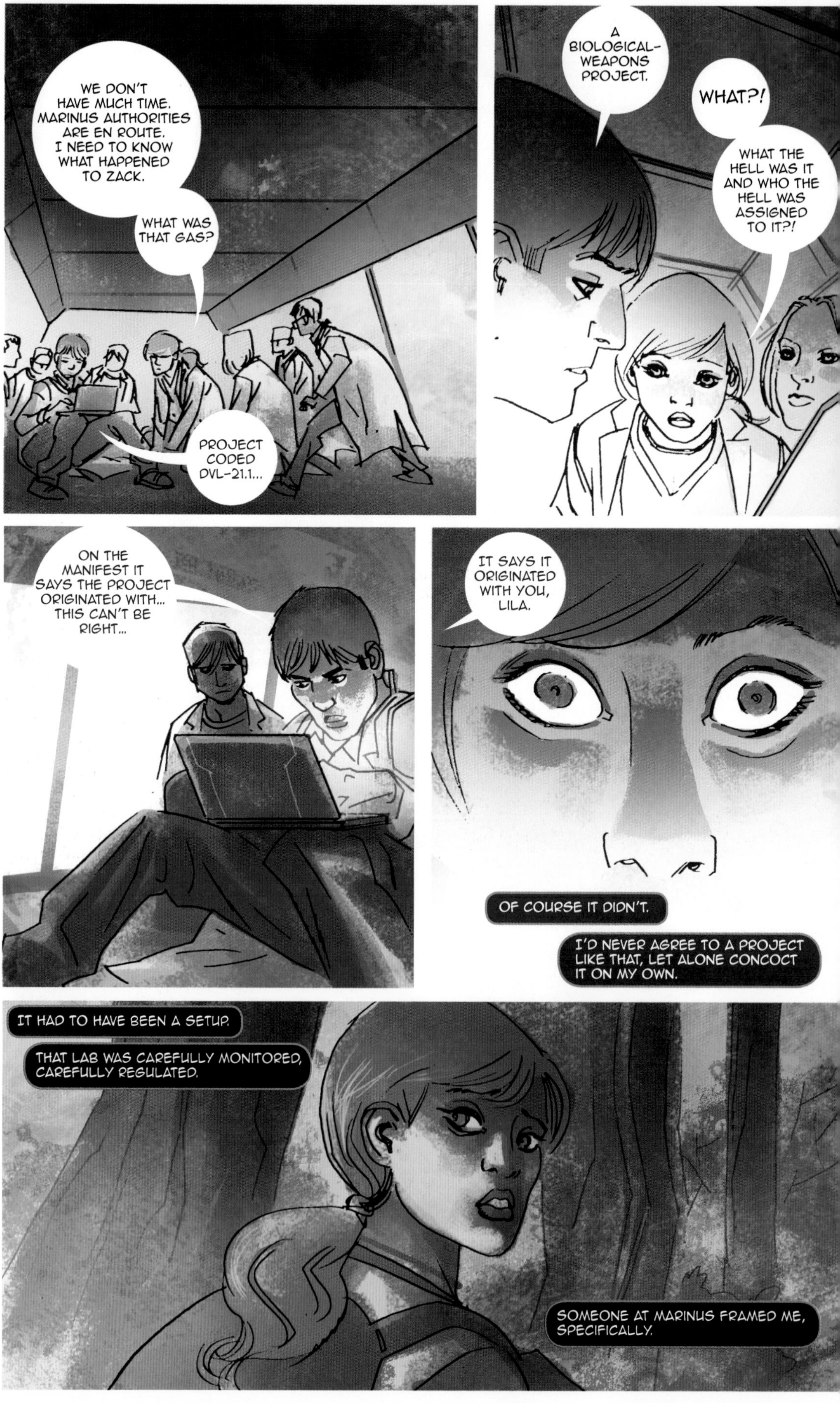
WE DON'T HAVE MUCH TIME. MARINUS AUTHORITIES ARE EN ROUTE. I NEED TO KNOW WHAT HAPPENED TO ZACK.
WHAT WAS THAT GAS?
PROJECT CODED DVL-21.1...
A BIOLOGICAL-WEAPONS PROJECT.
WHAT?!
WHAT THE HELL WAS IT AND WHO THE HELL WAS ASSIGNED TO IT?!
ON THE MANIFEST IT SAYS THE PROJECT ORIGINATED WITH... THIS CAN'T BE RIGHT...
IT SAYS IT ORIGINATED WITH YOU, LILA.
OF COURSE IT DIDN'T.
I'D NEVER AGREE TO A PROJECT LIKE THAT, LET ALONE CONCOCT IT ON MY OWN.
IT HAD TO HAVE BEEN A SETUP.
THAT LAB WAS CAREFULLY MONITORED, CAREFULLY REGULATED.
SOMEONE AT MARINUS FRAMED ME, SPECIFICALLY.

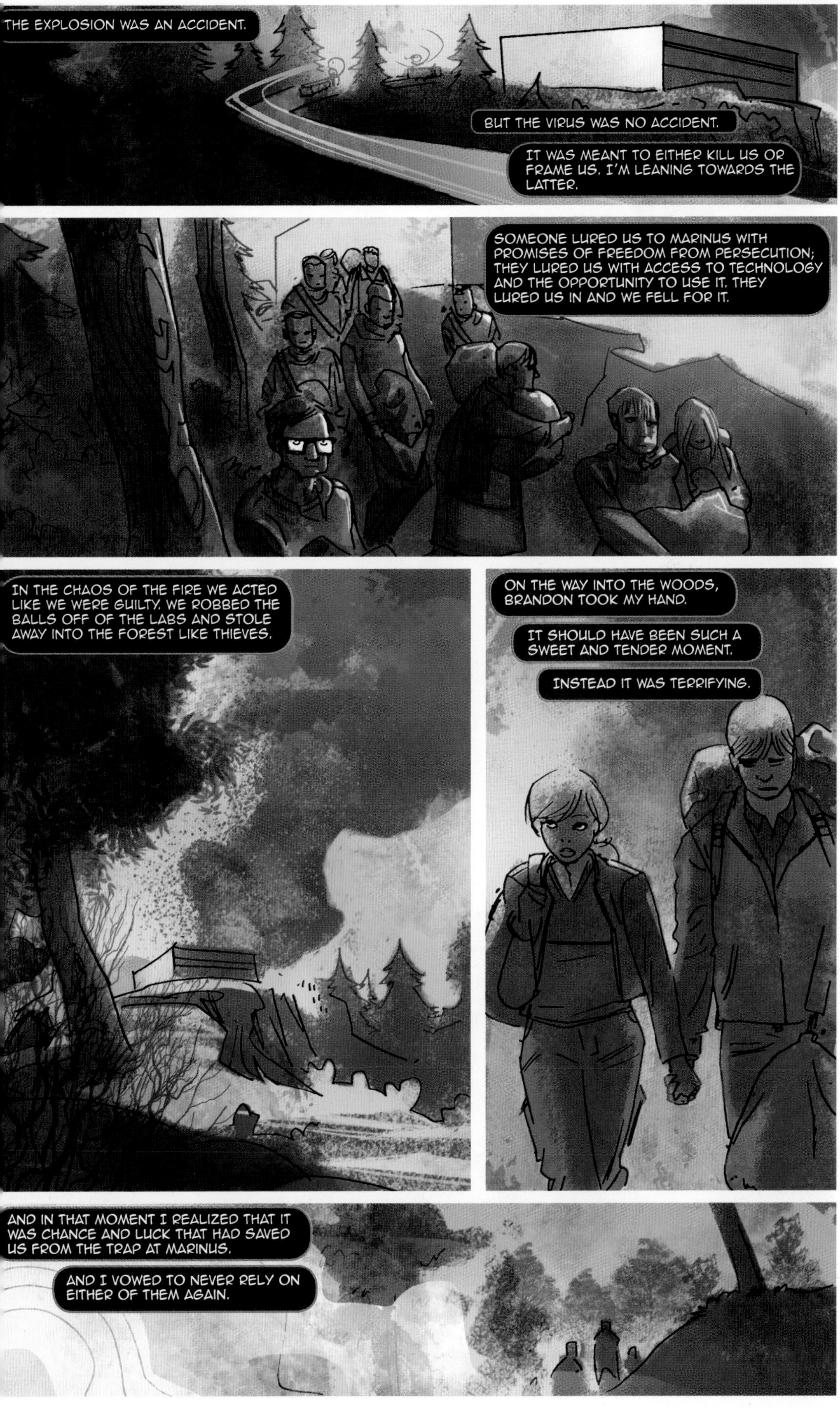
THE EXPLOSION WAS AN ACCIDENT.
BUT THE VIRUS WAS NO ACCIDENT.
IT WAS MEANT TO EITHER KILL US OR FRAME US. I'M LEANING TOWARDS THE LATTER.
SOMEONE LURED US TO MARINUS WITH PROMISES OF FREEDOM FROM PERSECUTION; THEY LURED US WITH ACCESS TO TECHNOLOGY AND THE OPPORTUNITY TO USE IT. THEY LURED US IN AND WE FELL FOR IT.
IN THE CHAOS OF THE FIRE WE ACTED LIKE WE WERE GUILTY. WE ROBBED THE BALLS OFF OF THE LABS AND STOLE AWAY INTO THE FOREST LIKE THIEVES.
ON THE WAY INTO THE WOODS, BRANDON TOOK MY HAND.
IT SHOULD HAVE BEEN SUCH A SWEET AND TENDER MOMENT.
INSTEAD IT WAS TERRIFYING.
AND IN THAT MOMENT I REALIZED THAT IT WAS CHANCE AND LUCK THAT HAD SAVED US FROM THE TRAP AT MARINUS.
AND I VOWED TO NEVER RELY ON EITHER OF THEM AGAIN.

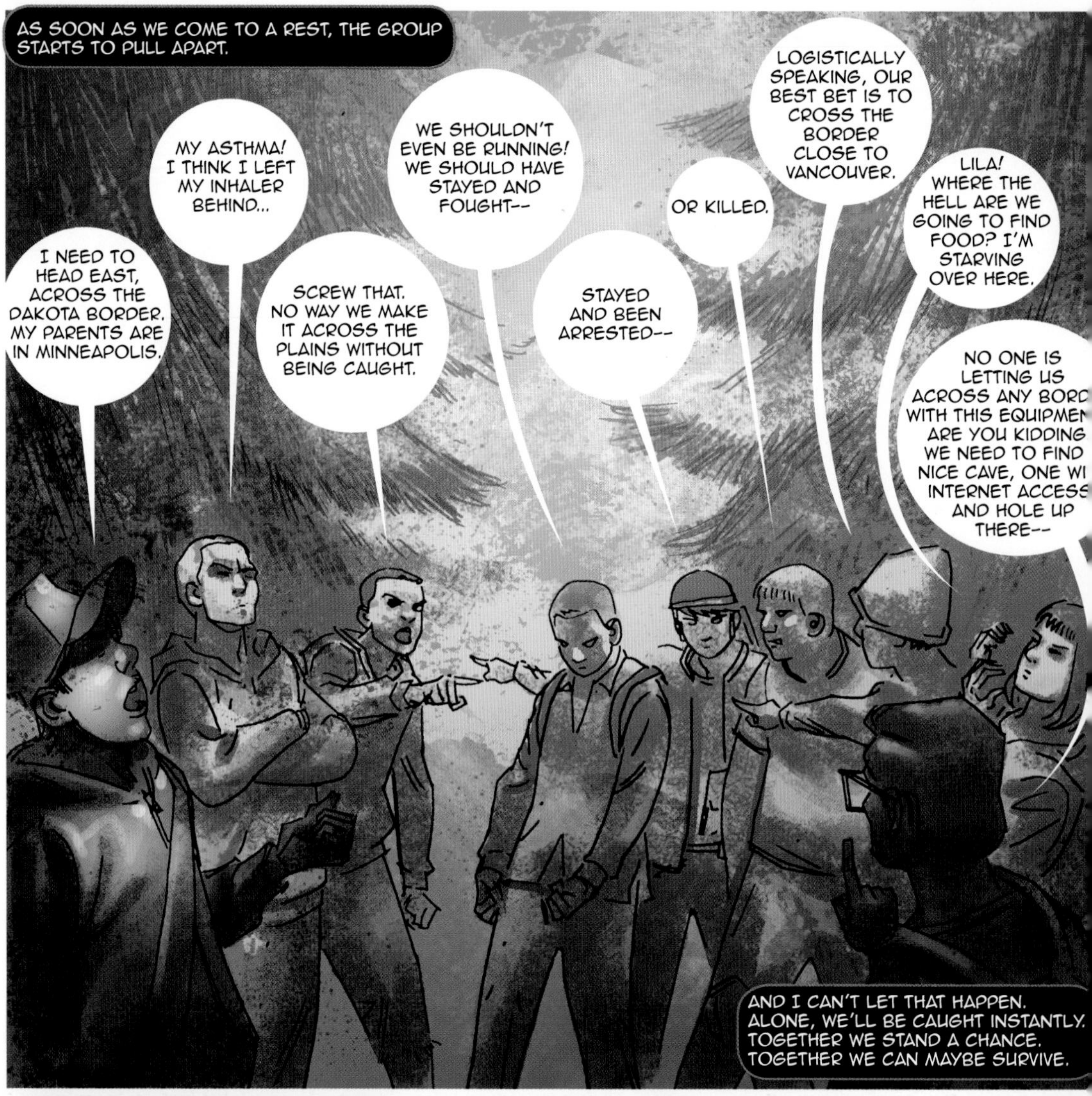
AS SOON AS WE COME TO A REST, THE GROUP STARTS TO PULL APART.
I NEED TO HEAD EAST, ACROSS THE DAKOTA BORDER. MY PARENTS ARE IN MINNEAPOLIS.
MY ASTHMA! I THINK I LEFT MY INHALER BEHIND...
SCREW THAT. NO WAY WE MAKE IT ACROSS THE PLAINS WITHOUT BEING CAUGHT.
WE SHOULDN'T EVEN BE RUNNING! WE SHOULD HAVE STAYED AND FOUGHT--
STAYED AND BEEN ARRESTED--
OR KILLED.
LOGISTICALLY SPEAKING, OUR BEST BET IS TO CROSS THE BORDER CLOSE TO VANCOUVER.
LILA! WHERE THE HELL ARE WE GOING TO FIND FOOD? I'M STARVING OVER HERE.
NO ONE IS LETTING US ACROSS ANY BORD WITH THIS EQUIPMEN ARE YOU KIDDING WE NEED TO FIND NICE CAVE, ONE WI INTERNET ACCESS AND HOLE UP THERE--
AND I CAN'T LET THAT HAPPEN. ALONE, WE'LL BE CAUGHT INSTANTLY. TOGETHER WE STAND A CHANCE. TOGETHER WE CAN MAYBE SURVIVE.

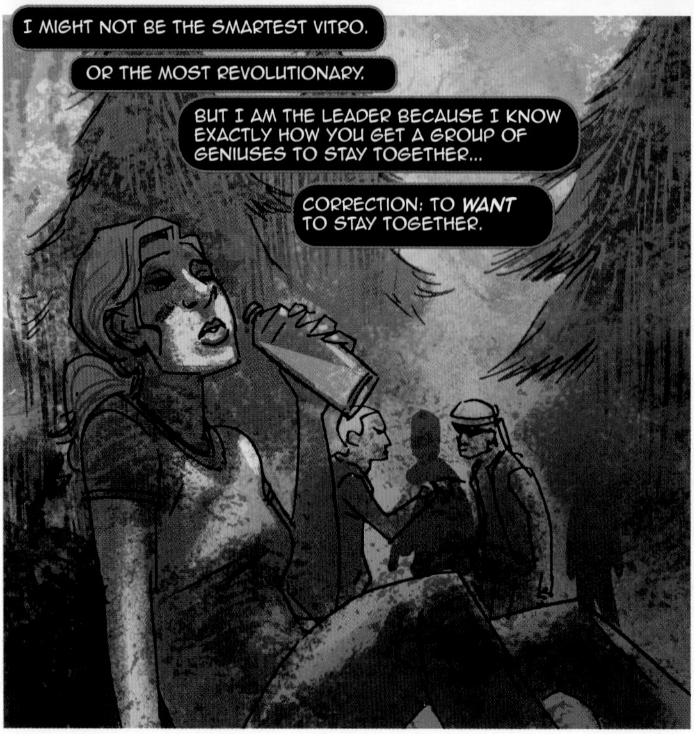
I MIGHT NOT BE THE SMARTEST VITRO.
OR THE MOST REVOLUTIONARY.
BUT I AM THE LEADER BECAUSE I KNOW EXACTLY HOW YOU GET A GROUP OF GENIUSES TO STAY TOGETHER...
CORRECTION: TO *WANT* TO STAY TOGETHER.

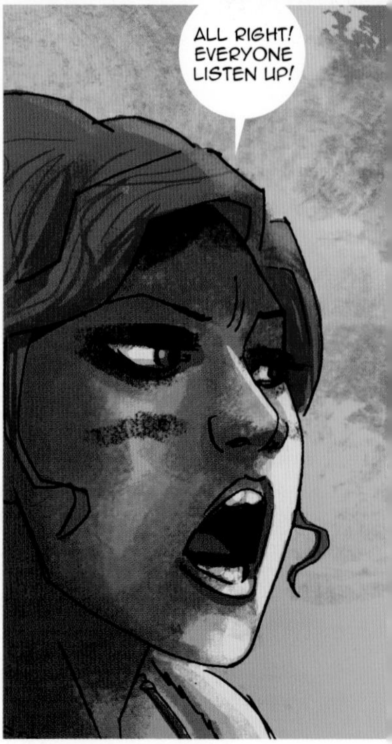
ALL RIGHT! EVERYONE LISTEN UP!

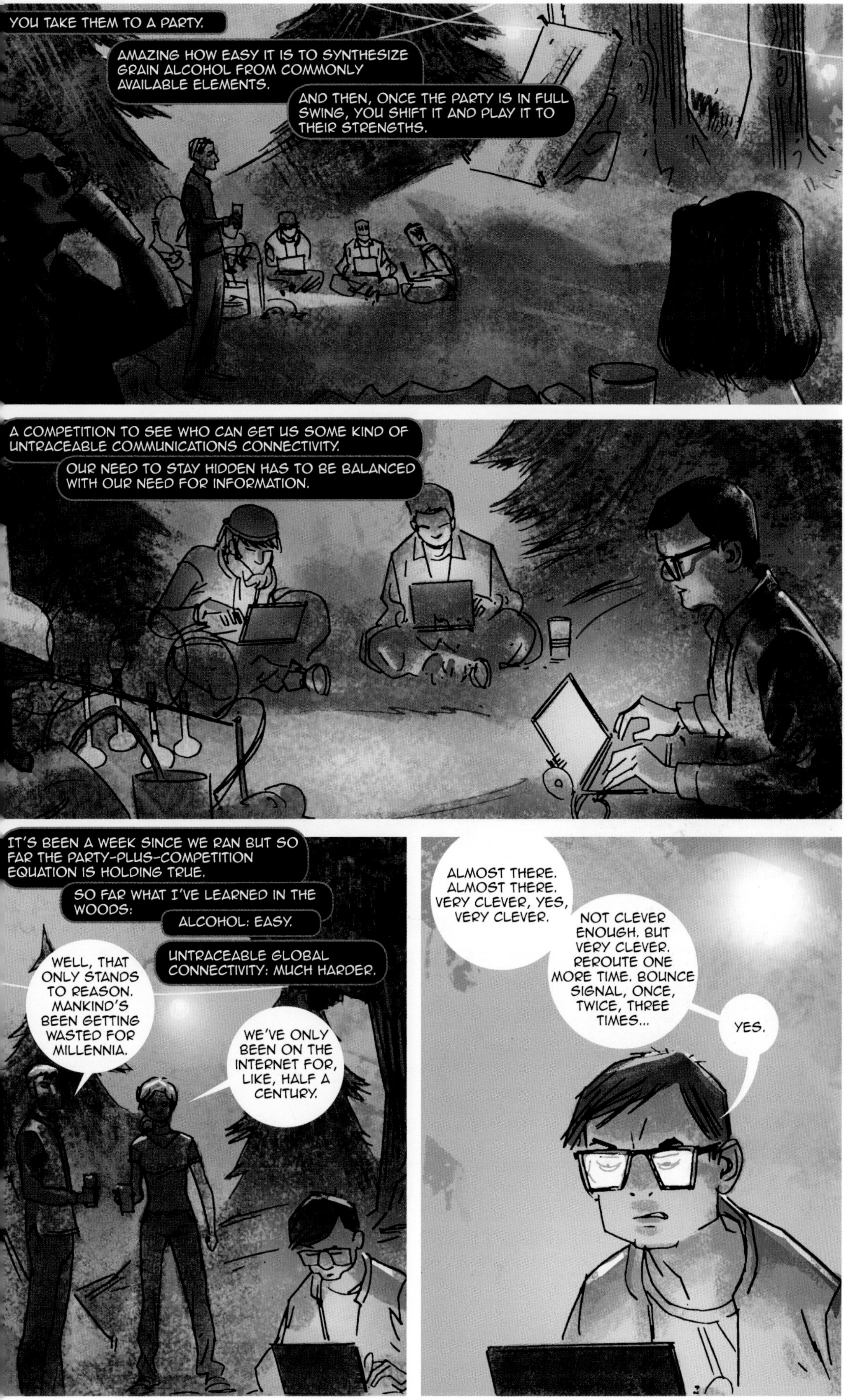

YOU TAKE THEM TO A PARTY.
AMAZING HOW EASY IT IS TO SYNTHESIZE GRAIN ALCOHOL FROM COMMONLY AVAILABLE ELEMENTS.
AND THEN, ONCE THE PARTY IS IN FULL SWING, YOU SHIFT IT AND PLAY IT TO THEIR STRENGTHS.
A COMPETITION TO SEE WHO CAN GET US SOME KIND OF UNTRACEABLE COMMUNICATIONS CONNECTIVITY.
OUR NEED TO STAY HIDDEN HAS TO BE BALANCED WITH OUR NEED FOR INFORMATION.
IT'S BEEN A WEEK SINCE WE RAN BUT SO FAR THE PARTY-PLUS-COMPETITION EQUATION IS HOLDING TRUE.
SO FAR WHAT I'VE LEARNED IN THE WOODS:
ALCOHOL: EASY.
UNTRACEABLE GLOBAL CONNECTIVITY: MUCH HARDER.
WELL, THAT ONLY STANDS TO REASON. MANKIND'S BEEN GETTING WASTED FOR MILLENNIA.
WE'VE ONLY BEEN ON THE INTERNET FOR, LIKE, HALF A CENTURY.
ALMOST THERE. ALMOST THERE. VERY CLEVER, YES, VERY CLEVER.
NOT CLEVER ENOUGH. BUT VERY CLEVER. REROUTE ONE MORE TIME. BOUNCE SIGNAL, ONCE, TWICE, THREE TIMES...
YES.

I GOT IT!

OH MAN, *NEIL* GOT IT! THAT SUCKS.

YOU CAN ALL SUCK MY DICK.

BOUNCED OFF A WEB OF OUTDATED, OUT-OF-SERVICE SATELLITES, MANY OF WHICH ARE IN RAPIDLY DETERIORATING ORBIT.

100% UNTRACEABLE. THOUGH THE CONNECTION WILL ONLY LAST FOR ABOUT THREE HOURS.

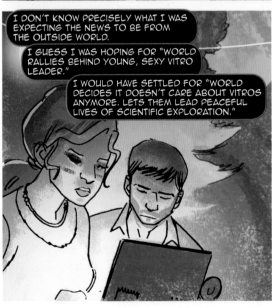

I DON'T KNOW PRECISELY WHAT I WAS EXPECTING THE NEWS TO BE FROM THE OUTSIDE WORLD.

I GUESS I WAS HOPING FOR "WORLD RALLIES BEHIND YOUNG, SEXY VITRO LEADER."

I WOULD HAVE SETTLED FOR "WORLD DECIDES IT DOESN'T CARE ABOUT VITROS ANYMORE. LETS THEM LEAD PEACEFUL LIVES OF SCIENTIFIC EXPLORATION."

SO YEAH. THIS IS REALLY NOT IN KEEPING WITH THOSE EXPECTATIONS.

SHIT. HELL. SHIT.

NEWS YOU CAN USE

Vitro Terrorists Being Rounded Up Across The Globe

VITROS CAPTURED

Vitro "Cell" In Custody In San Diego

Vitro Caught On The Run

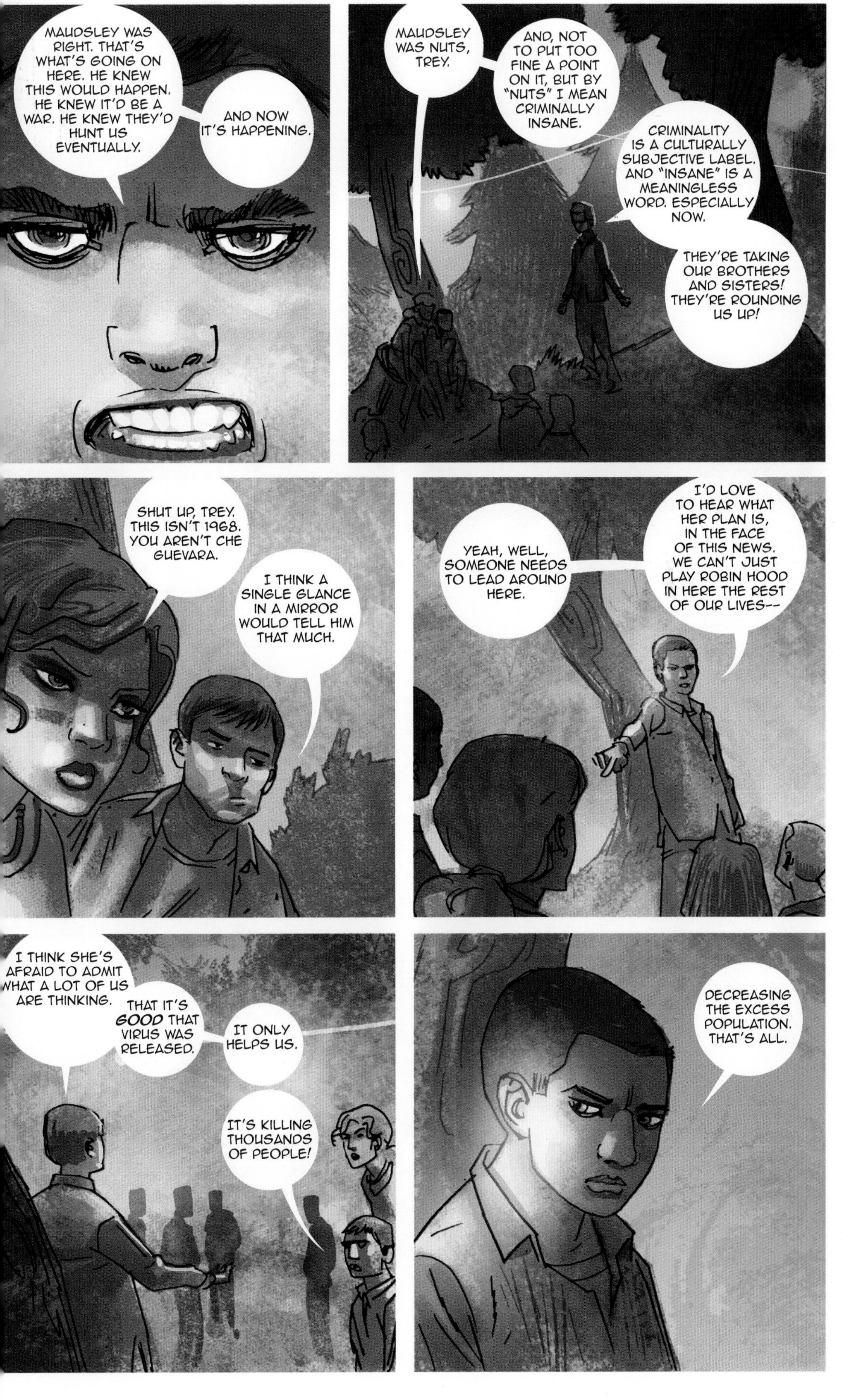
MAUDSLEY WAS RIGHT. THAT'S WHAT'S GOING ON HERE. HE KNEW THIS WOULD HAPPEN. HE KNEW IT'D BE A WAR. HE KNEW THEY'D HUNT US EVENTUALLY.
AND NOW IT'S HAPPENING.
MAUDSLEY WAS NUTS, TREY.
AND, NOT TO PUT TOO FINE A POINT ON IT, BUT BY "NUTS" I MEAN CRIMINALLY INSANE.
CRIMINALITY IS A CULTURALLY SUBJECTIVE LABEL. AND "INSANE" IS A MEANINGLESS WORD. ESPECIALLY NOW.
THEY'RE TAKING OUR BROTHERS AND SISTERS! THEY'RE ROUNDING US UP!
SHUT UP, TREY. THIS ISN'T 1968. YOU AREN'T CHE GUEVARA.
I THINK A SINGLE GLANCE IN A MIRROR WOULD TELL HIM THAT MUCH.
YEAH, WELL, SOMEONE NEEDS TO LEAD AROUND HERE.
I'D LOVE TO HEAR WHAT HER PLAN IS, IN THE FACE OF THIS NEWS. WE CAN'T JUST PLAY ROBIN HOOD IN HERE THE REST OF OUR LIVES--
I THINK SHE'S AFRAID TO ADMIT WHAT A LOT OF US ARE THINKING.
THAT IT'S *GOOD* THAT VIRUS WAS RELEASED.
IT ONLY HELPS US.
IT'S KILLING THOUSANDS OF PEOPLE!
DECREASING THE EXCESS POPULATION. THAT'S ALL.

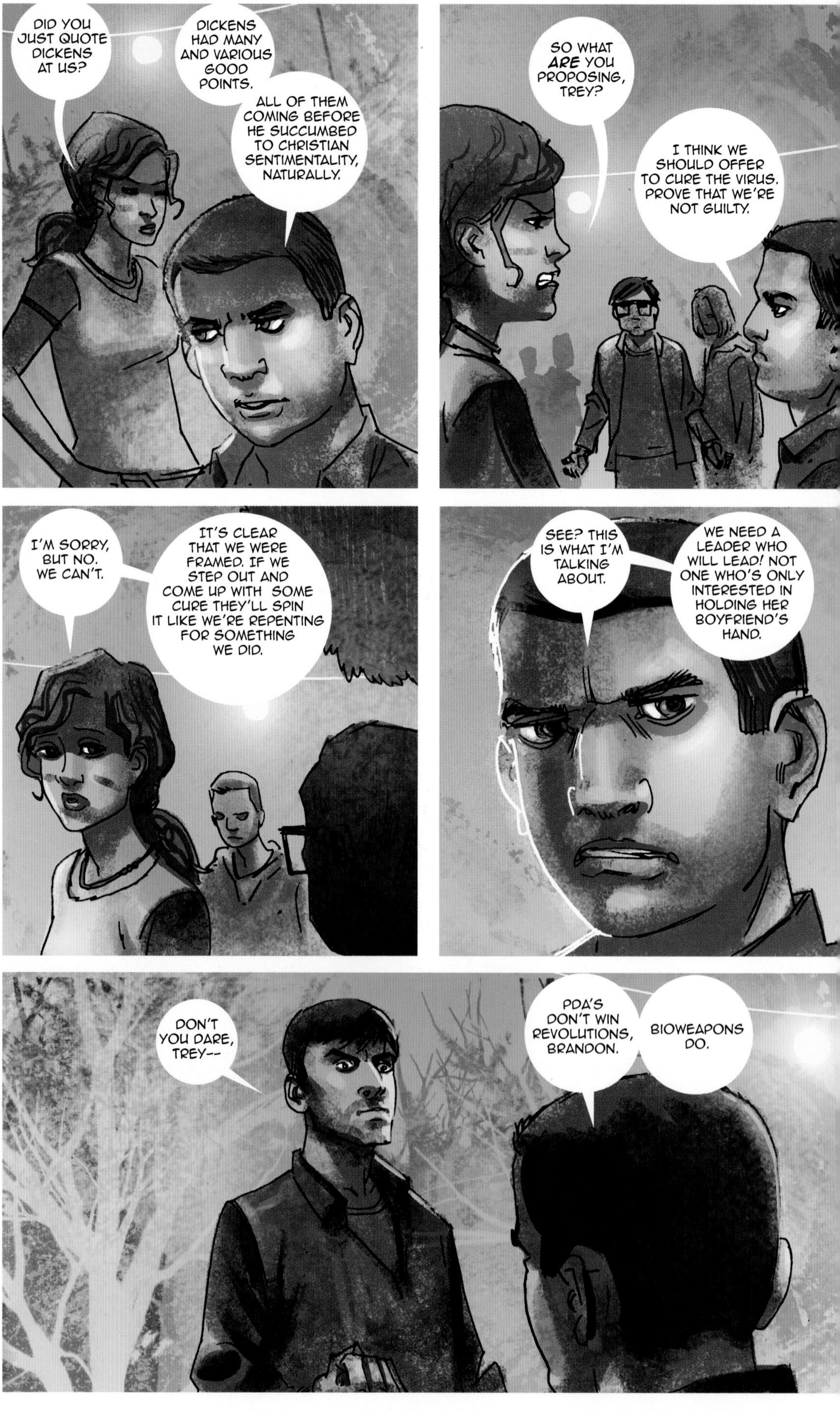
DID YOU JUST QUOTE DICKENS AT US?
DICKENS HAD MANY AND VARIOUS GOOD POINTS.
ALL OF THEM COMING BEFORE HE SUCCUMBED TO CHRISTIAN SENTIMENTALITY, NATURALLY.
SO WHAT *ARE* YOU PROPOSING, TREY?
I THINK WE SHOULD OFFER TO CURE THE VIRUS. PROVE THAT WE'RE NOT GUILTY.
I'M SORRY, BUT NO. WE CAN'T.
IT'S CLEAR THAT WE WERE FRAMED. IF WE STEP OUT AND COME UP WITH SOME CURE THEY'LL SPIN IT LIKE WE'RE REPENTING FOR SOMETHING WE DID.
SEE? THIS IS WHAT I'M TALKING ABOUT.
WE NEED A LEADER WHO WILL LEAD! NOT ONE WHO'S ONLY INTERESTED IN HOLDING HER BOYFRIEND'S HAND.
DON'T YOU DARE, TREY--
PDA'S DON'T WIN REVOLUTIONS, BRANDON.
BIOWEAPONS DO.

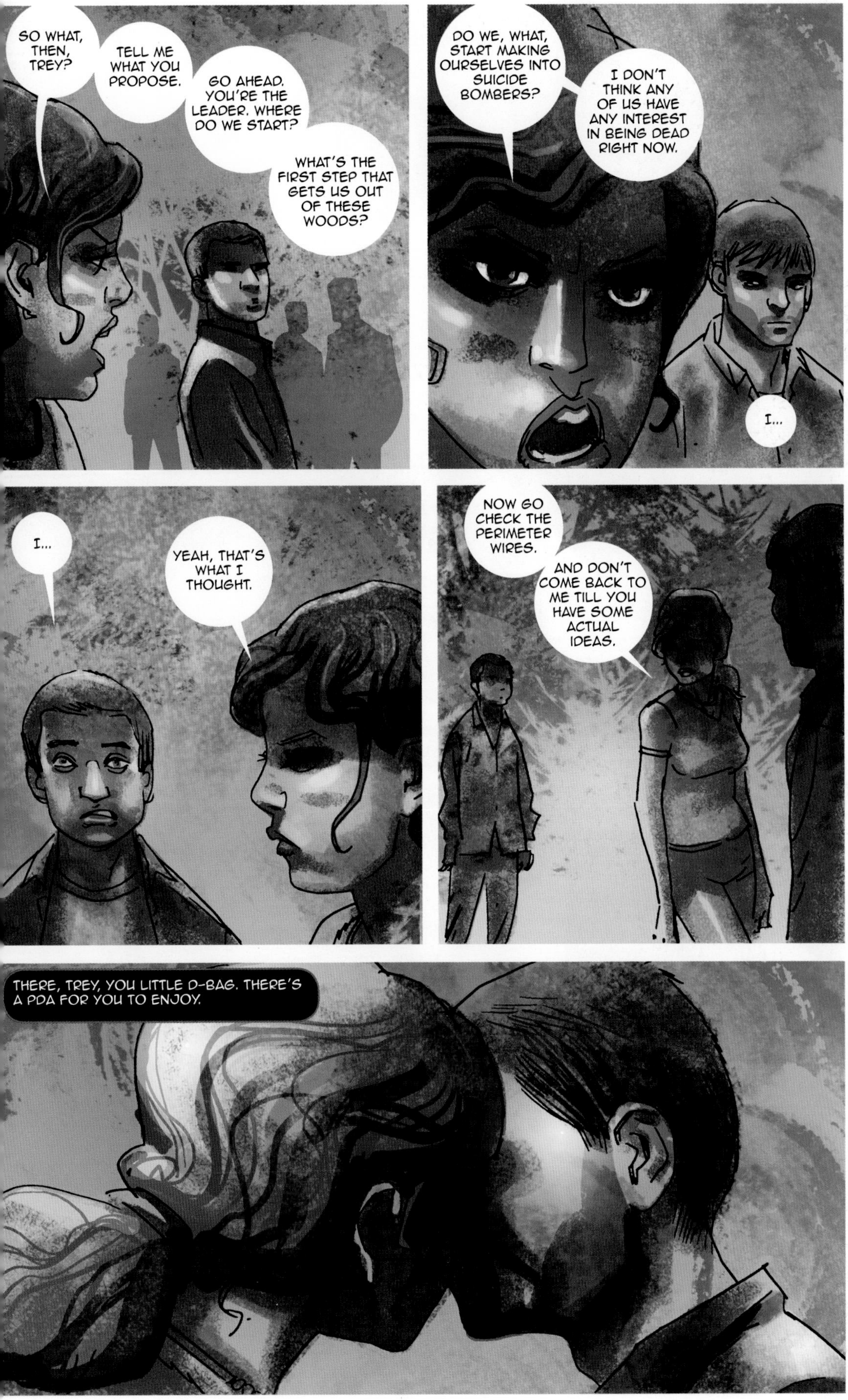
SO WHAT, THEN, TREY?
TELL ME WHAT YOU PROPOSE.
GO AHEAD. YOU'RE THE LEADER. WHERE DO WE START?
WHAT'S THE FIRST STEP THAT GETS US OUT OF THESE WOODS?
DO WE, WHAT, START MAKING OURSELVES INTO SUICIDE BOMBERS?
I DON'T THINK ANY OF US HAVE ANY INTEREST IN BEING DEAD RIGHT NOW.
I...
I...
YEAH, THAT'S WHAT I THOUGHT.
NOW GO CHECK THE PERIMETER WIRES.
AND DON'T COME BACK TO ME TILL YOU HAVE SOME ACTUAL IDEAS.
THERE, TREY, YOU LITTLE D-BAG. THERE'S A PDA FOR YOU TO ENJOY.

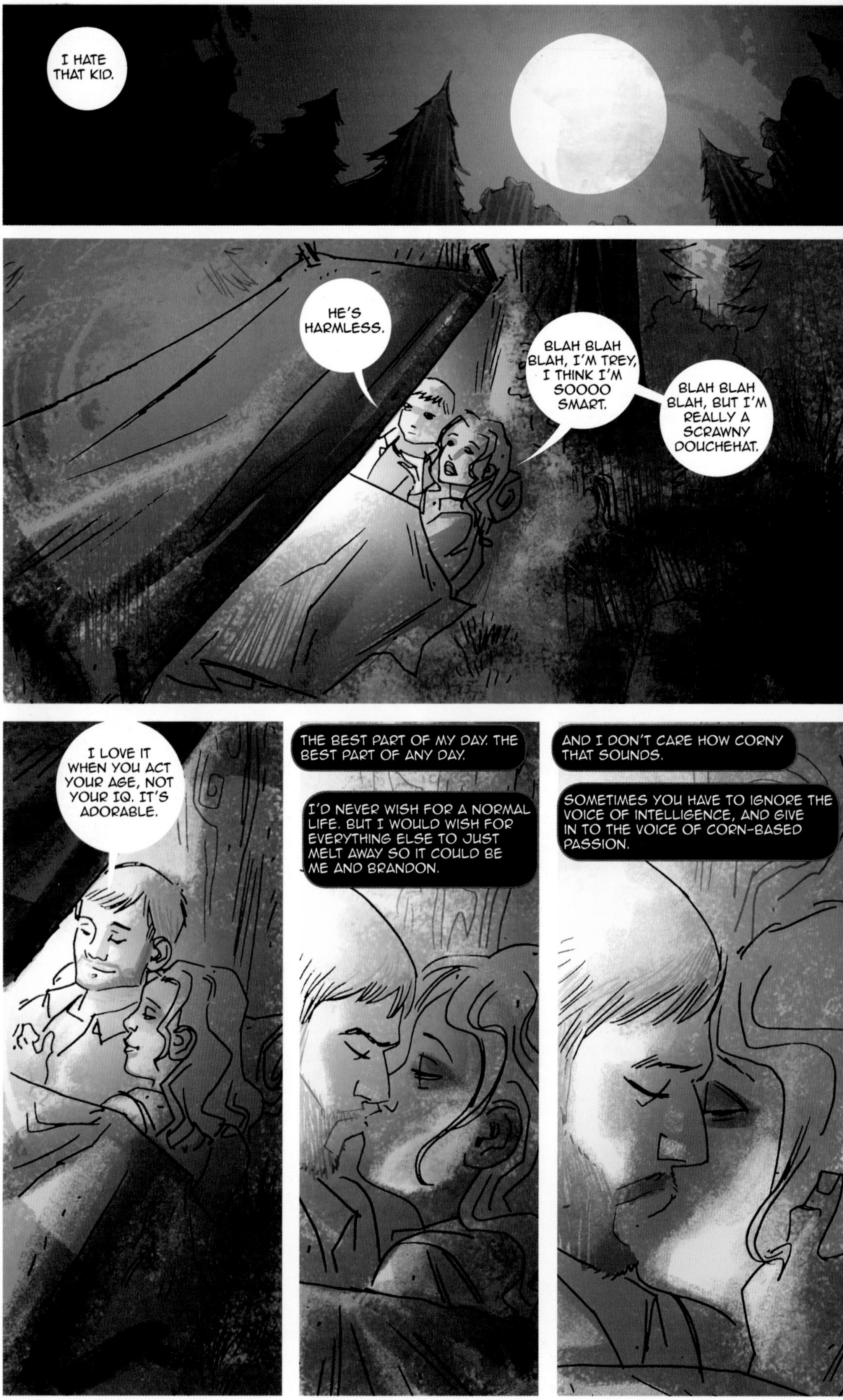
I HATE THAT KID.
HE'S HARMLESS.
BLAH BLAH BLAH, I'M TREY, I THINK I'M SOOOO SMART.
BLAH BLAH BLAH, BUT I'M REALLY A SCRAWNY DOUCHEHAT.
I LOVE IT WHEN YOU ACT YOUR AGE, NOT YOUR IQ. IT'S ADORABLE.
THE BEST PART OF MY DAY. THE BEST PART OF ANY DAY.
I'D NEVER WISH FOR A NORMAL LIFE. BUT I WOULD WISH FOR EVERYTHING ELSE TO JUST MELT AWAY SO IT COULD BE ME AND BRANDON.
AND I DON'T CARE HOW CORNY THAT SOUNDS.
SOMETIMES YOU HAVE TO IGNORE THE VOICE OF INTELLIGENCE, AND GIVE IN TO THE VOICE OF CORN-BASED PASSION.

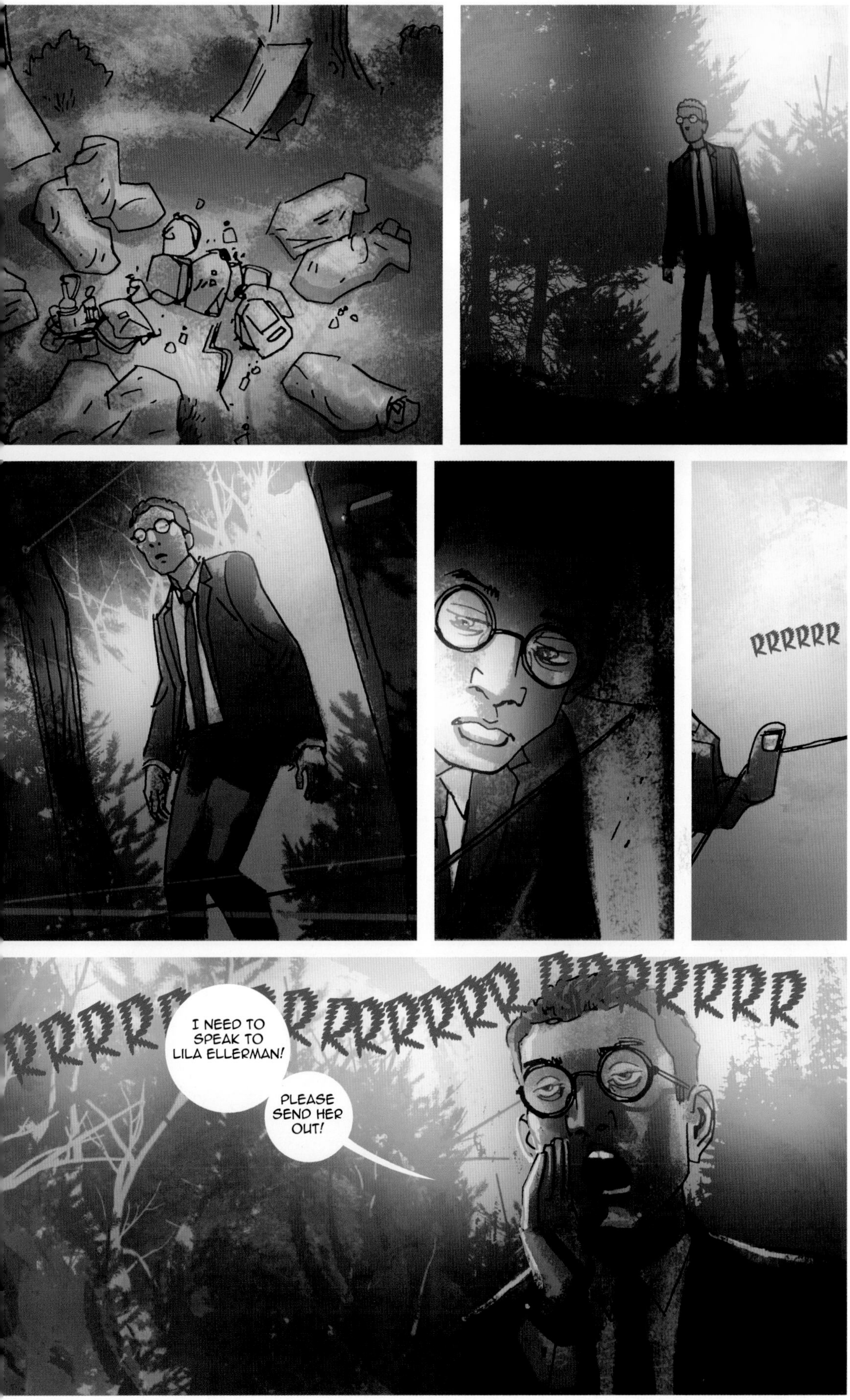
RRRRRR
RRRRRRRRRRRRRRRRRRRRRR
I NEED TO SPEAK TO LILA ELLERMAN!
PLEASE SEND HER OUT!

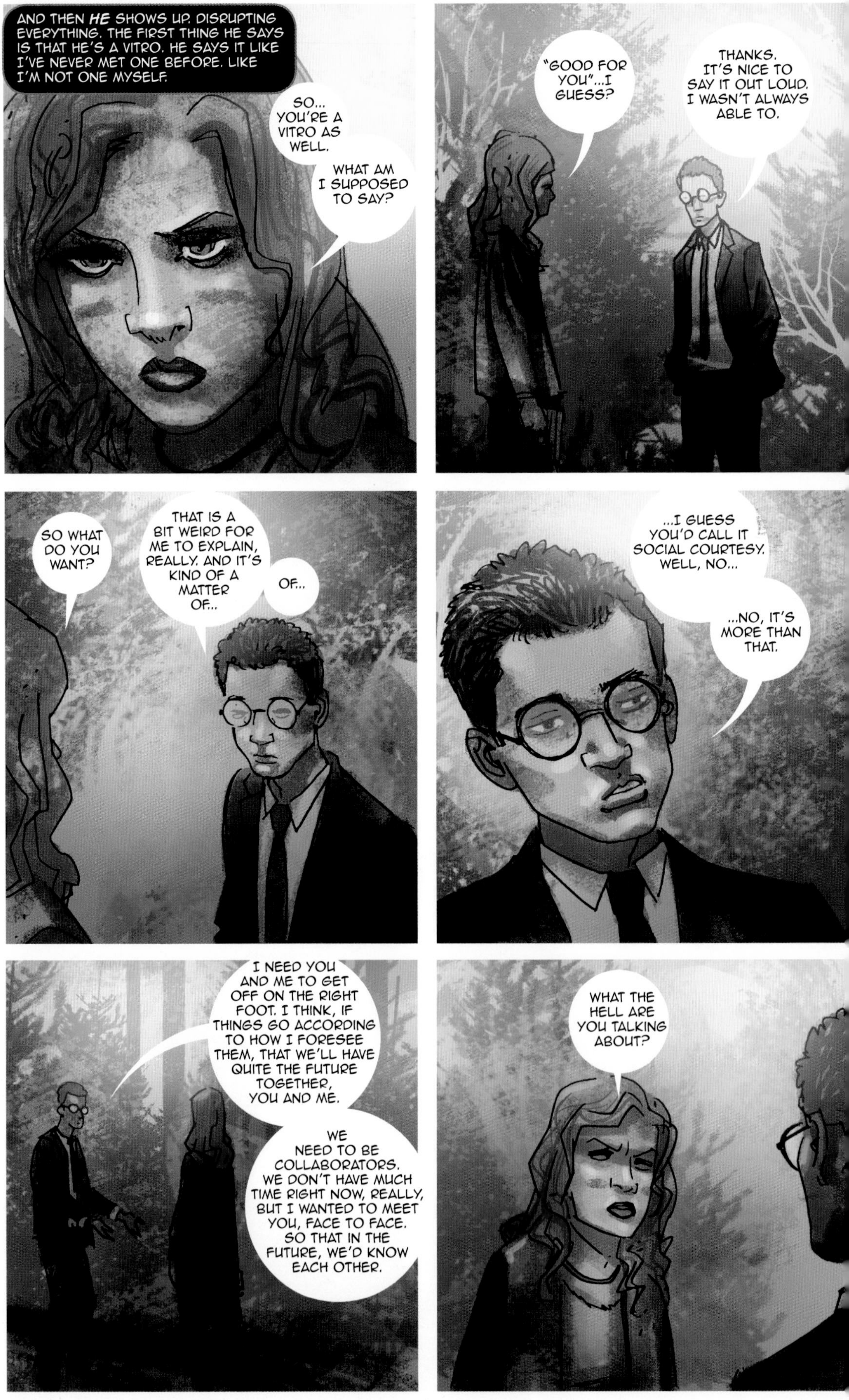

AND THEN **HE** SHOWS UP. DISRUPTING EVERYTHING. THE FIRST THING HE SAYS IS THAT HE'S A VITRO. HE SAYS IT LIKE I'VE NEVER MET ONE BEFORE. LIKE I'M NOT ONE MYSELF.
SO... YOU'RE A VITRO AS WELL.
WHAT AM I SUPPOSED TO SAY?
"GOOD FOR YOU"...I GUESS?
THANKS. IT'S NICE TO SAY IT OUT LOUD. I WASN'T ALWAYS ABLE TO.
SO WHAT DO YOU WANT?
THAT IS A BIT WEIRD FOR ME TO EXPLAIN, REALLY. AND IT'S KIND OF A MATTER OF...
OF...
...I GUESS YOU'D CALL IT SOCIAL COURTESY. WELL, NO...
...NO, IT'S MORE THAN THAT.
I NEED YOU AND ME TO GET OFF ON THE RIGHT FOOT. I THINK, IF THINGS GO ACCORDING TO HOW I FORESEE THEM, THAT WE'LL HAVE QUITE THE FUTURE TOGETHER, YOU AND ME.
WE NEED TO BE COLLABORATORS. WE DON'T HAVE MUCH TIME RIGHT NOW, REALLY, BUT I WANTED TO MEET YOU, FACE TO FACE. SO THAT IN THE FUTURE, WE'D KNOW EACH OTHER.
WHAT THE HELL ARE YOU TALKING ABOUT?

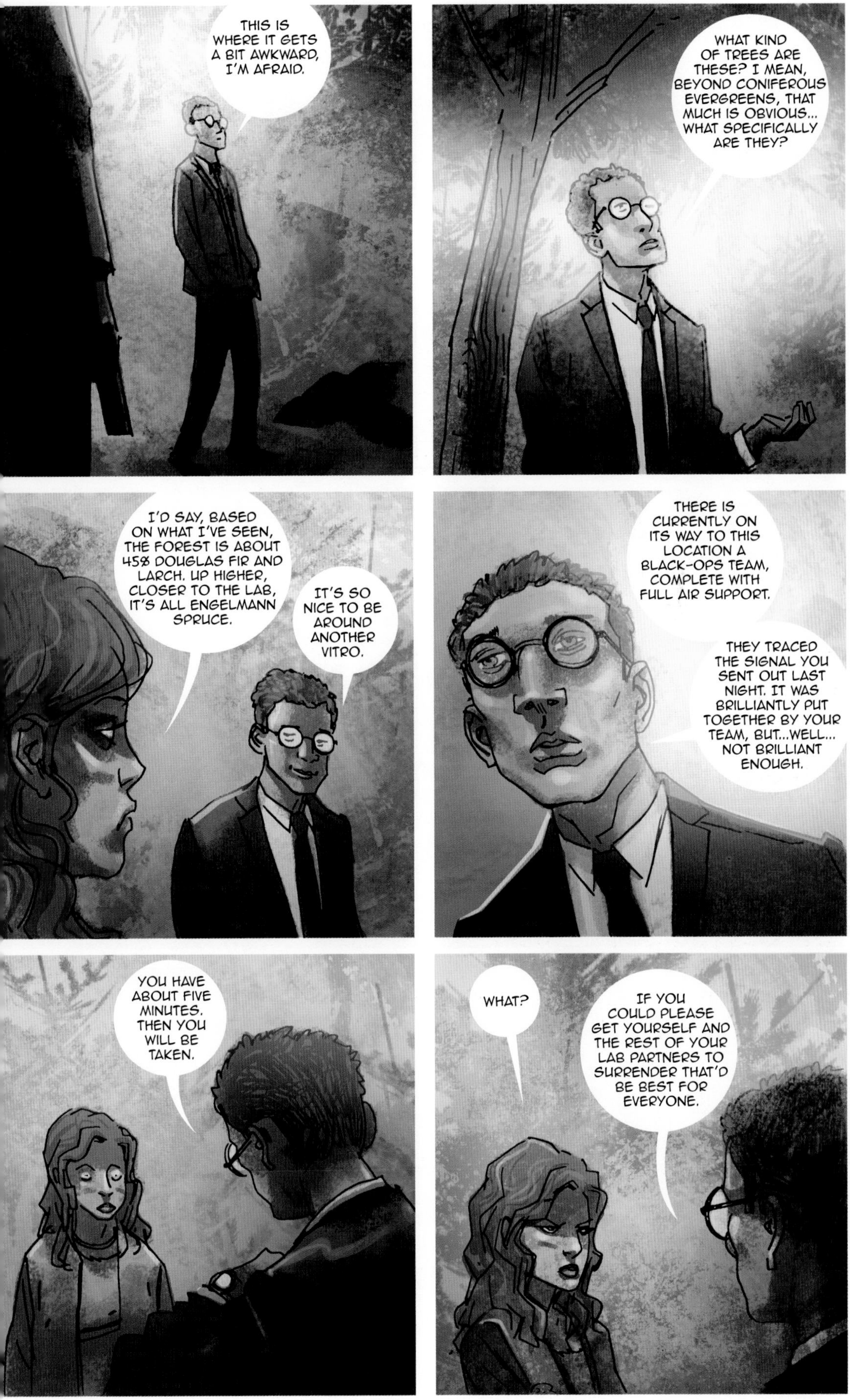
THIS IS WHERE IT GETS A BIT AWKWARD, I'M AFRAID.
WHAT KIND OF TREES ARE THESE? I MEAN, BEYOND CONIFEROUS EVERGREENS, THAT MUCH IS OBVIOUS... WHAT SPECIFICALLY ARE THEY?
I'D SAY, BASED ON WHAT I'VE SEEN, THE FOREST IS ABOUT 45% DOUGLAS FIR AND LARCH. UP HIGHER, CLOSER TO THE LAB, IT'S ALL ENGELMANN SPRUCE.
IT'S SO NICE TO BE AROUND ANOTHER VITRO.
THERE IS CURRENTLY ON ITS WAY TO THIS LOCATION A BLACK-OPS TEAM, COMPLETE WITH FULL AIR SUPPORT.
THEY TRACED THE SIGNAL YOU SENT OUT LAST NIGHT. IT WAS BRILLIANTLY PUT TOGETHER BY YOUR TEAM, BUT...WELL... NOT BRILLIANT ENOUGH.
YOU HAVE ABOUT FIVE MINUTES. THEN YOU WILL BE TAKEN.
WHAT?
IF YOU COULD PLEASE GET YOURSELF AND THE REST OF YOUR LAB PARTNERS TO SURRENDER THAT'D BE BEST FOR EVERYONE.

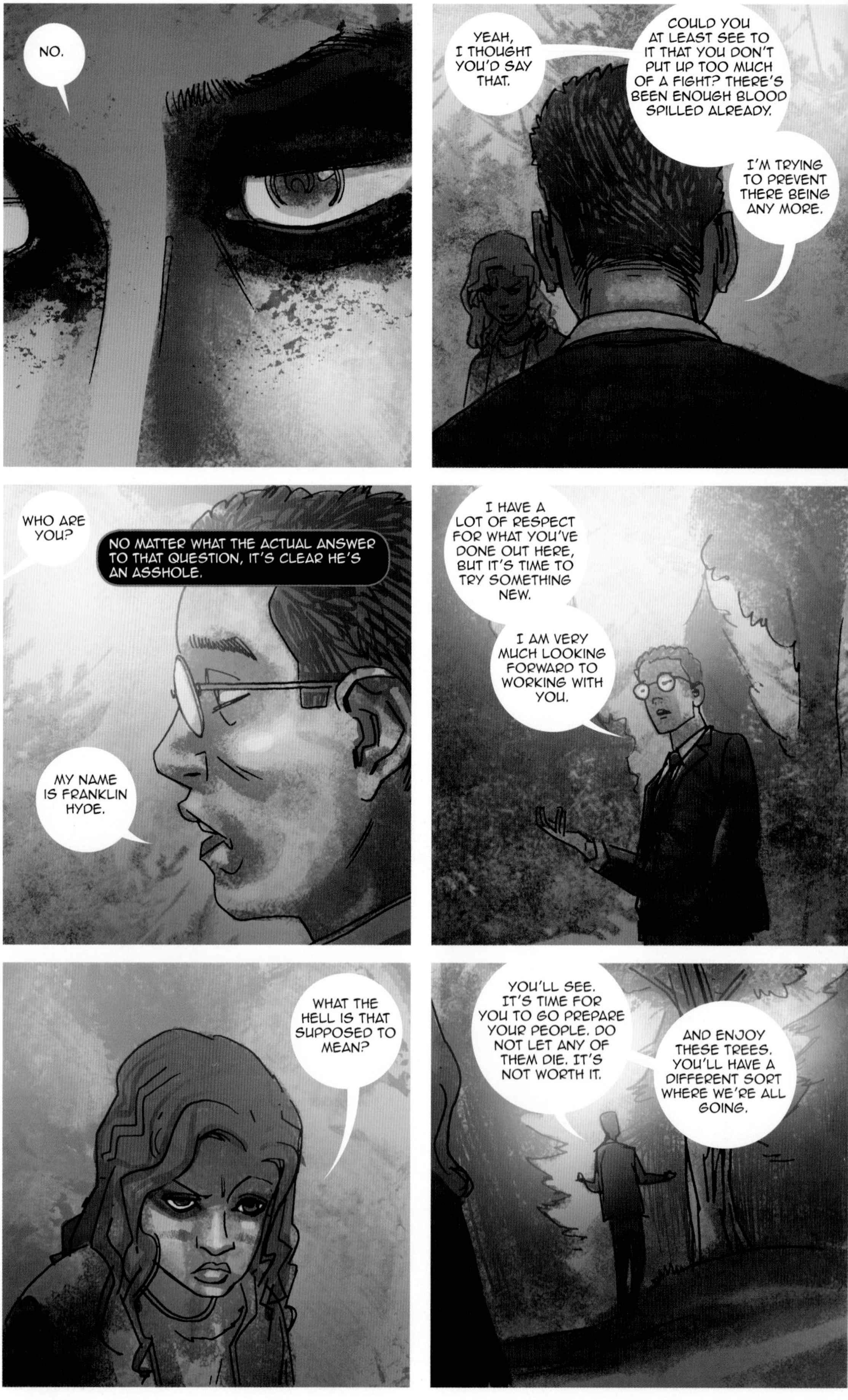
NO.
YEAH, I THOUGHT YOU'D SAY THAT.
COULD YOU AT LEAST SEE TO IT THAT YOU DON'T PUT UP TOO MUCH OF A FIGHT? THERE'S BEEN ENOUGH BLOOD SPILLED ALREADY.
I'M TRYING TO PREVENT THERE BEING ANY MORE.
WHO ARE YOU?
NO MATTER WHAT THE ACTUAL ANSWER TO THAT QUESTION, IT'S CLEAR HE'S AN ASSHOLE.
MY NAME IS FRANKLIN HYDE.
I HAVE A LOT OF RESPECT FOR WHAT YOU'VE DONE OUT HERE, BUT IT'S TIME TO TRY SOMETHING NEW.
I AM VERY MUCH LOOKING FORWARD TO WORKING WITH YOU.
WHAT THE HELL IS THAT SUPPOSED TO MEAN?
YOU'LL SEE. IT'S TIME FOR YOU TO GO PREPARE YOUR PEOPLE. DO NOT LET ANY OF THEM DIE. IT'S NOT WORTH IT.
AND ENJOY THESE TREES. YOU'LL HAVE A DIFFERENT SORT WHERE WE'RE ALL GOING.

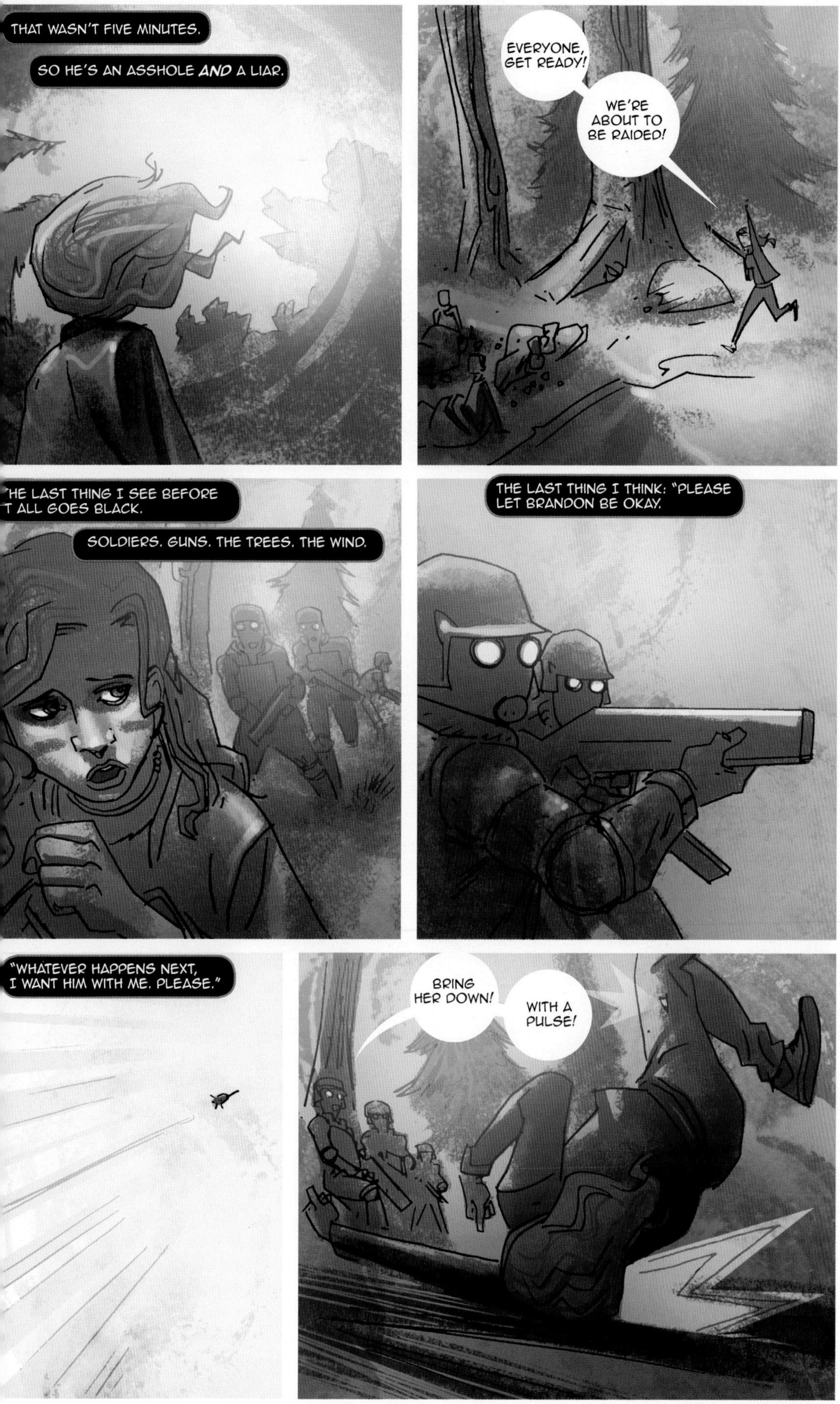
THAT WASN'T FIVE MINUTES.
SO HE'S AN ASSHOLE AND A LIAR.
EVERYONE, GET READY!
WE'RE ABOUT TO BE RAIDED!
HE LAST THING I SEE BEFORE T ALL GOES BLACK.
SOLDIERS. GUNS. THE TREES. THE WIND.
THE LAST THING I THINK: "PLEASE LET BRANDON BE OKAY.
"WHATEVER HAPPENS NEXT, I WANT HIM WITH ME. PLEASE."
BRING HER DOWN!
WITH A PULSE!

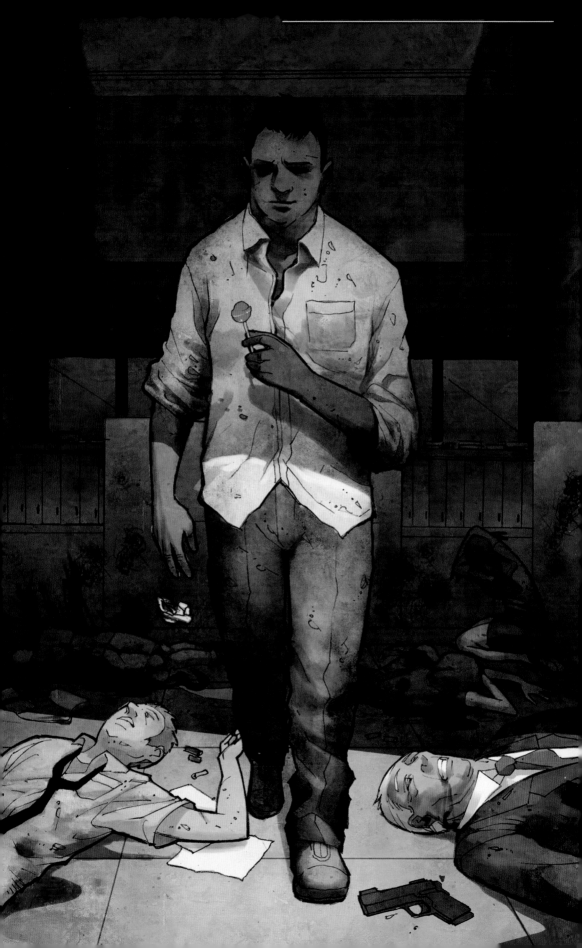

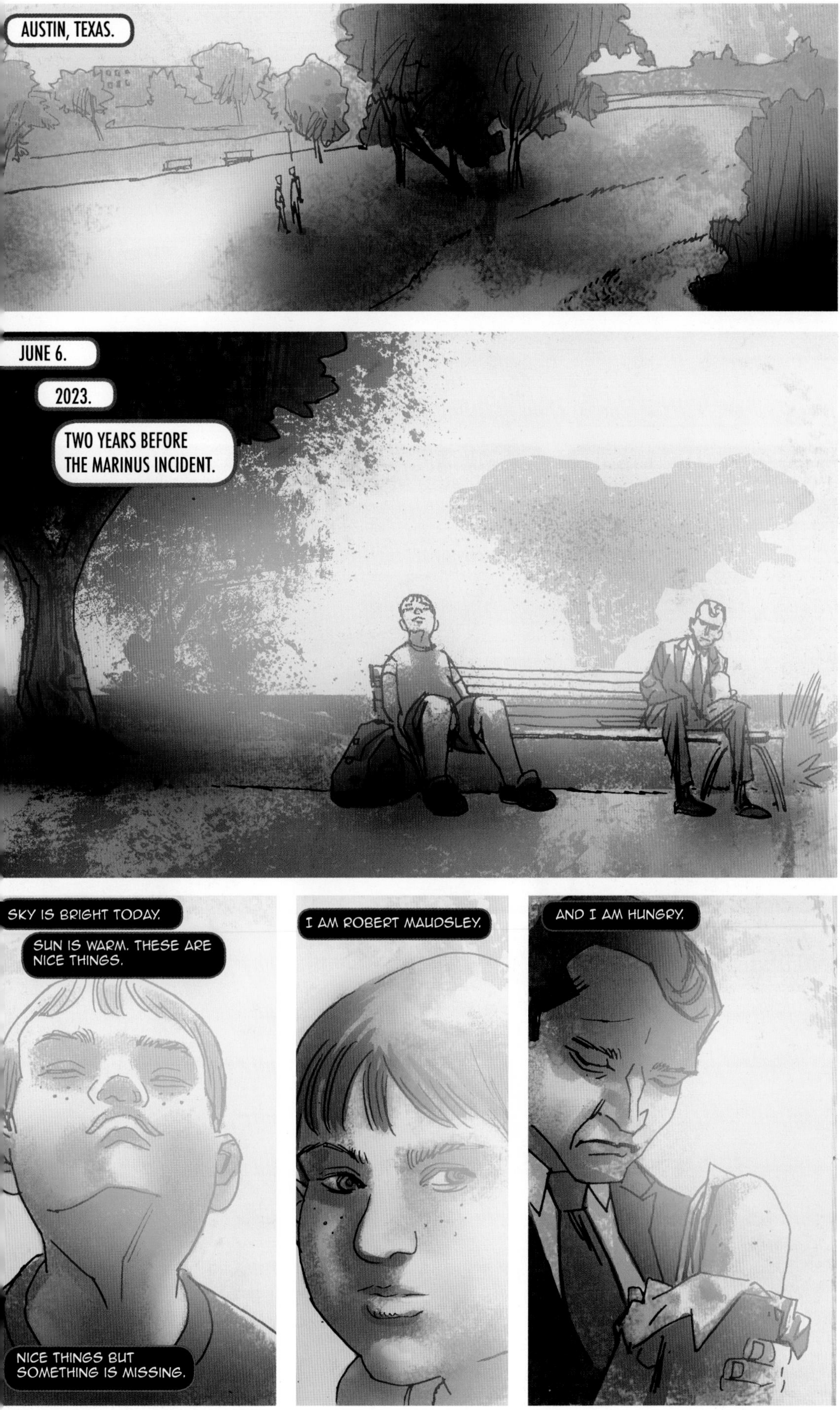
AUSTIN, TEXAS.
JUNE 6.
2023.
TWO YEARS BEFORE THE MARINUS INCIDENT.
SKY IS BRIGHT TODAY.
SUN IS WARM. THESE ARE NICE THINGS.
NICE THINGS BUT SOMETHING IS MISSING.
I AM ROBERT MAUDSLEY.
AND I AM HUNGRY.

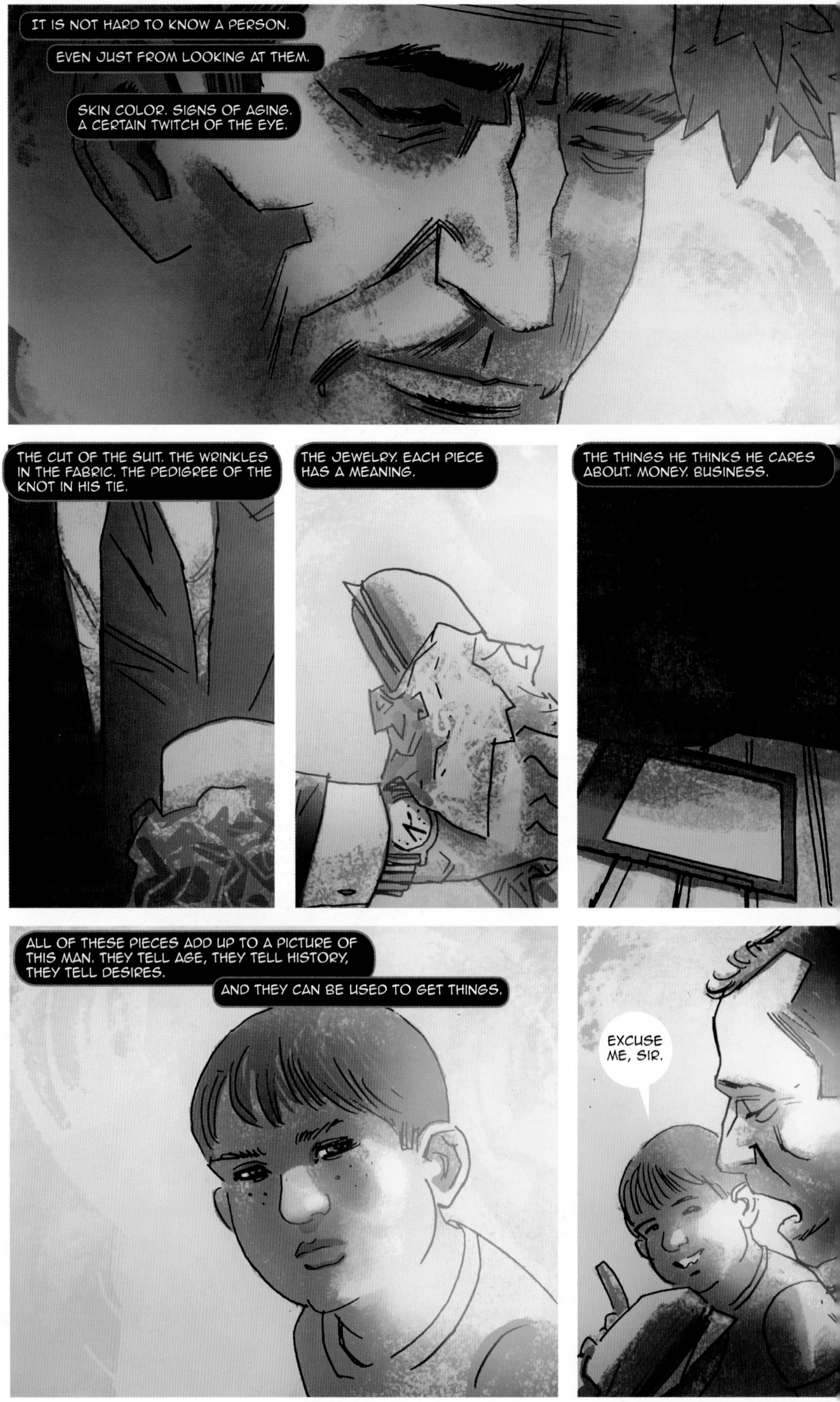
IT IS NOT HARD TO KNOW A PERSON.
EVEN JUST FROM LOOKING AT THEM.
SKIN COLOR. SIGNS OF AGING. A CERTAIN TWITCH OF THE EYE.
THE CUT OF THE SUIT. THE WRINKLES IN THE FABRIC. THE PEDIGREE OF THE KNOT IN HIS TIE.
THE JEWELRY. EACH PIECE HAS A MEANING.
THE THINGS HE THINKS HE CARES ABOUT. MONEY. BUSINESS.
ALL OF THESE PIECES ADD UP TO A PICTURE OF THIS MAN. THEY TELL AGE, THEY TELL HISTORY, THEY TELL DESIRES.
AND THEY CAN BE USED TO GET THINGS.
EXCUSE ME, SIR.

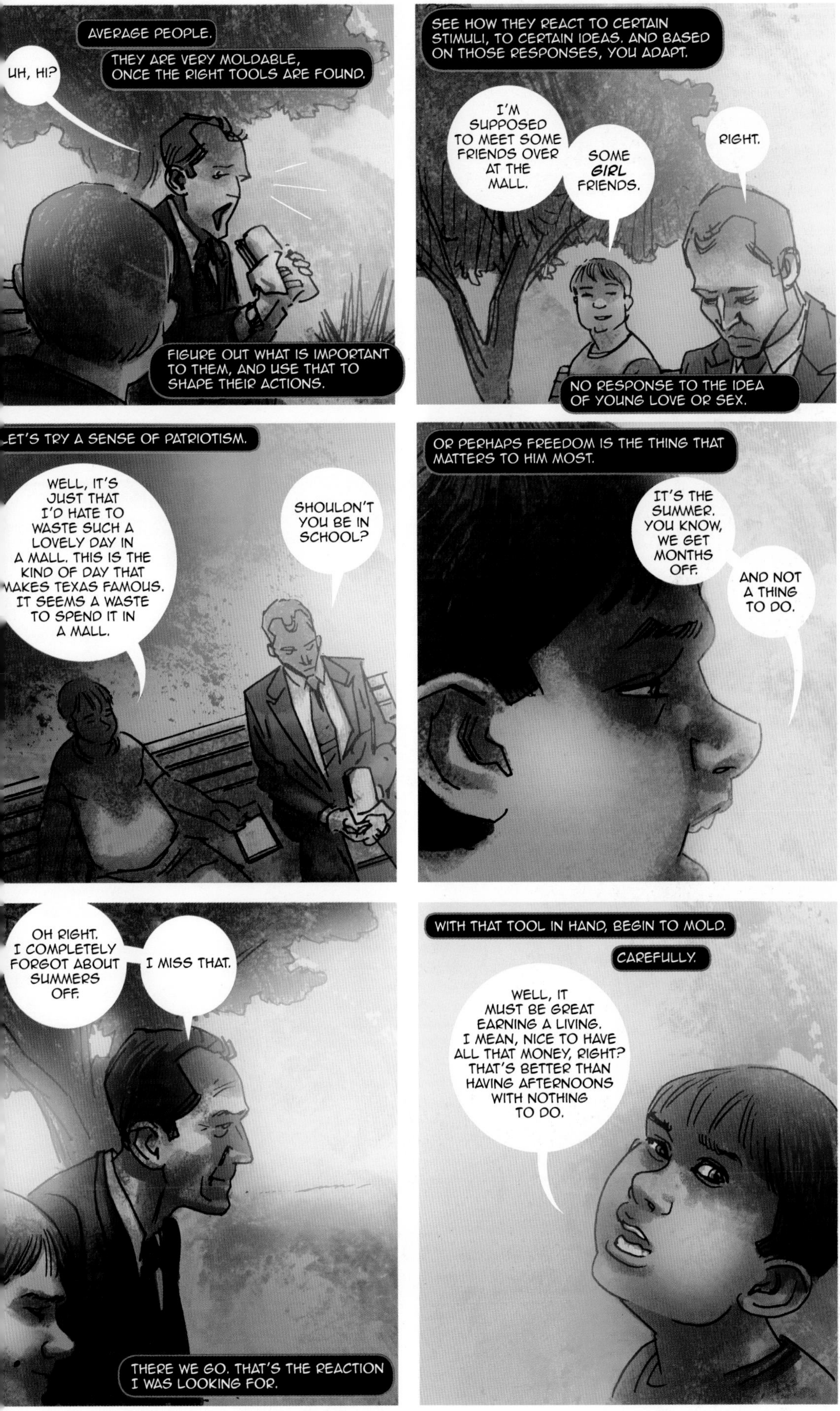
AVERAGE PEOPLE.
THEY ARE VERY MOLDABLE, ONCE THE RIGHT TOOLS ARE FOUND.
UH, HI?
FIGURE OUT WHAT IS IMPORTANT TO THEM, AND USE THAT TO SHAPE THEIR ACTIONS.
SEE HOW THEY REACT TO CERTAIN STIMULI, TO CERTAIN IDEAS. AND BASED ON THOSE RESPONSES, YOU ADAPT.
I'M SUPPOSED TO MEET SOME FRIENDS OVER AT THE MALL.
SOME **GIRL** FRIENDS.
RIGHT.
NO RESPONSE TO THE IDEA OF YOUNG LOVE OR SEX.
LET'S TRY A SENSE OF PATRIOTISM.
WELL, IT'S JUST THAT I'D HATE TO WASTE SUCH A LOVELY DAY IN A MALL. THIS IS THE KIND OF DAY THAT MAKES TEXAS FAMOUS. IT SEEMS A WASTE TO SPEND IT IN A MALL.
SHOULDN'T YOU BE IN SCHOOL?
OR PERHAPS FREEDOM IS THE THING THAT MATTERS TO HIM MOST.
IT'S THE SUMMER. YOU KNOW, WE GET MONTHS OFF.
AND NOT A THING TO DO.
OH RIGHT. I COMPLETELY FORGOT ABOUT SUMMERS OFF.
I MISS THAT.
THERE WE GO. THAT'S THE REACTION I WAS LOOKING FOR.
WITH THAT TOOL IN HAND, BEGIN TO MOLD.
CAREFULLY.
WELL, IT MUST BE GREAT EARNING A LIVING. I MEAN, NICE TO HAVE ALL THAT MONEY, RIGHT? THAT'S BETTER THAN HAVING AFTERNOONS WITH NOTHING TO DO.

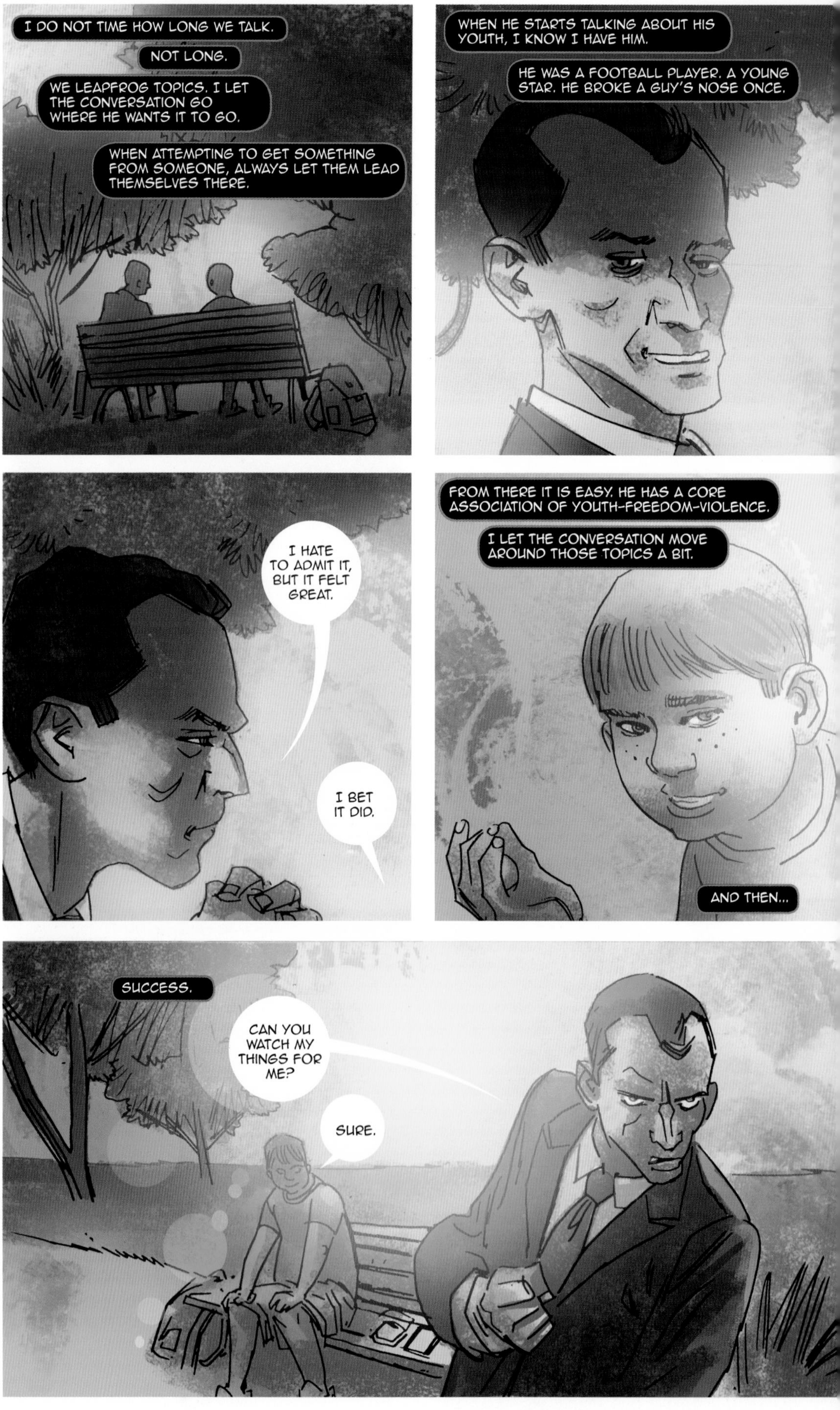
I DO NOT TIME HOW LONG WE TALK.
NOT LONG.
WE LEAPFROG TOPICS. I LET THE CONVERSATION GO WHERE HE WANTS IT TO GO.
WHEN ATTEMPTING TO GET SOMETHING FROM SOMEONE, ALWAYS LET THEM LEAD THEMSELVES THERE.
WHEN HE STARTS TALKING ABOUT HIS YOUTH, I KNOW I HAVE HIM.
HE WAS A FOOTBALL PLAYER. A YOUNG STAR. HE BROKE A GUY'S NOSE ONCE.
I HATE TO ADMIT IT, BUT IT FELT GREAT.
I BET IT DID.
FROM THERE IT IS EASY. HE HAS A CORE ASSOCIATION OF YOUTH-FREEDOM-VIOLENCE.
I LET THE CONVERSATION MOVE AROUND THOSE TOPICS A BIT.
AND THEN...
SUCCESS.
CAN YOU WATCH MY THINGS FOR ME?
SURE.

WELL.

THAT IS HOW IT IS DONE.

AND IT IS A BEAUTIFUL DAY.
YES, A BEAUTIFUL DAY.

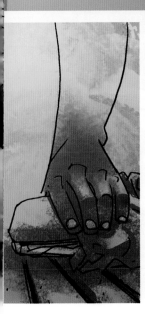

AND I AM NO LONGER HUNGRY.

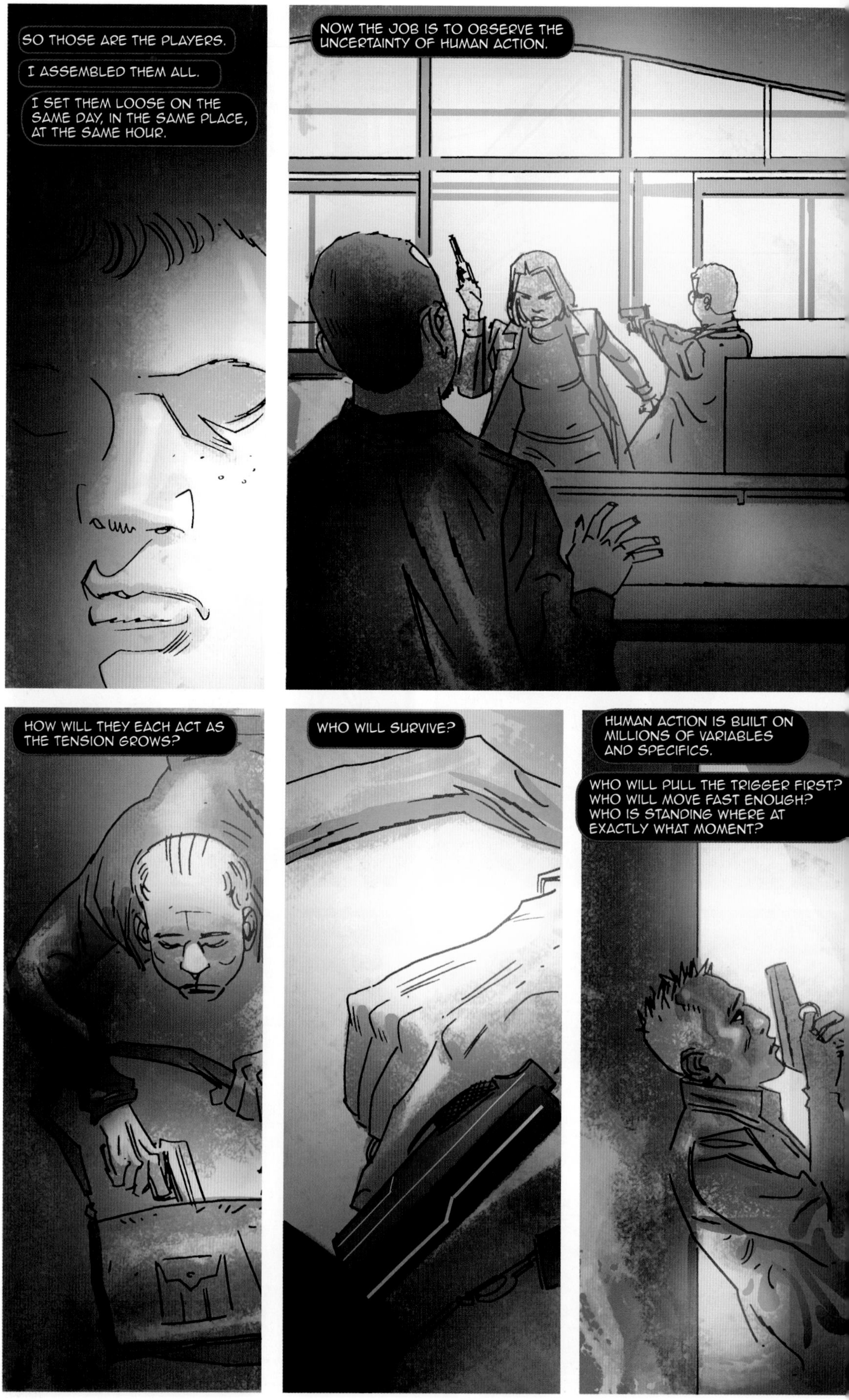
SO THOSE ARE THE PLAYERS.
I ASSEMBLED THEM ALL.
I SET THEM LOOSE ON THE SAME DAY, IN THE SAME PLACE, AT THE SAME HOUR.
NOW THE JOB IS TO OBSERVE THE UNCERTAINTY OF HUMAN ACTION.
HOW WILL THEY EACH ACT AS THE TENSION GROWS?
WHO WILL SURVIVE?
HUMAN ACTION IS BUILT ON MILLIONS OF VARIABLES AND SPECIFICS.
WHO WILL PULL THE TRIGGER FIRST? WHO WILL MOVE FAST ENOUGH? WHO IS STANDING WHERE AT EXACTLY WHAT MOMENT?

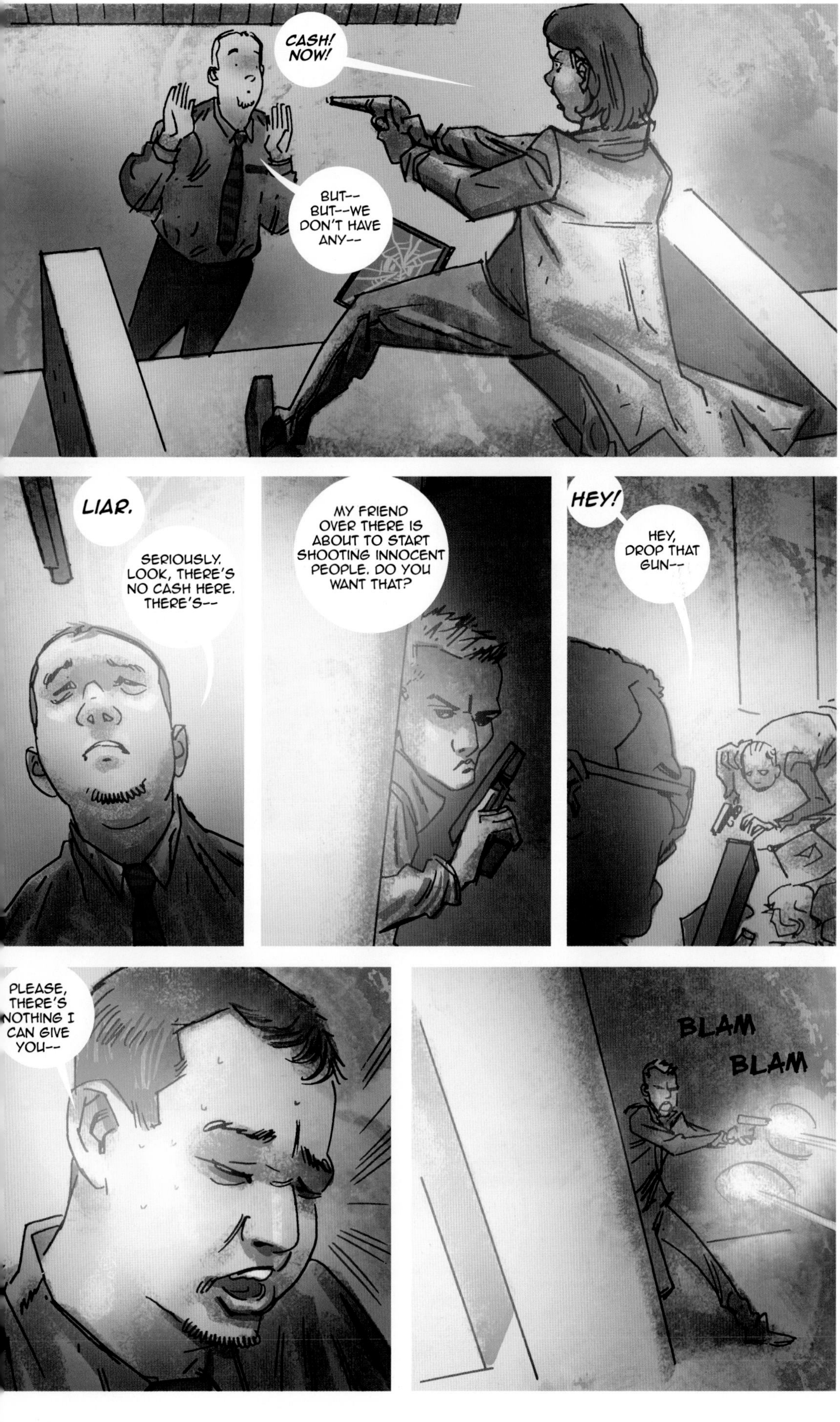
CASH! NOW!
BUT-- BUT--WE DON'T HAVE ANY--
LIAR.
SERIOUSLY. LOOK, THERE'S NO CASH HERE. THERE'S--
MY FRIEND OVER THERE IS ABOUT TO START SHOOTING INNOCENT PEOPLE. DO YOU WANT THAT?
HEY!
HEY, DROP THAT GUN--
PLEASE, THERE'S NOTHING I CAN GIVE YOU--
BLAM
BLAM

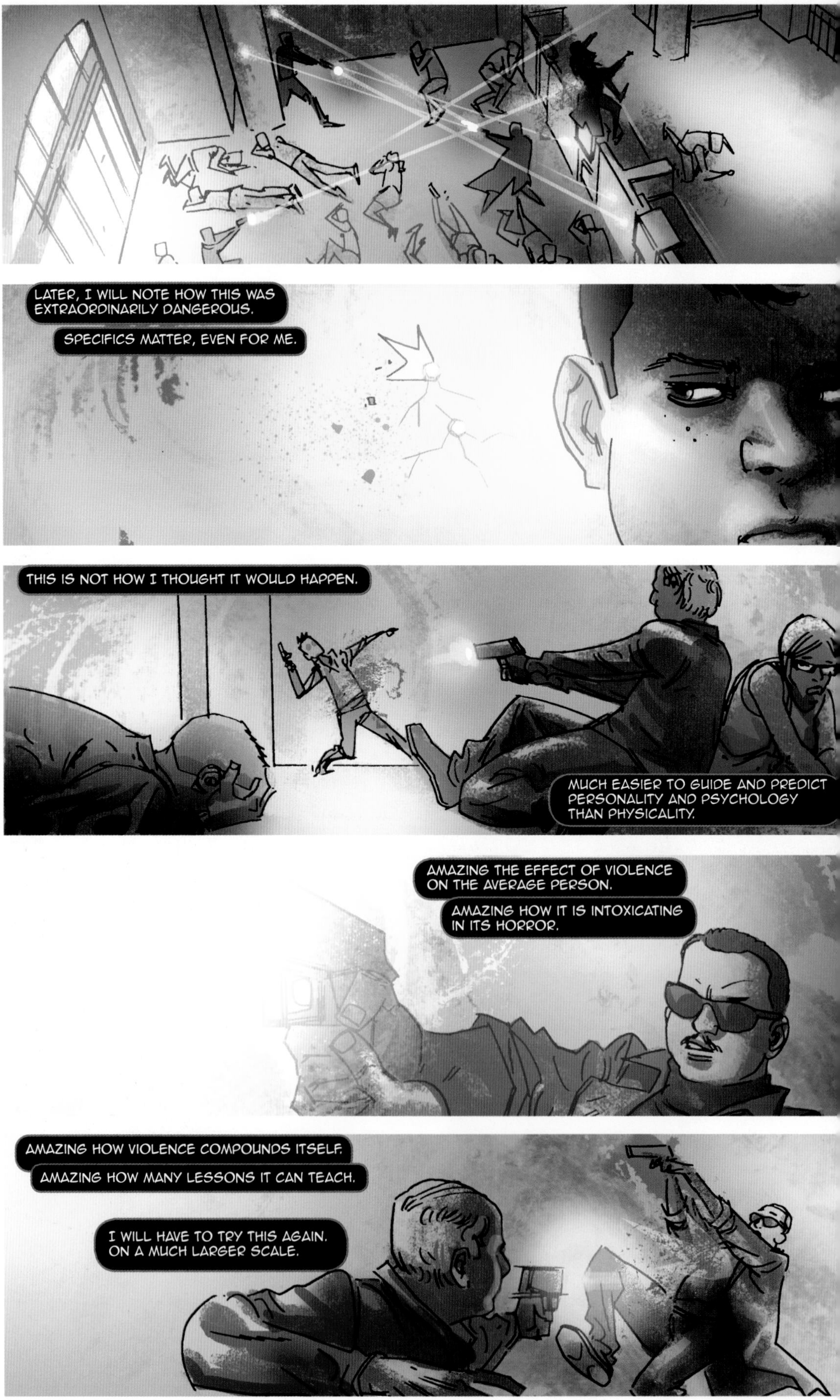
LATER, I WILL NOTE HOW THIS WAS EXTRAORDINARILY DANGEROUS.
SPECIFICS MATTER, EVEN FOR ME.
THIS IS NOT HOW I THOUGHT IT WOULD HAPPEN.
MUCH EASIER TO GUIDE AND PREDICT PERSONALITY AND PSYCHOLOGY THAN PHYSICALITY.
AMAZING THE EFFECT OF VIOLENCE ON THE AVERAGE PERSON.
AMAZING HOW IT IS INTOXICATING IN ITS HORROR.
AMAZING HOW VIOLENCE COMPOUNDS ITSELF.
AMAZING HOW MANY LESSONS IT CAN TEACH.
I WILL HAVE TO TRY THIS AGAIN. ON A MUCH LARGER SCALE.

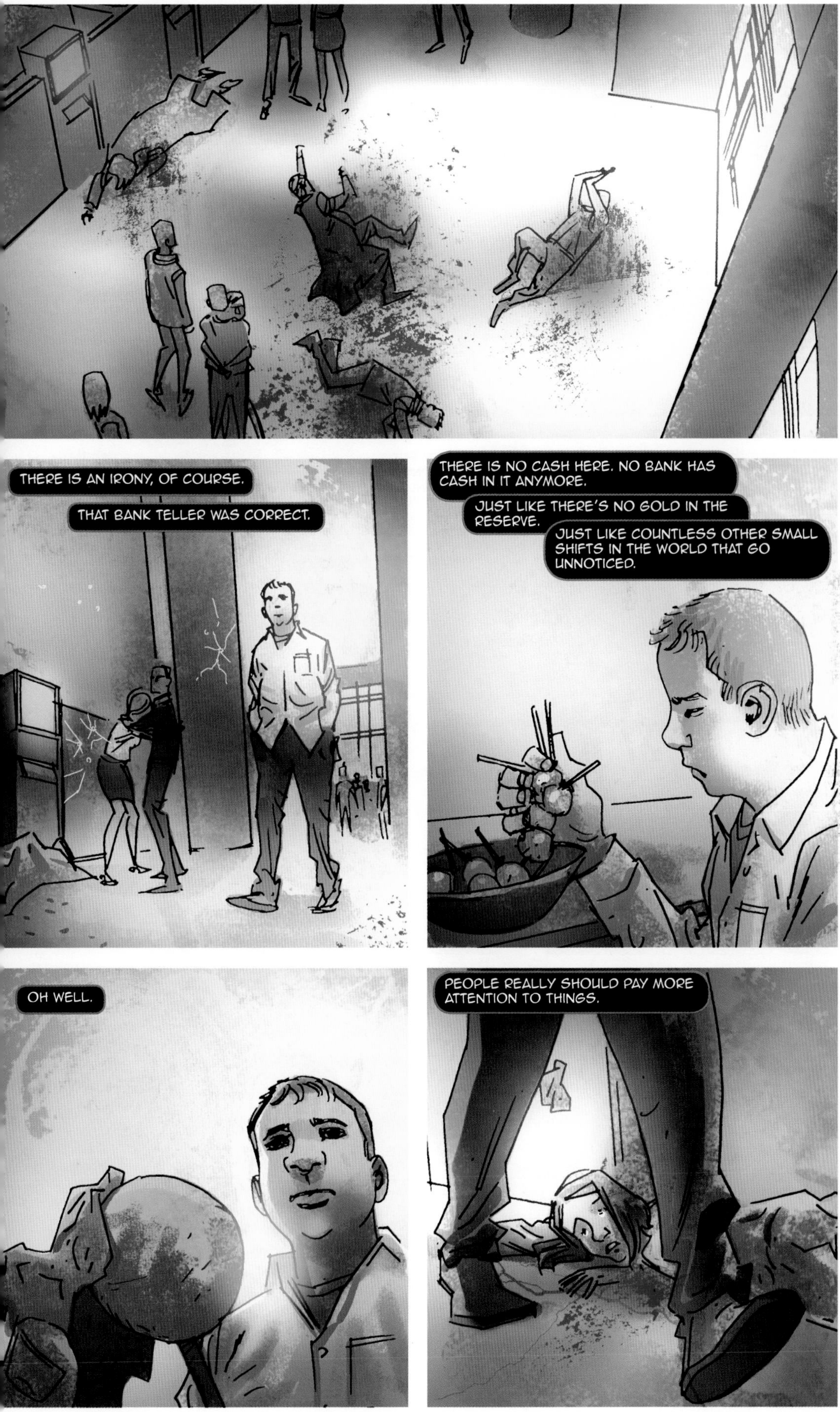
THERE IS AN IRONY, OF COURSE.
THAT BANK TELLER WAS CORRECT.
THERE IS NO CASH HERE. NO BANK HAS CASH IN IT ANYMORE.
JUST LIKE THERE'S NO GOLD IN THE RESERVE.
JUST LIKE COUNTLESS OTHER SMALL SHIFTS IN THE WORLD THAT GO UNNOTICED.
OH WELL.
PEOPLE REALLY SHOULD PAY MORE ATTENTION TO THINGS.

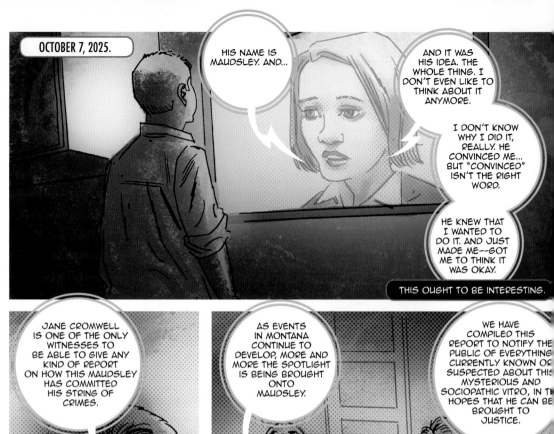

OCTOBER 7, 2025.

HIS NAME IS MAUDSLEY. AND...

AND IT WAS HIS IDEA. THE WHOLE THING. I DON'T EVEN LIKE TO THINK ABOUT IT ANYMORE.

I DON'T KNOW WHY I DID IT, REALLY. HE CONVINCED ME... BUT "CONVINCED" ISN'T THE RIGHT WORD.

HE KNEW THAT I WANTED TO DO IT. AND JUST MADE ME--GOT ME TO THINK IT WAS OKAY.

THIS OUGHT TO BE INTERESTING.

JANE CROMWELL IS ONE OF THE ONLY WITNESSES TO BE ABLE TO GIVE ANY KIND OF REPORT ON HOW THIS MAUDSLEY HAS COMMITTED HIS STRING OF CRIMES.

AS EVENTS IN MONTANA CONTINUE TO DEVELOP, MORE AND MORE THE SPOTLIGHT IS BEING BROUGHT ONTO MAUDSLEY.

WE HAVE COMPILED THIS REPORT TO NOTIFY THE PUBLIC OF EVERYTHING CURRENTLY KNOWN OR SUSPECTED ABOUT THIS MYSTERIOUS AND SOCIOPATHIC VITRO, IN T HOPES THAT HE CAN BE BROUGHT TO JUSTICE.

BORN LIKE ALL THE VITROS FROM A BATCH OF IN-VITRO CURES FOR A RARE AND FATAL GENETIC DISEASE THAT ORIGINATED IN THIS MEDICAL RESEARCH FACILITY...

...ROBERT MAUDSLEY WAS ONE OF THE FIRST TO SHOW THE UNEXPECTED SIDE EFFECT OF RAPIDLY INCREASED INTELLIGENCE UPON REACHING EARLY PUBERTY.

AND HIS PARENTS WERE THE FIRST OF THE VITRO PARENTS TO ACKNOWLEDGE THE STRANGE THINGS HAPPENING TO THEIR CHILDREN.

PICTURED HERE, ROBE MAUDSLEY WITH HIS PARENTS, DANIEL AND CATHERINE.

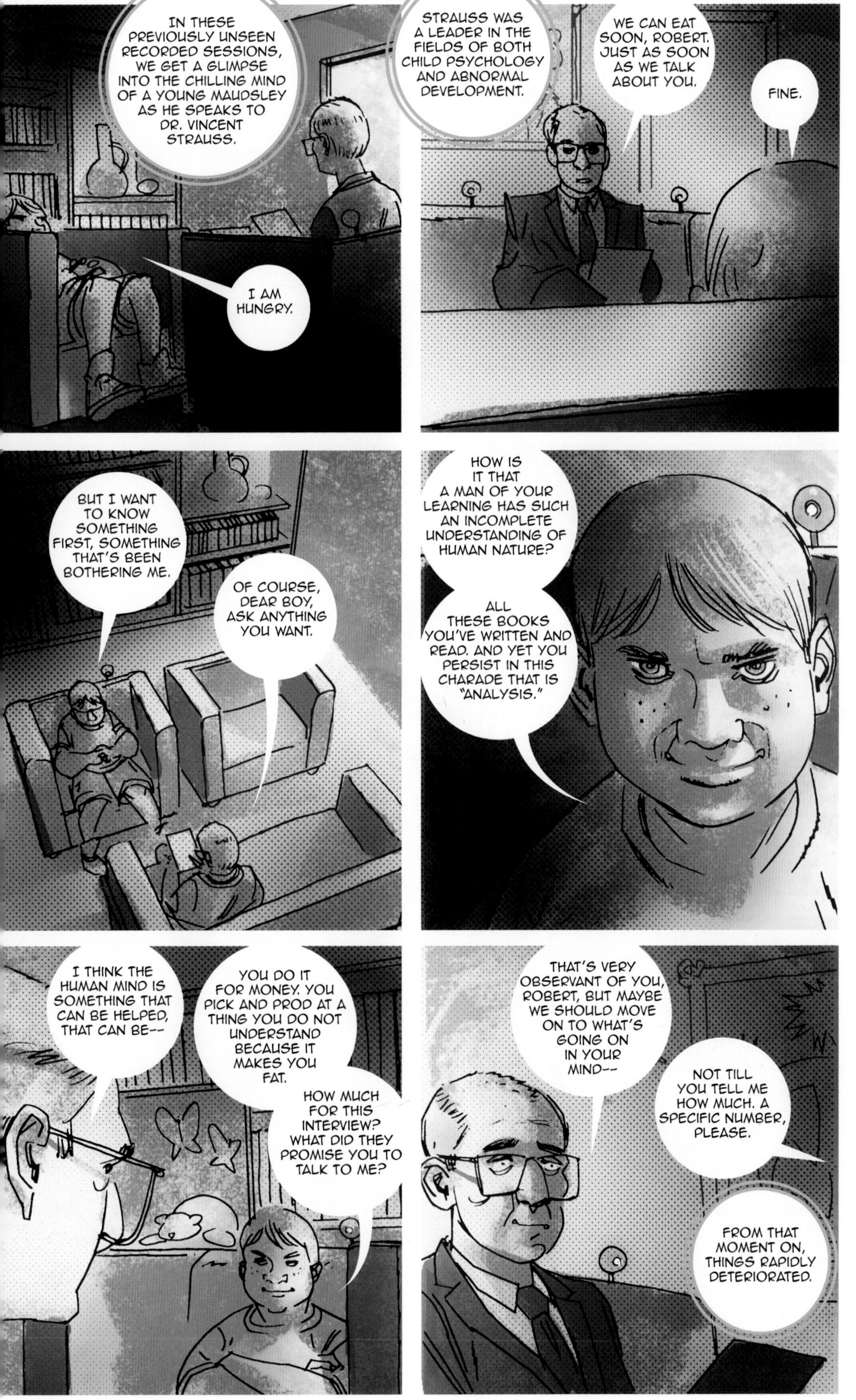
IN THESE PREVIOUSLY UNSEEN RECORDED SESSIONS, WE GET A GLIMPSE INTO THE CHILLING MIND OF A YOUNG MAUDSLEY AS HE SPEAKS TO DR. VINCENT STRAUSS.
I AM HUNGRY.
STRAUSS WAS A LEADER IN THE FIELDS OF BOTH CHILD PSYCHOLOGY AND ABNORMAL DEVELOPMENT.
WE CAN EAT SOON, ROBERT. JUST AS SOON AS WE TALK ABOUT YOU.
FINE.
BUT I WANT TO KNOW SOMETHING FIRST, SOMETHING THAT'S BEEN BOTHERING ME.
OF COURSE, DEAR BOY, ASK ANYTHING YOU WANT.
HOW IS IT THAT A MAN OF YOUR LEARNING HAS SUCH AN INCOMPLETE UNDERSTANDING OF HUMAN NATURE?
ALL THESE BOOKS YOU'VE WRITTEN AND READ. AND YET YOU PERSIST IN THIS CHARADE THAT IS "ANALYSIS."
I THINK THE HUMAN MIND IS SOMETHING THAT CAN BE HELPED, THAT CAN BE--
YOU DO IT FOR MONEY. YOU PICK AND PROD AT A THING YOU DO NOT UNDERSTAND BECAUSE IT MAKES YOU FAT.
HOW MUCH FOR THIS INTERVIEW? WHAT DID THEY PROMISE YOU TO TALK TO ME?
THAT'S VERY OBSERVANT OF YOU, ROBERT, BUT MAYBE WE SHOULD MOVE ON TO WHAT'S GOING ON IN YOUR MIND--
NOT TILL YOU TELL ME HOW MUCH. A SPECIFIC NUMBER, PLEASE.
FROM THAT MOMENT ON, THINGS RAPIDLY DETERIORATED.

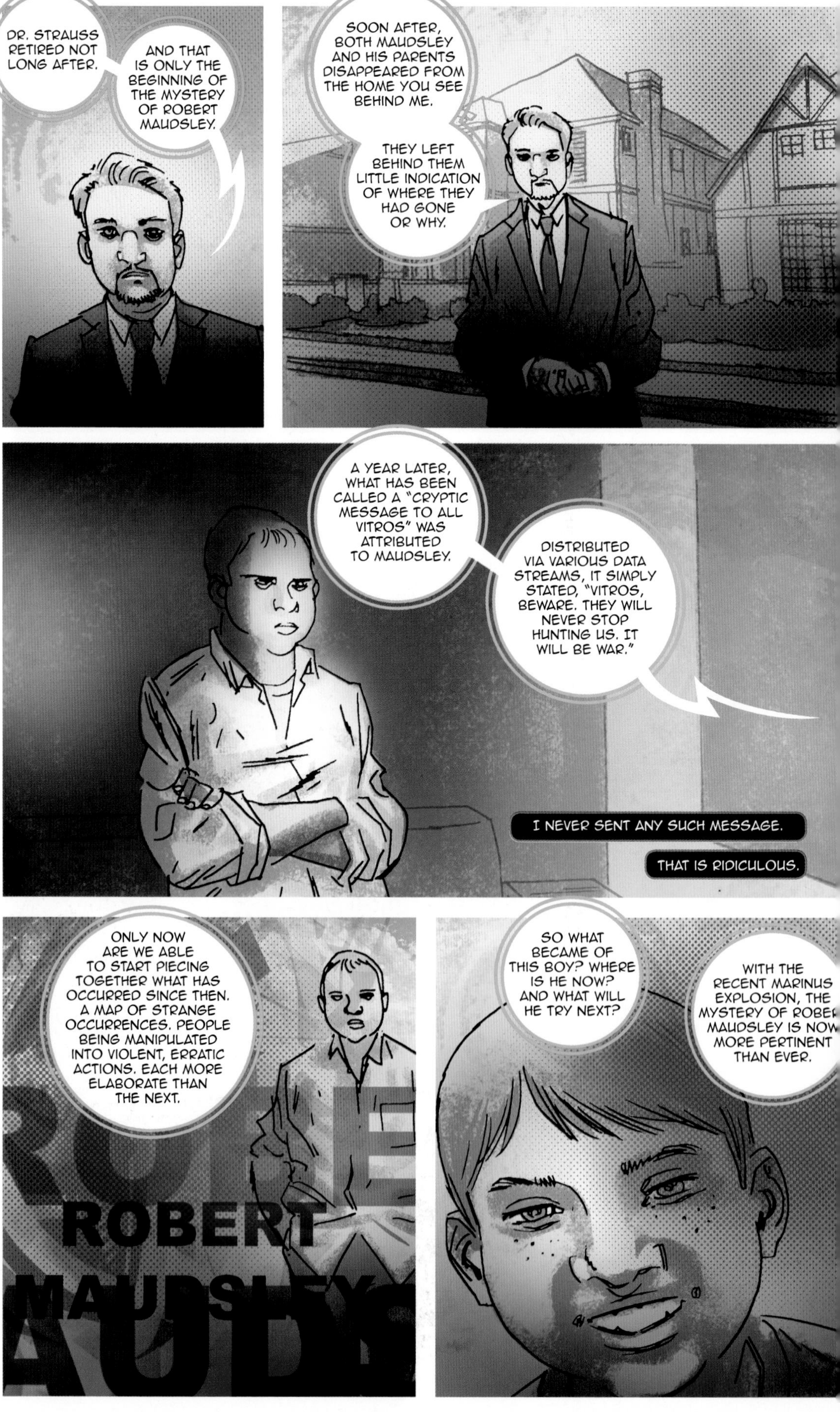
DR. STRAUSS RETIRED NOT LONG AFTER.
AND THAT IS ONLY THE BEGINNING OF THE MYSTERY OF ROBERT MAUDSLEY.
SOON AFTER, BOTH MAUDSLEY AND HIS PARENTS DISAPPEARED FROM THE HOME YOU SEE BEHIND ME.
THEY LEFT BEHIND THEM LITTLE INDICATION OF WHERE THEY HAD GONE OR WHY.
A YEAR LATER, WHAT HAS BEEN CALLED A "CRYPTIC MESSAGE TO ALL VITROS" WAS ATTRIBUTED TO MAUDSLEY.
DISTRIBUTED VIA VARIOUS DATA STREAMS, IT SIMPLY STATED, "VITROS, BEWARE. THEY WILL NEVER STOP HUNTING US. IT WILL BE WAR."
I NEVER SENT ANY SUCH MESSAGE.
THAT IS RIDICULOUS.
ONLY NOW ARE WE ABLE TO START PIECING TOGETHER WHAT HAS OCCURRED SINCE THEN. A MAP OF STRANGE OCCURRENCES. PEOPLE BEING MANIPULATED INTO VIOLENT, ERRATIC ACTIONS. EACH MORE ELABORATE THAN THE NEXT.
ROBERT
MAUDSLEY
SO WHAT BECAME OF THIS BOY? WHERE IS HE NOW? AND WHAT WILL HE TRY NEXT?
WITH THE RECENT MARINUS EXPLOSION, THE MYSTERY OF ROBER MAUDSLEY IS NOW MORE PERTINENT THAN EVER.

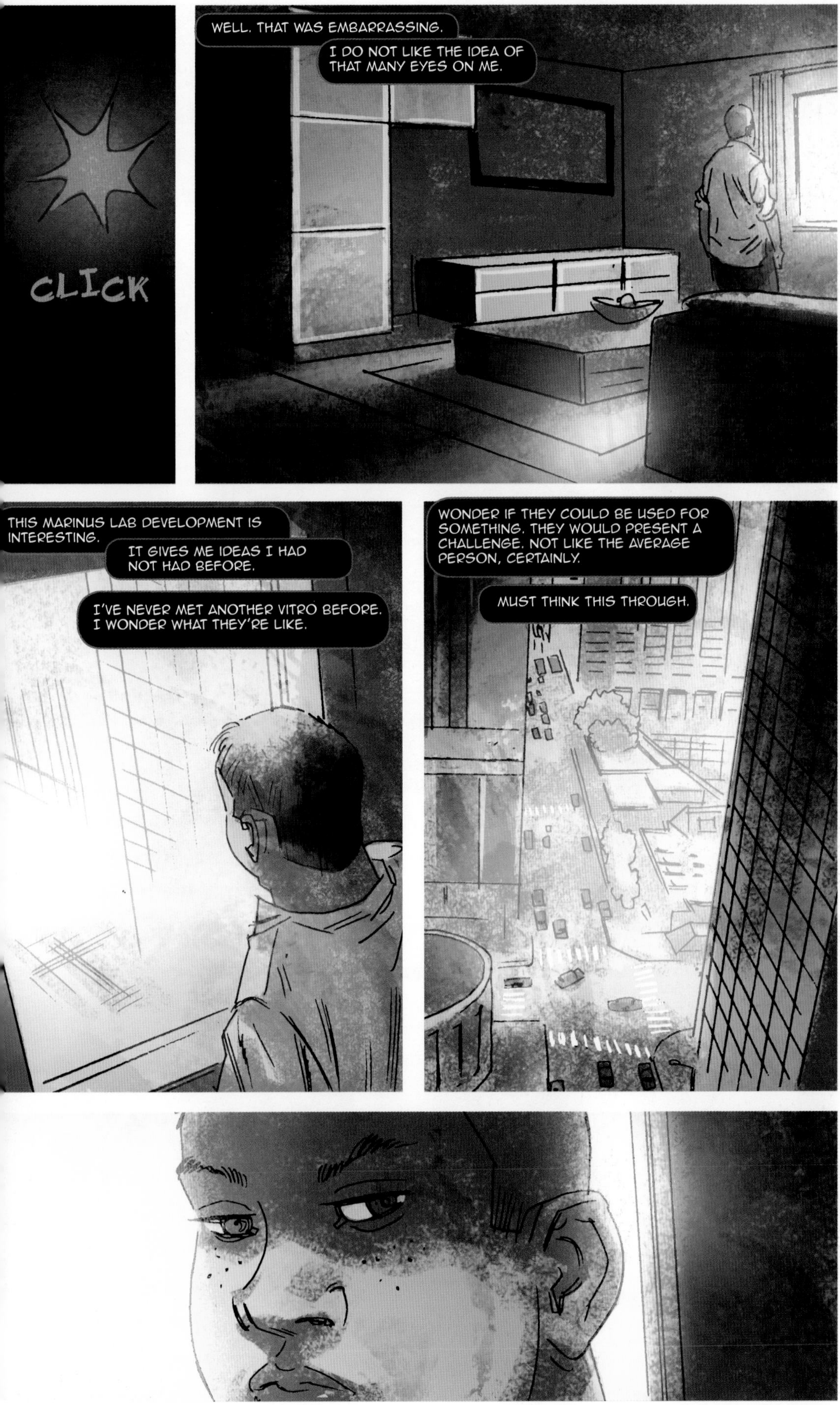
CLICK
WELL. THAT WAS EMBARRASSING.
I DO NOT LIKE THE IDEA OF THAT MANY EYES ON ME.
THIS MARINUS LAB DEVELOPMENT IS INTERESTING.
IT GIVES ME IDEAS I HAD NOT HAD BEFORE.
I'VE NEVER MET ANOTHER VITRO BEFORE. I WONDER WHAT THEY'RE LIKE.
WONDER IF THEY COULD BE USED FOR SOMETHING. THEY WOULD PRESENT A CHALLENGE. NOT LIKE THE AVERAGE PERSON, CERTAINLY.
MUST THINK THIS THROUGH.

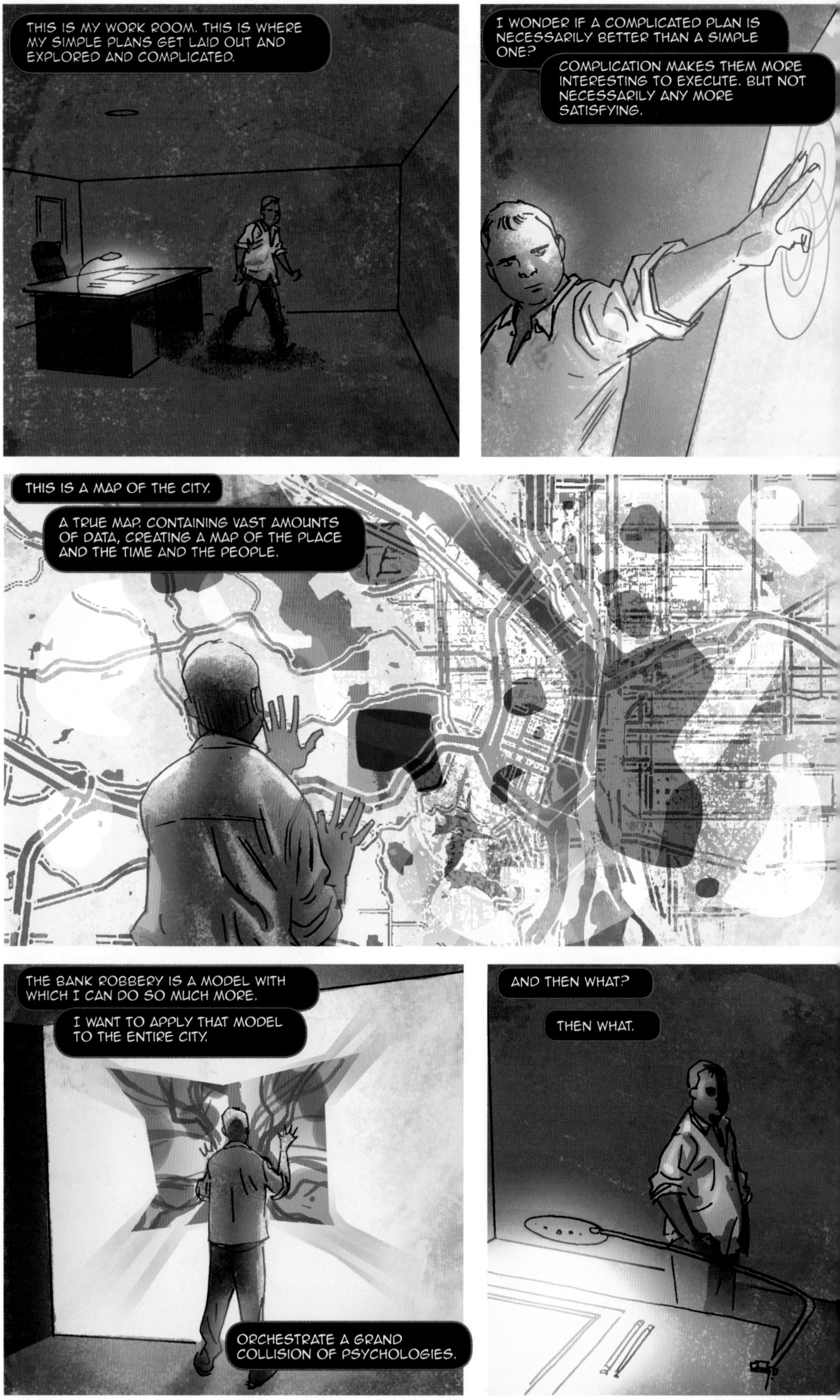
THIS IS MY WORK ROOM. THIS IS WHERE MY SIMPLE PLANS GET LAID OUT AND EXPLORED AND COMPLICATED.
I WONDER IF A COMPLICATED PLAN IS NECESSARILY BETTER THAN A SIMPLE ONE?
COMPLICATION MAKES THEM MORE INTERESTING TO EXECUTE. BUT NOT NECESSARILY ANY MORE SATISFYING.
THIS IS A MAP OF THE CITY.
A TRUE MAP. CONTAINING VAST AMOUNTS OF DATA, CREATING A MAP OF THE PLACE AND THE TIME AND THE PEOPLE.
THE BANK ROBBERY IS A MODEL WITH WHICH I CAN DO SO MUCH MORE.
I WANT TO APPLY THAT MODEL TO THE ENTIRE CITY.
ORCHESTRATE A GRAND COLLISION OF PSYCHOLOGIES.
AND THEN WHAT?
THEN WHAT.

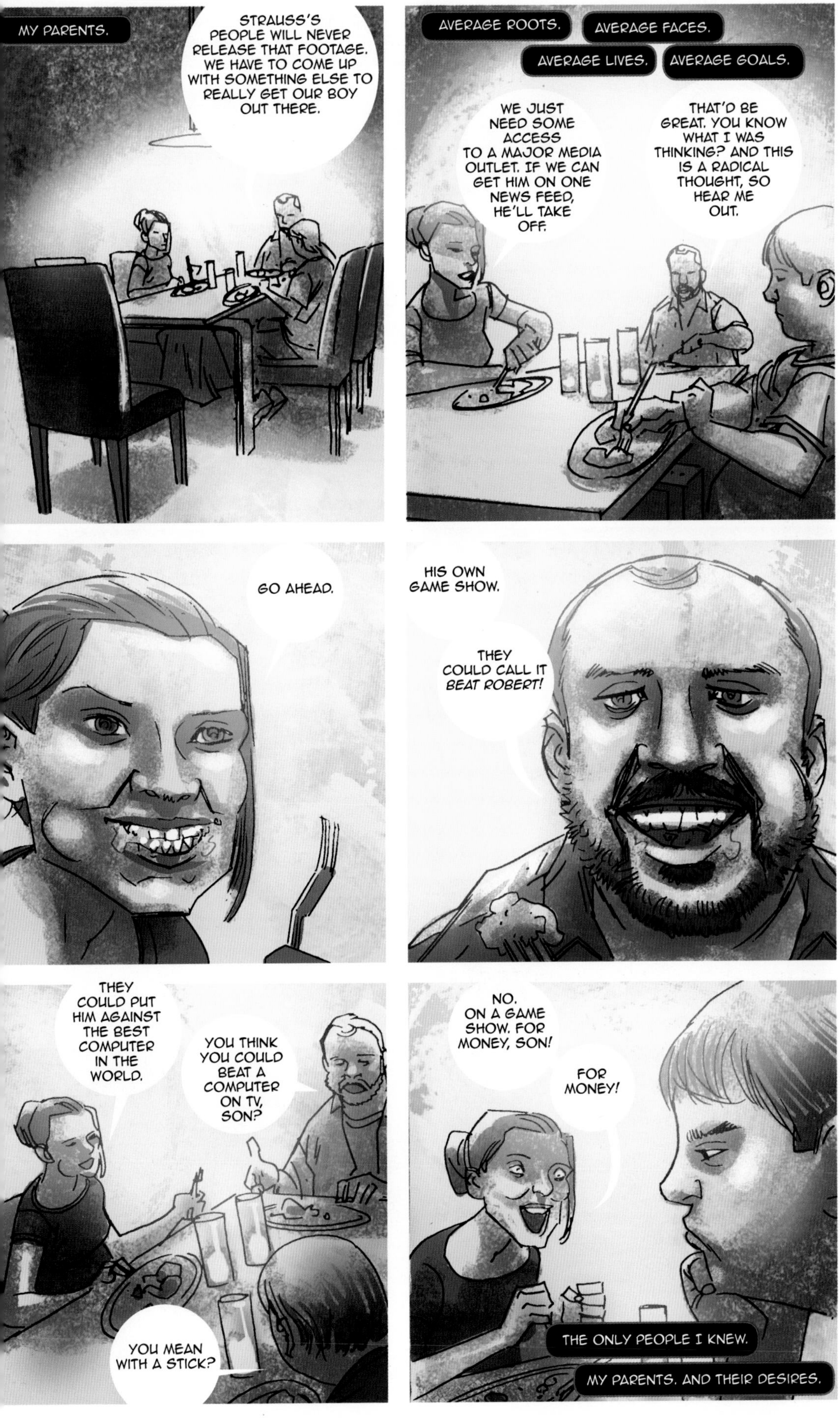

MY PARENTS.
STRAUSS'S PEOPLE WILL NEVER RELEASE THAT FOOTAGE. WE HAVE TO COME UP WITH SOMETHING ELSE TO REALLY GET OUR BOY OUT THERE.
AVERAGE ROOTS.
AVERAGE FACES.
AVERAGE LIVES.
AVERAGE GOALS.
WE JUST NEED SOME ACCESS TO A MAJOR MEDIA OUTLET. IF WE CAN GET HIM ON ONE NEWS FEED, HE'LL TAKE OFF.
THAT'D BE GREAT. YOU KNOW WHAT I WAS THINKING? AND THIS IS A RADICAL THOUGHT, SO HEAR ME OUT.
GO AHEAD.
HIS OWN GAME SHOW.
THEY COULD CALL IT *BEAT ROBERT!*
THEY COULD PUT HIM AGAINST THE BEST COMPUTER IN THE WORLD.
YOU THINK YOU COULD BEAT A COMPUTER ON TV, SON?
YOU MEAN WITH A STICK?
NO. ON A GAME SHOW. FOR MONEY, SON!
FOR MONEY!
THE ONLY PEOPLE I KNEW.
MY PARENTS. AND THEIR DESIRES.

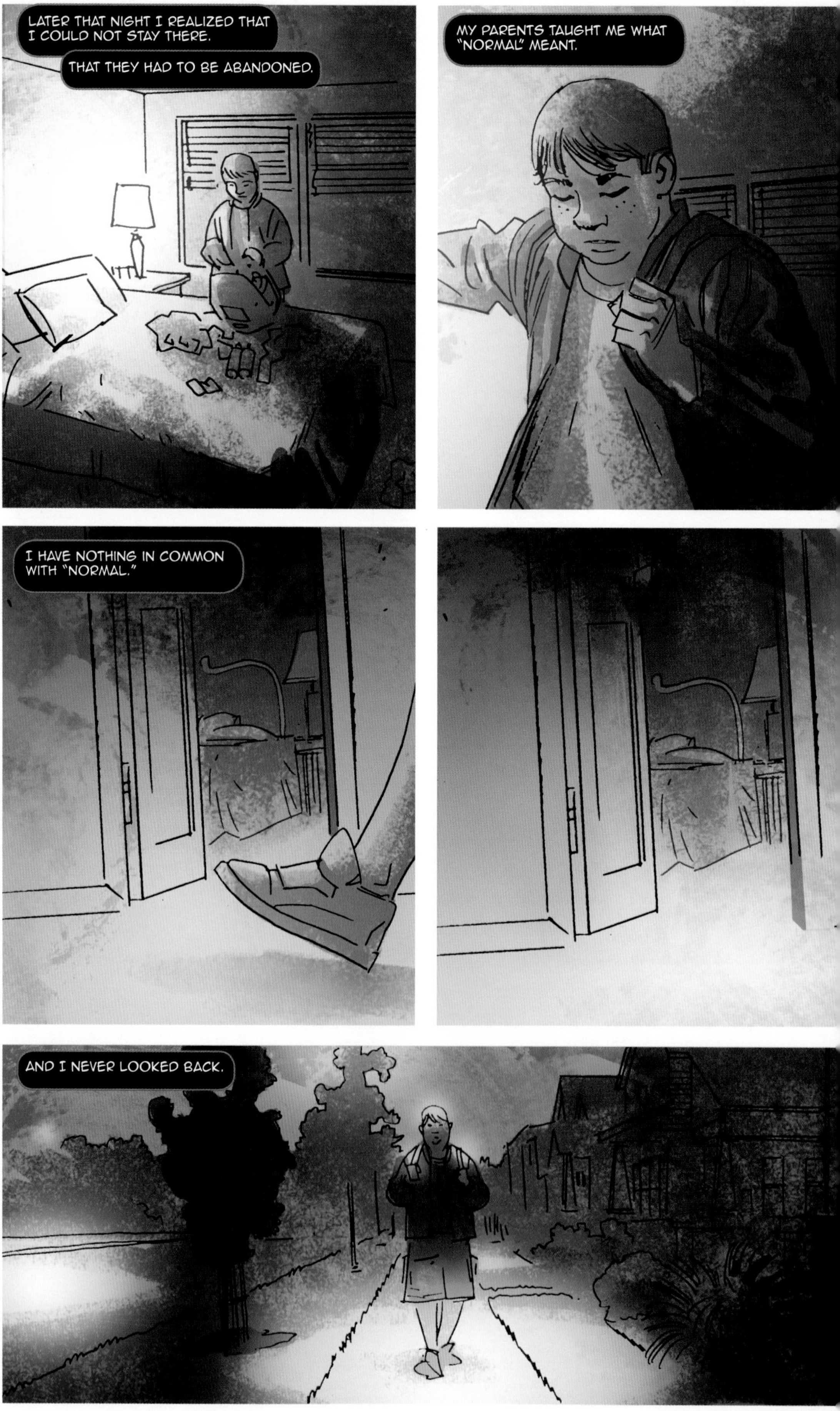
LATER THAT NIGHT I REALIZED THAT I COULD NOT STAY THERE.
THAT THEY HAD TO BE ABANDONED.
MY PARENTS TAUGHT ME WHAT "NORMAL" MEANT.
I HAVE NOTHING IN COMMON WITH "NORMAL."
AND I NEVER LOOKED BACK.

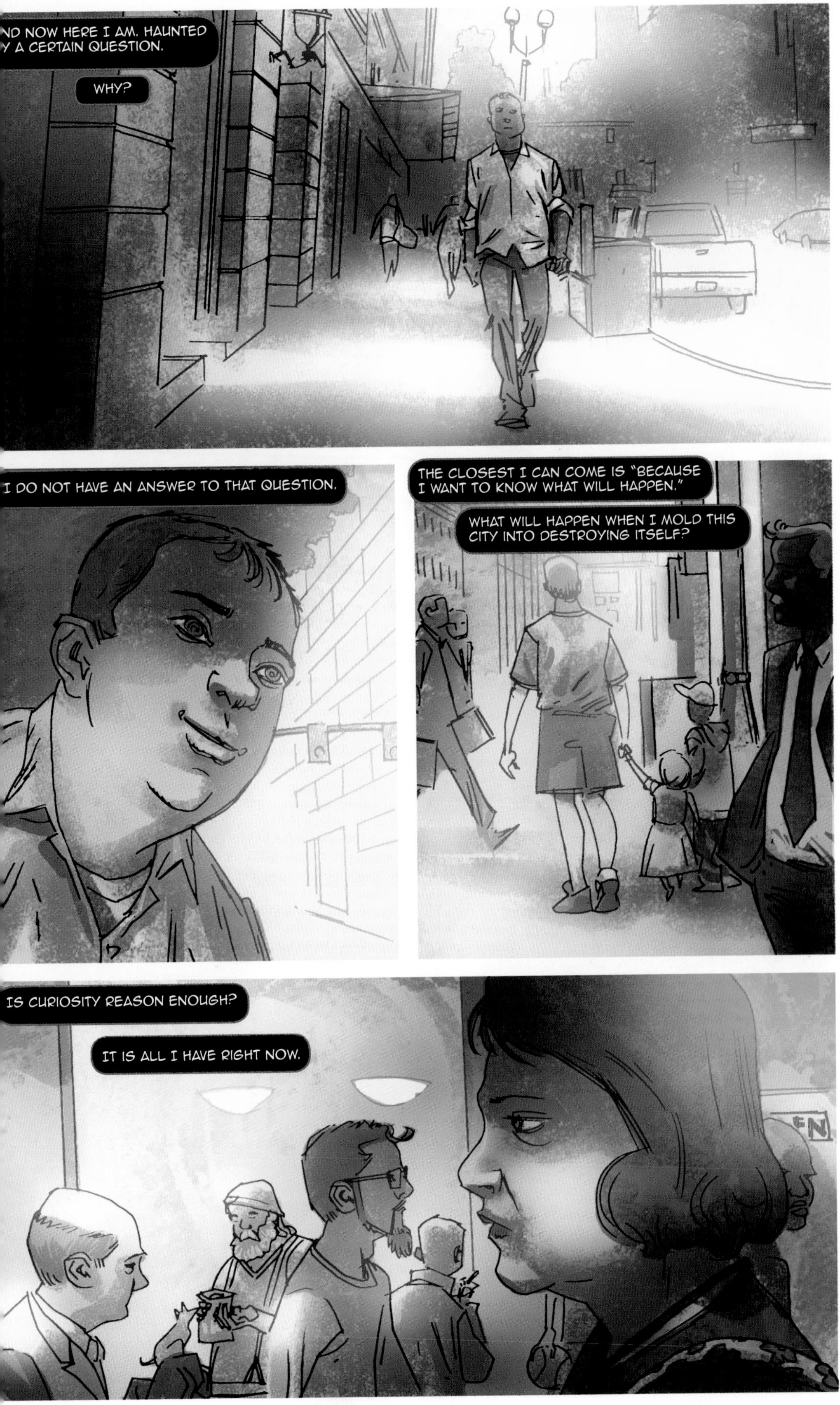
ND NOW HERE I AM. HAUNTED
Y A CERTAIN QUESTION.
WHY?
I DO NOT HAVE AN ANSWER TO THAT QUESTION.
THE CLOSEST I CAN COME IS "BECAUSE I WANT TO KNOW WHAT WILL HAPPEN."
WHAT WILL HAPPEN WHEN I MOLD THIS CITY INTO DESTROYING ITSELF?
IS CURIOSITY REASON ENOUGH?
IT IS ALL I HAVE RIGHT NOW.

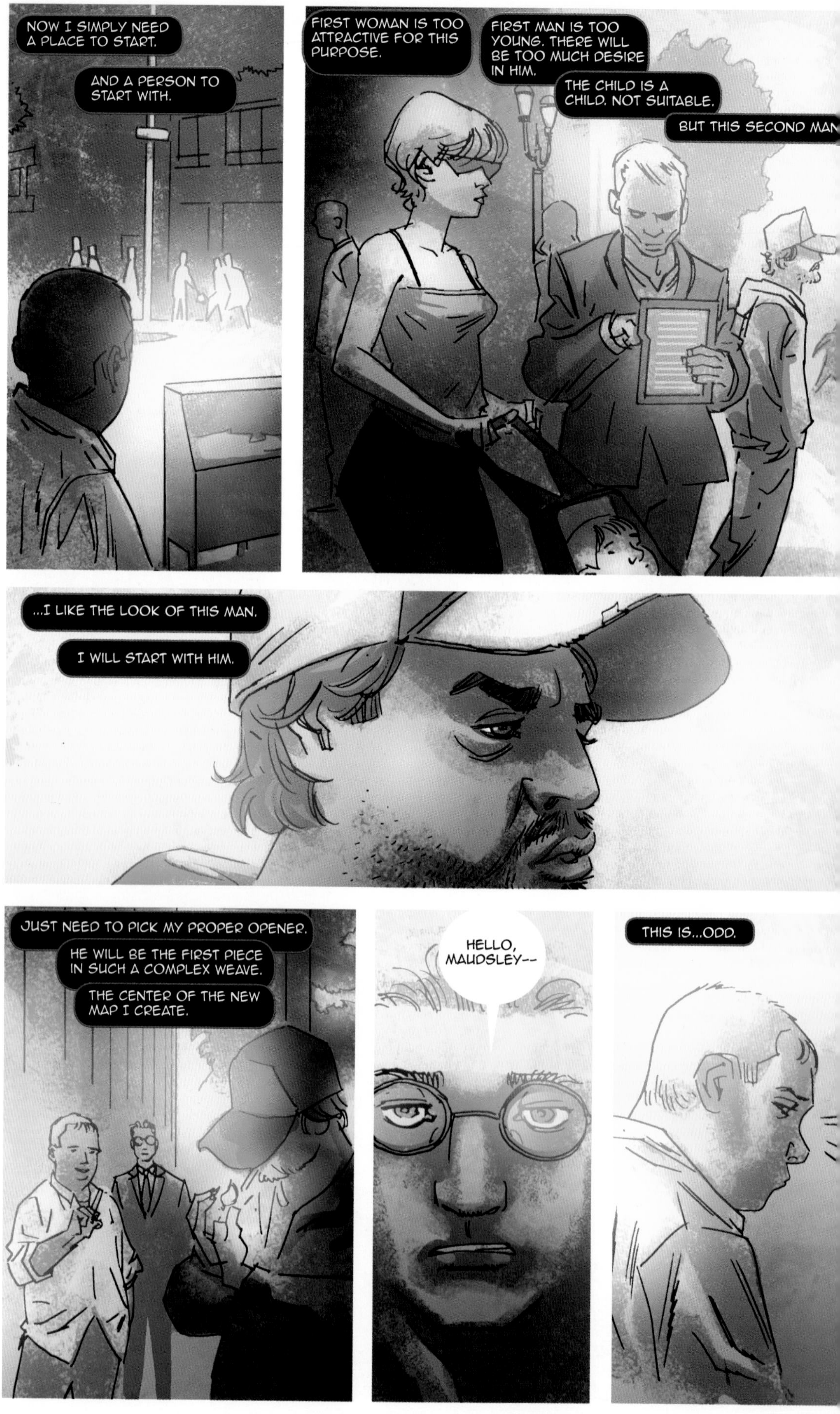
NOW I SIMPLY NEED A PLACE TO START.
AND A PERSON TO START WITH.
FIRST WOMAN IS TOO ATTRACTIVE FOR THIS PURPOSE.
FIRST MAN IS TOO YOUNG. THERE WILL BE TOO MUCH DESIRE IN HIM.
THE CHILD IS A CHILD. NOT SUITABLE.
BUT THIS SECOND MAN
...I LIKE THE LOOK OF THIS MAN.
I WILL START WITH HIM.
JUST NEED TO PICK MY PROPER OPENER.
HE WILL BE THE FIRST PIECE IN SUCH A COMPLEX WEAVE.
THE CENTER OF THE NEW MAP I CREATE.
HELLO, MAUDSLEY--
THIS IS...ODD.

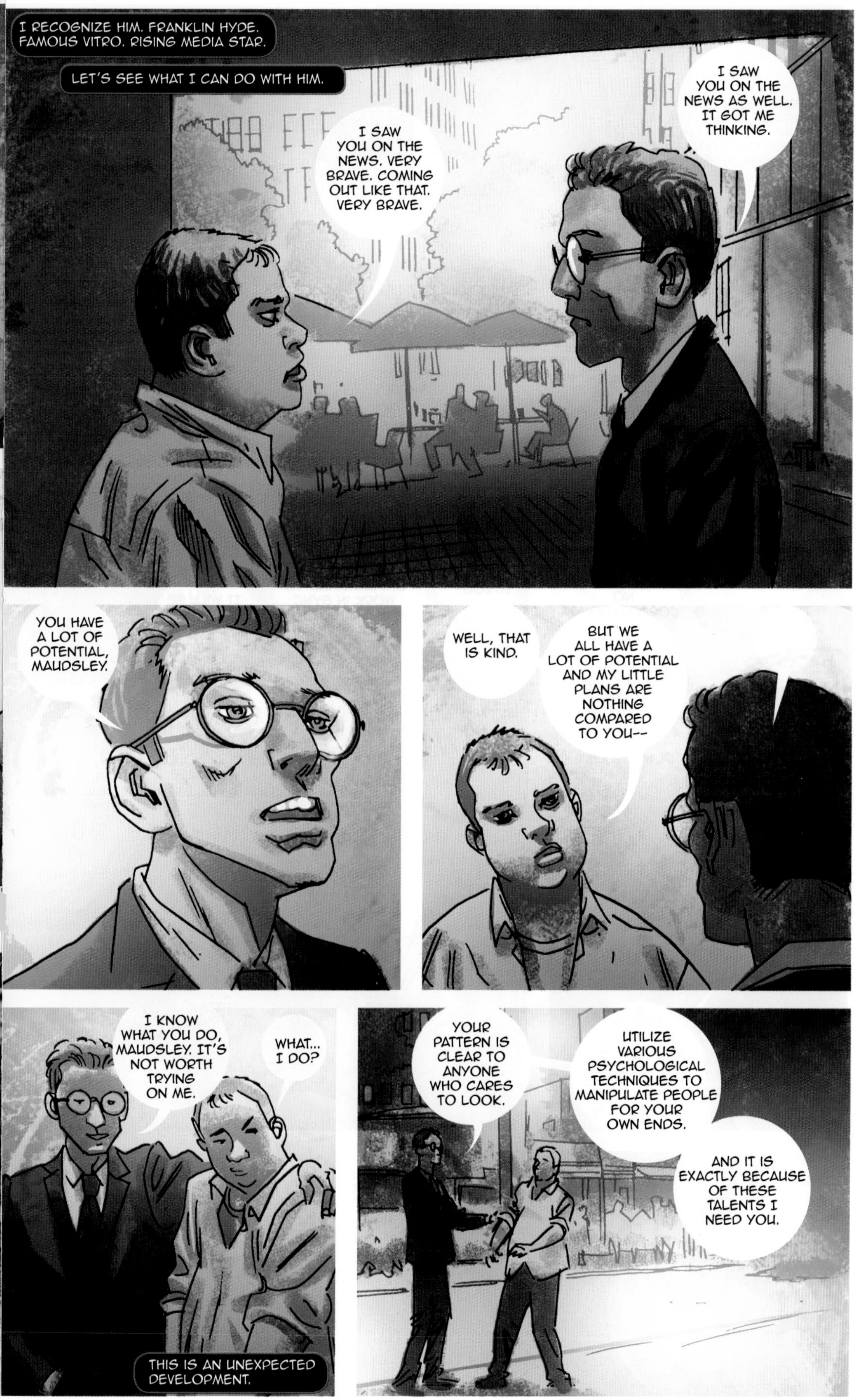
I RECOGNIZE HIM. FRANKLIN HYDE. FAMOUS VITRO. RISING MEDIA STAR.
LET'S SEE WHAT I CAN DO WITH HIM.
I SAW YOU ON THE NEWS. VERY BRAVE. COMING OUT LIKE THAT. VERY BRAVE.
I SAW YOU ON THE NEWS AS WELL. IT GOT ME THINKING.
YOU HAVE A LOT OF POTENTIAL, MAUDSLEY.
WELL, THAT IS KIND.
BUT WE ALL HAVE A LOT OF POTENTIAL AND MY LITTLE PLANS ARE NOTHING COMPARED TO YOU--
I KNOW WHAT YOU DO, MAUDSLEY. IT'S NOT WORTH TRYING ON ME.
WHAT... I DO?
THIS IS AN UNEXPECTED DEVELOPMENT.
YOUR PATTERN IS CLEAR TO ANYONE WHO CARES TO LOOK.
UTILIZE VARIOUS PSYCHOLOGICAL TECHNIQUES TO MANIPULATE PEOPLE FOR YOUR OWN ENDS.
AND IT IS EXACTLY BECAUSE OF THESE TALENTS I NEED YOU.

CHAPTER FOUR

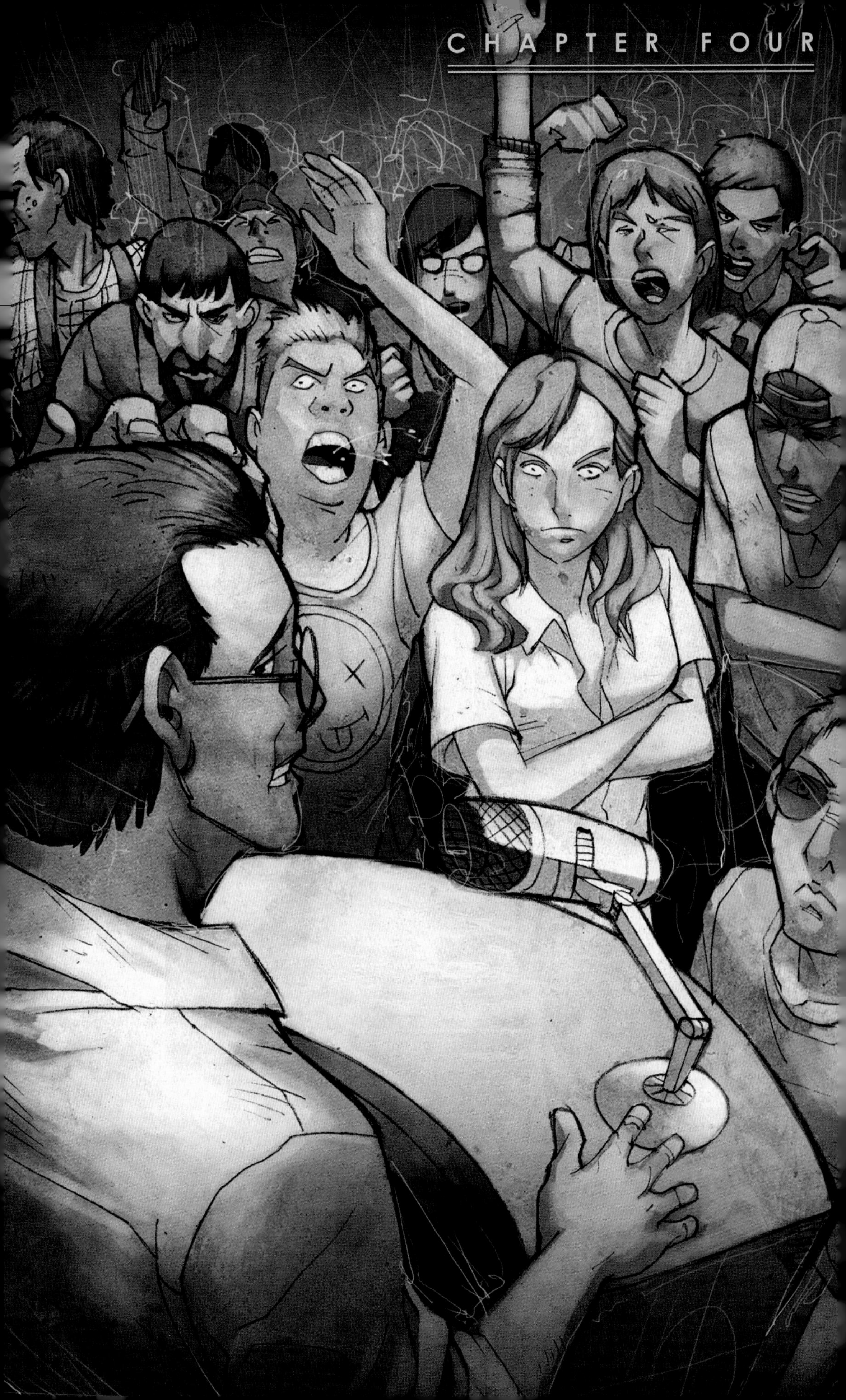

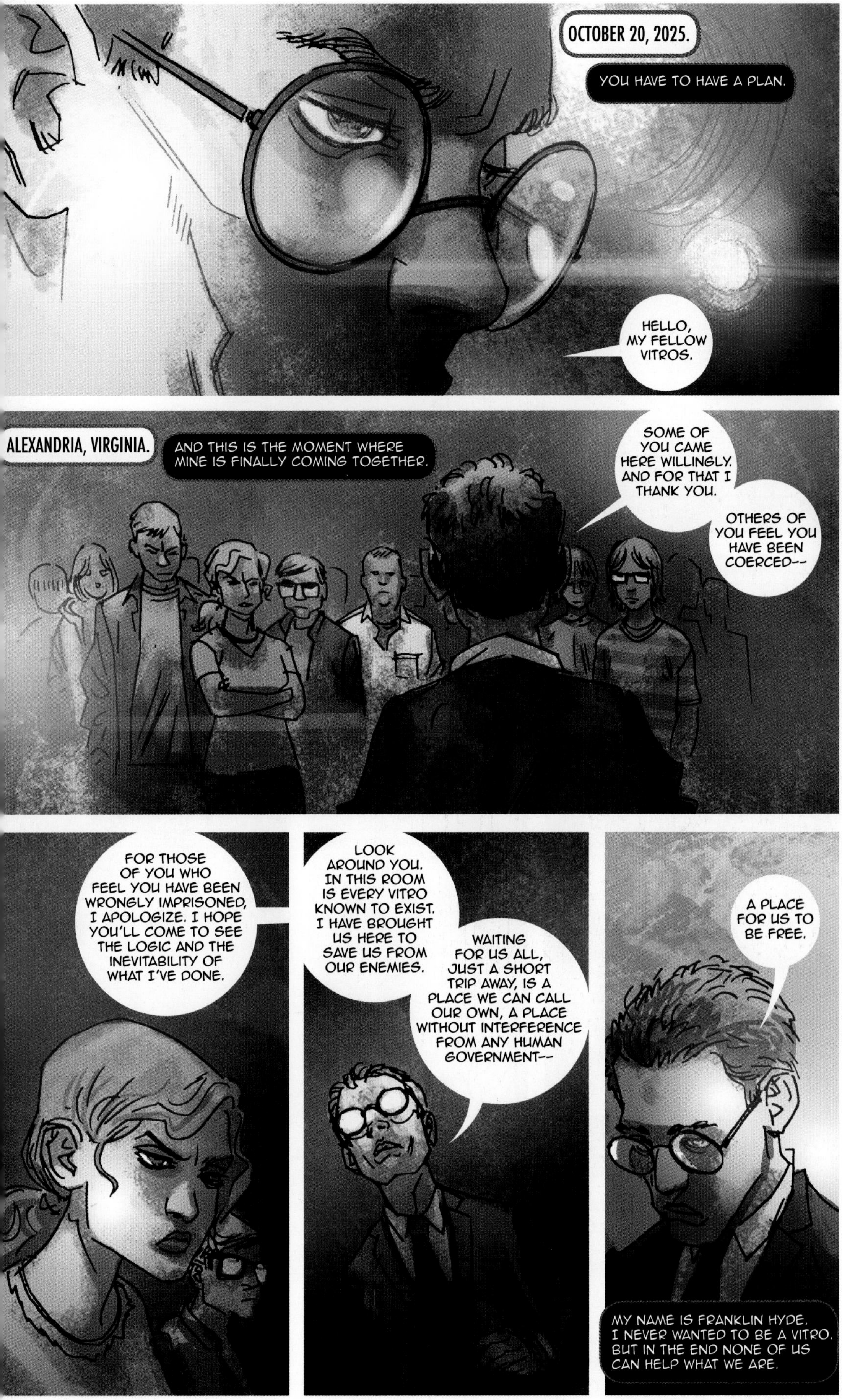
OCTOBER 20, 2025.
YOU HAVE TO HAVE A PLAN.
HELLO, MY FELLOW VITROS.
ALEXANDRIA, VIRGINIA.
AND THIS IS THE MOMENT WHERE MINE IS FINALLY COMING TOGETHER.
SOME OF YOU CAME HERE WILLINGLY. AND FOR THAT I THANK YOU.
OTHERS OF YOU FEEL YOU HAVE BEEN COERCED--
FOR THOSE OF YOU WHO FEEL YOU HAVE BEEN WRONGLY IMPRISONED, I APOLOGIZE. I HOPE YOU'LL COME TO SEE THE LOGIC AND THE INEVITABILITY OF WHAT I'VE DONE.
LOOK AROUND YOU. IN THIS ROOM IS EVERY VITRO KNOWN TO EXIST. I HAVE BROUGHT US HERE TO SAVE US FROM OUR ENEMIES.
WAITING FOR US ALL, JUST A SHORT TRIP AWAY, IS A PLACE WE CAN CALL OUR OWN, A PLACE WITHOUT INTERFERENCE FROM ANY HUMAN GOVERNMENT--
A PLACE FOR US TO BE FREE.
MY NAME IS FRANKLIN HYDE. I NEVER WANTED TO BE A VITRO. BUT IN THE END NONE OF US CAN HELP WHAT WE ARE.

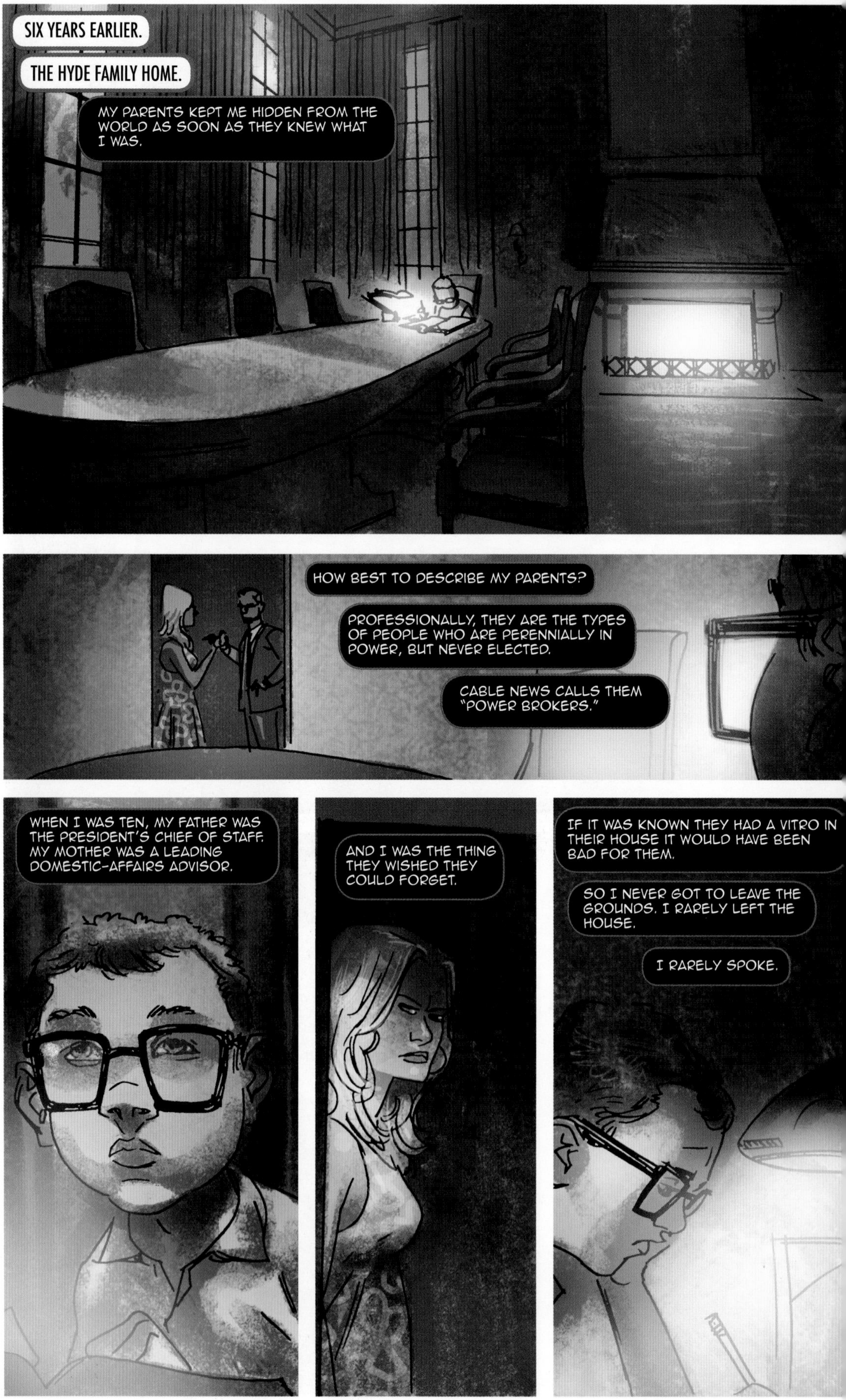
SIX YEARS EARLIER.
THE HYDE FAMILY HOME.
MY PARENTS KEPT ME HIDDEN FROM THE WORLD AS SOON AS THEY KNEW WHAT I WAS.
HOW BEST TO DESCRIBE MY PARENTS?
PROFESSIONALLY, THEY ARE THE TYPES OF PEOPLE WHO ARE PERENNIALLY IN POWER, BUT NEVER ELECTED.
CABLE NEWS CALLS THEM "POWER BROKERS."
WHEN I WAS TEN, MY FATHER WAS THE PRESIDENT'S CHIEF OF STAFF. MY MOTHER WAS A LEADING DOMESTIC-AFFAIRS ADVISOR.
AND I WAS THE THING THEY WISHED THEY COULD FORGET.
IF IT WAS KNOWN THEY HAD A VITRO IN THEIR HOUSE IT WOULD HAVE BEEN BAD FOR THEM.
SO I NEVER GOT TO LEAVE THE GROUNDS. I RARELY LEFT THE HOUSE.
I RARELY SPOKE.

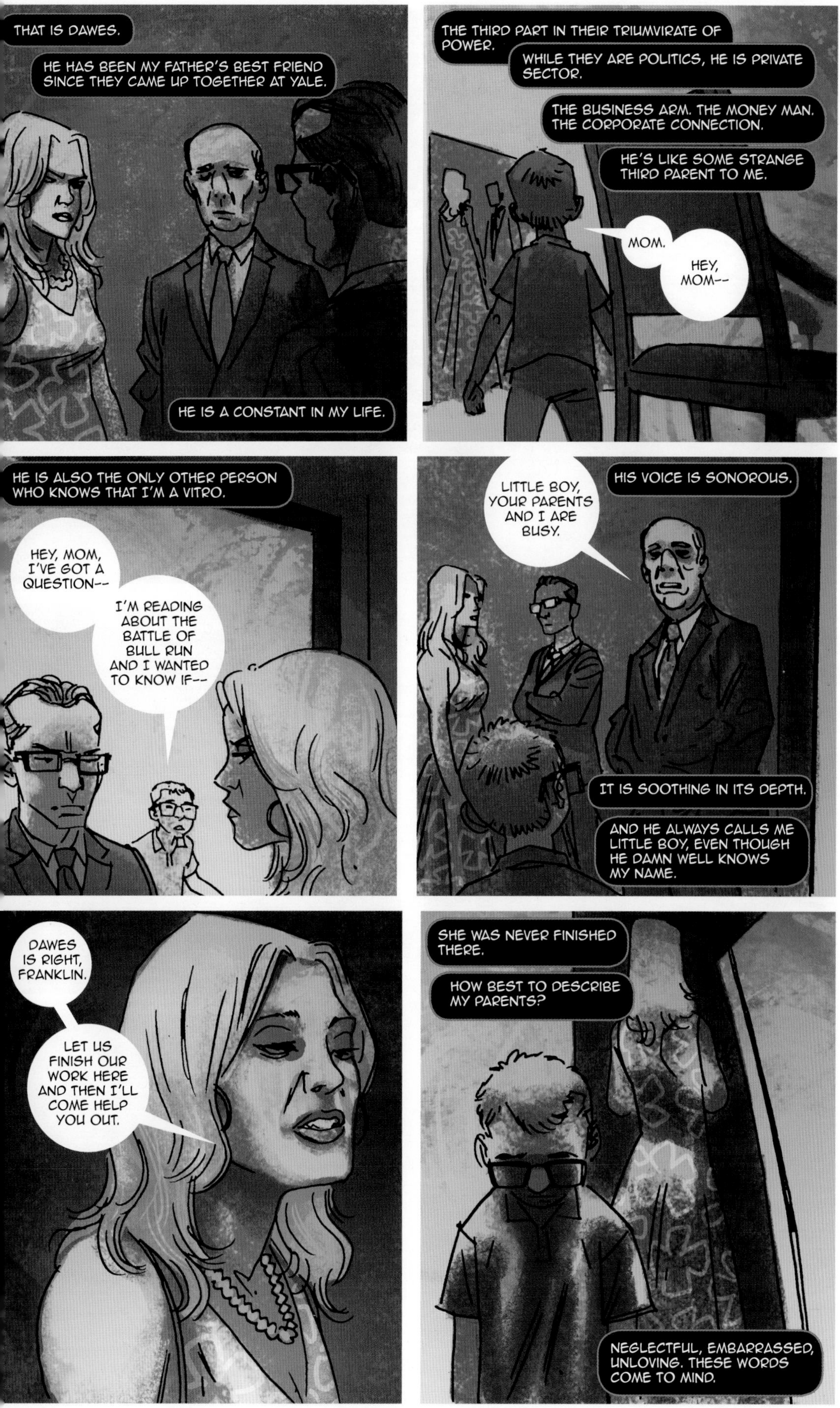
THAT IS DAWES.
HE HAS BEEN MY FATHER'S BEST FRIEND SINCE THEY CAME UP TOGETHER AT YALE.
HE IS A CONSTANT IN MY LIFE.
THE THIRD PART IN THEIR TRIUMVIRATE OF POWER.
WHILE THEY ARE POLITICS, HE IS PRIVATE SECTOR.
THE BUSINESS ARM. THE MONEY MAN. THE CORPORATE CONNECTION.
HE'S LIKE SOME STRANGE THIRD PARENT TO ME.
MOM.
HEY, MOM--
HE IS ALSO THE ONLY OTHER PERSON WHO KNOWS THAT I'M A VITRO.
HEY, MOM, I'VE GOT A QUESTION--
I'M READING ABOUT THE BATTLE OF BULL RUN AND I WANTED TO KNOW IF--
HIS VOICE IS SONOROUS.
LITTLE BOY, YOUR PARENTS AND I ARE BUSY.
IT IS SOOTHING IN ITS DEPTH.
AND HE ALWAYS CALLS ME LITTLE BOY, EVEN THOUGH HE DAMN WELL KNOWS MY NAME.
DAWES IS RIGHT, FRANKLIN.
LET US FINISH OUR WORK HERE AND THEN I'LL COME HELP YOU OUT.
SHE WAS NEVER FINISHED THERE.
HOW BEST TO DESCRIBE MY PARENTS?
NEGLECTFUL, EMBARRASSED, UNLOVING. THESE WORDS COME TO MIND.

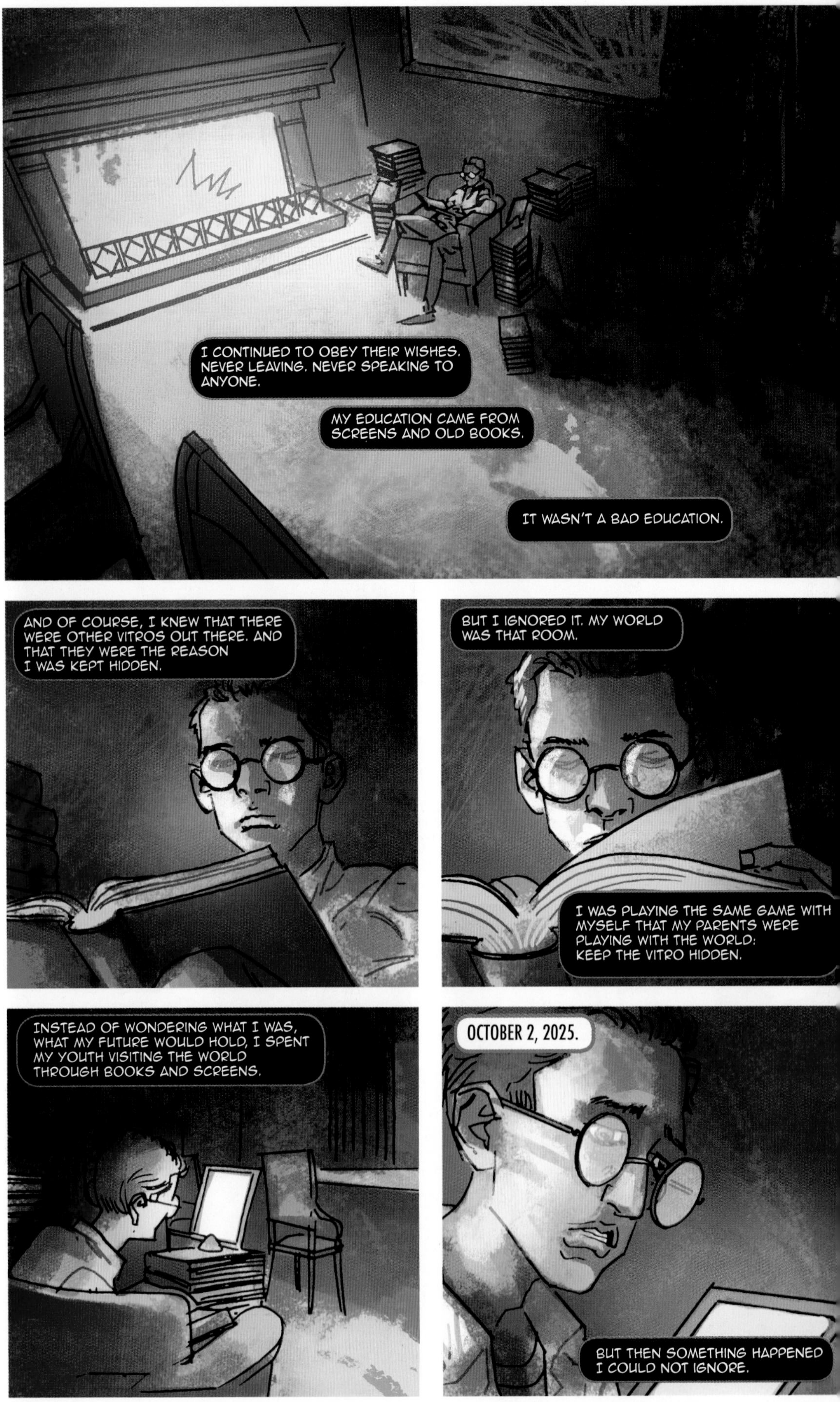
I CONTINUED TO OBEY THEIR WISHES. NEVER LEAVING. NEVER SPEAKING TO ANYONE.
MY EDUCATION CAME FROM SCREENS AND OLD BOOKS.
IT WASN'T A BAD EDUCATION.
AND OF COURSE, I KNEW THAT THERE WERE OTHER VITROS OUT THERE. AND THAT THEY WERE THE REASON I WAS KEPT HIDDEN.
BUT I IGNORED IT. MY WORLD WAS THAT ROOM.
I WAS PLAYING THE SAME GAME WITH MYSELF THAT MY PARENTS WERE PLAYING WITH THE WORLD: KEEP THE VITRO HIDDEN.
INSTEAD OF WONDERING WHAT I WAS, WHAT MY FUTURE WOULD HOLD, I SPENT MY YOUTH VISITING THE WORLD THROUGH BOOKS AND SCREENS.
OCTOBER 2, 2025.
BUT THEN SOMETHING HAPPENED I COULD NOT IGNORE.

MARINUS LAB ON FIRE

INCOMING NEWS ALERT

VITROS SUSPECTED OF ARSON.
WILL THERE BE A WAR ON VITROS?
CONGRESS CONVENES
EMERGENCY MEETING.

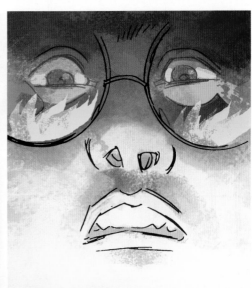

I HAD NEVER SAID THE WORD "VITRO" OUT LOUD BEFORE.

BUT SUDDENLY I FOUND MYSELF UNABLE TO STOP THINKING ABOUT IT. ABOUT *THEM.*

AND WITH THOSE THOUGHTS, RESENTMENTS I HAD HELD INSIDE ME FOR YEARS STARTED TO BUBBLE TO THE SURFACE.

WHAT IF THOSE OTHER VITROS WERE NEVER GIVEN A CHANCE, LIKE ME?

WHAT IF THEY HAD BEEN IGNORED, LIKE ME?

WHAT IF THEY HAD BEEN HELD DOWN, LIKE ME? WHAT IF THEY HAD PROFOUND UNTAPPED POTENTIAL, LIKE ME?

THE ANSWERS TO THOSE QUESTIONS WERE ALL THE SAME:

"OF COURSE. OF COURSE, THEY'RE LIKE ME."

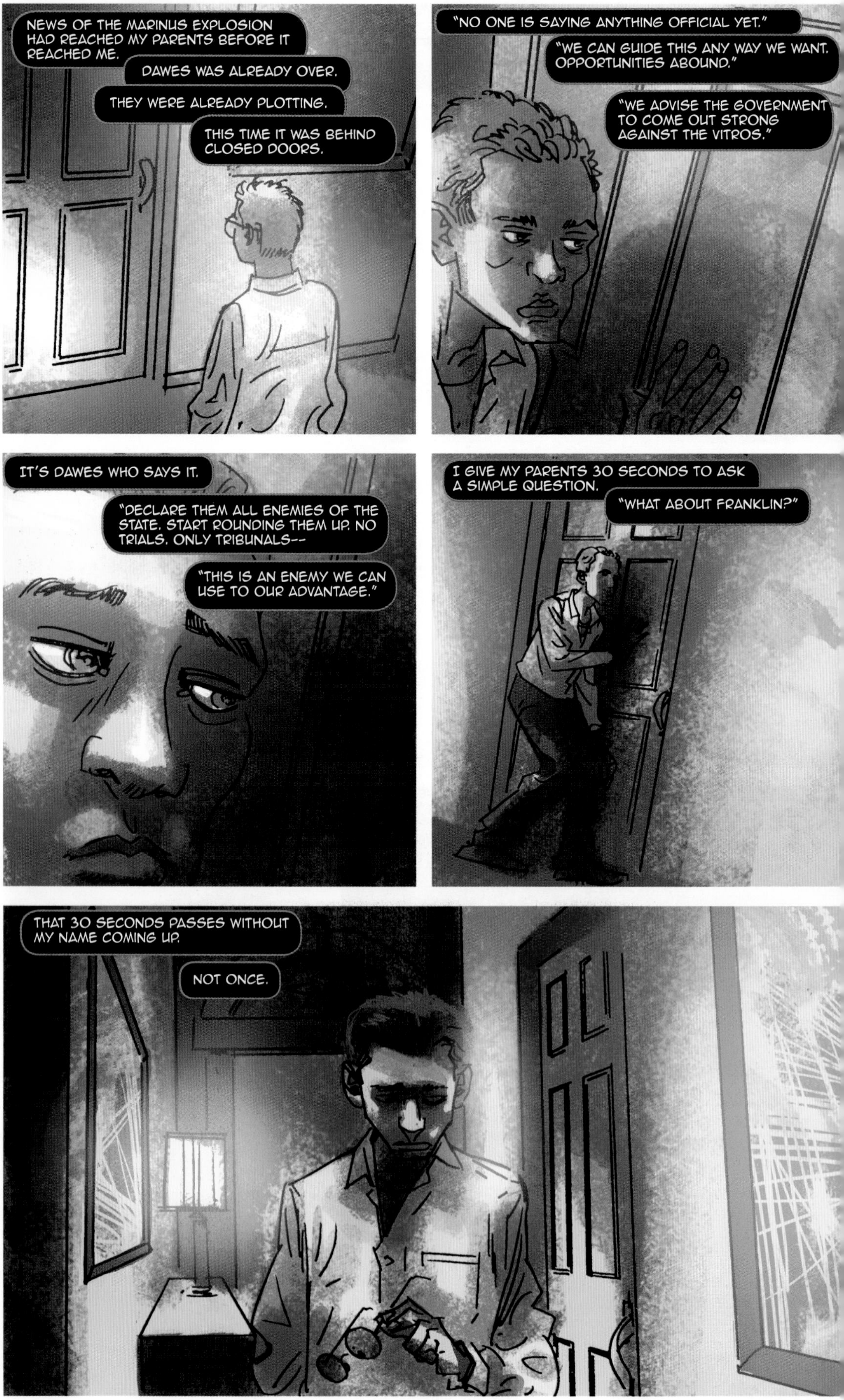
NEWS OF THE MARINUS EXPLOSION HAD REACHED MY PARENTS BEFORE IT REACHED ME.
DAWES WAS ALREADY OVER.
THEY WERE ALREADY PLOTTING.
THIS TIME IT WAS BEHIND CLOSED DOORS.
"NO ONE IS SAYING ANYTHING OFFICIAL YET."
"WE CAN GUIDE THIS ANY WAY WE WANT. OPPORTUNITIES ABOUND."
"WE ADVISE THE GOVERNMENT TO COME OUT STRONG AGAINST THE VITROS."
IT'S DAWES WHO SAYS IT.
"DECLARE THEM ALL ENEMIES OF THE STATE. START ROUNDING THEM UP. NO TRIALS. ONLY TRIBUNALS--
"THIS IS AN ENEMY WE CAN USE TO OUR ADVANTAGE."
I GIVE MY PARENTS 30 SECONDS TO ASK A SIMPLE QUESTION.
"WHAT ABOUT FRANKLIN?"
THAT 30 SECONDS PASSES WITHOUT MY NAME COMING UP.
NOT ONCE.

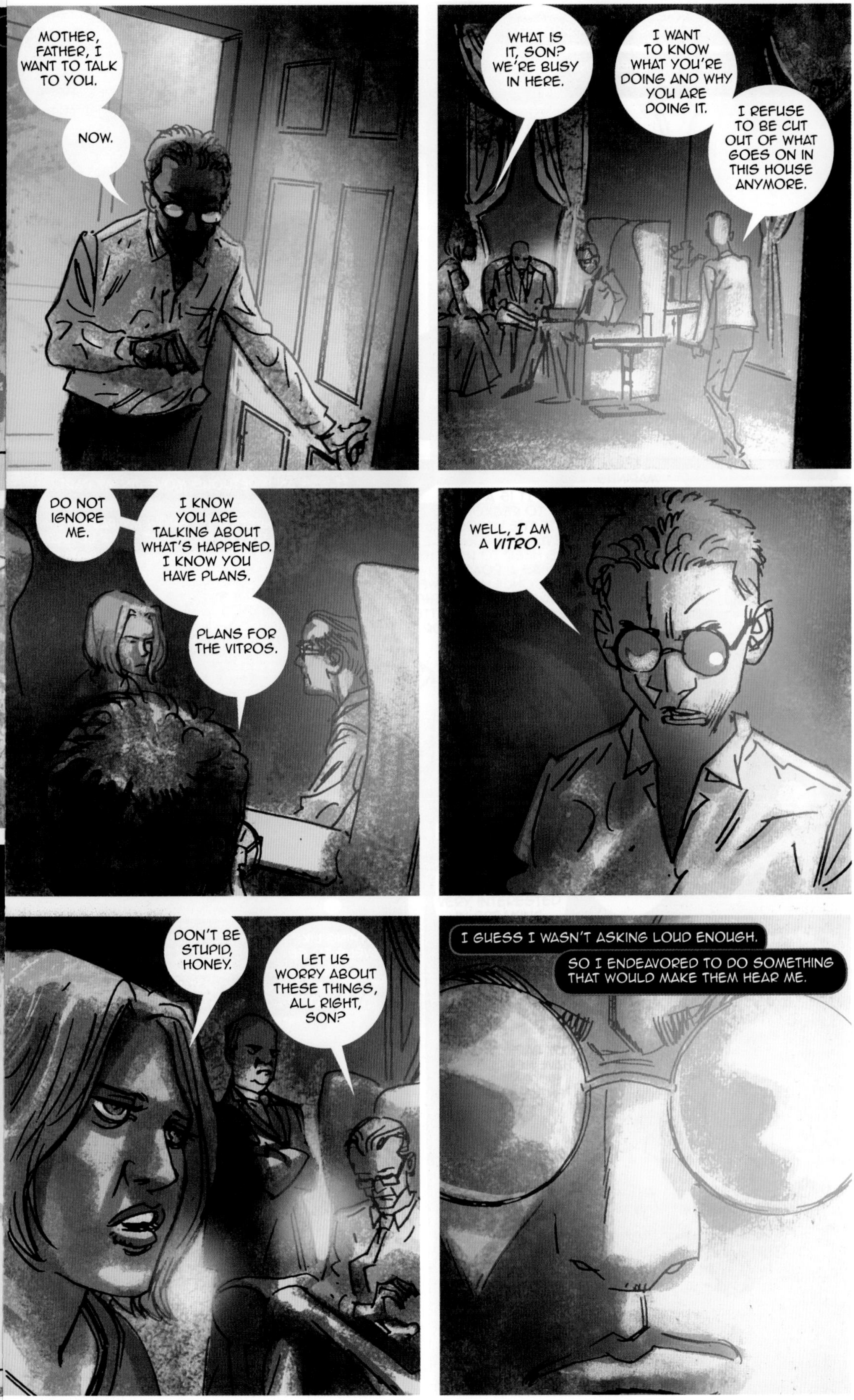
MOTHER, FATHER, I WANT TO TALK TO YOU.
NOW.
WHAT IS IT, SON? WE'RE BUSY IN HERE.
I WANT TO KNOW WHAT YOU'RE DOING AND WHY YOU ARE DOING IT.
I REFUSE TO BE CUT OUT OF WHAT GOES ON IN THIS HOUSE ANYMORE.
DO NOT IGNORE ME.
I KNOW YOU ARE TALKING ABOUT WHAT'S HAPPENED. I KNOW YOU HAVE PLANS.
PLANS FOR THE VITROS.
WELL, *I* AM A *VITRO*.
DON'T BE STUPID, HONEY.
LET US WORRY ABOUT THESE THINGS, ALL RIGHT, SON?
I GUESS I WASN'T ASKING LOUD ENOUGH.
SO I ENDEAVORED TO DO SOMETHING THAT WOULD MAKE THEM HEAR ME.

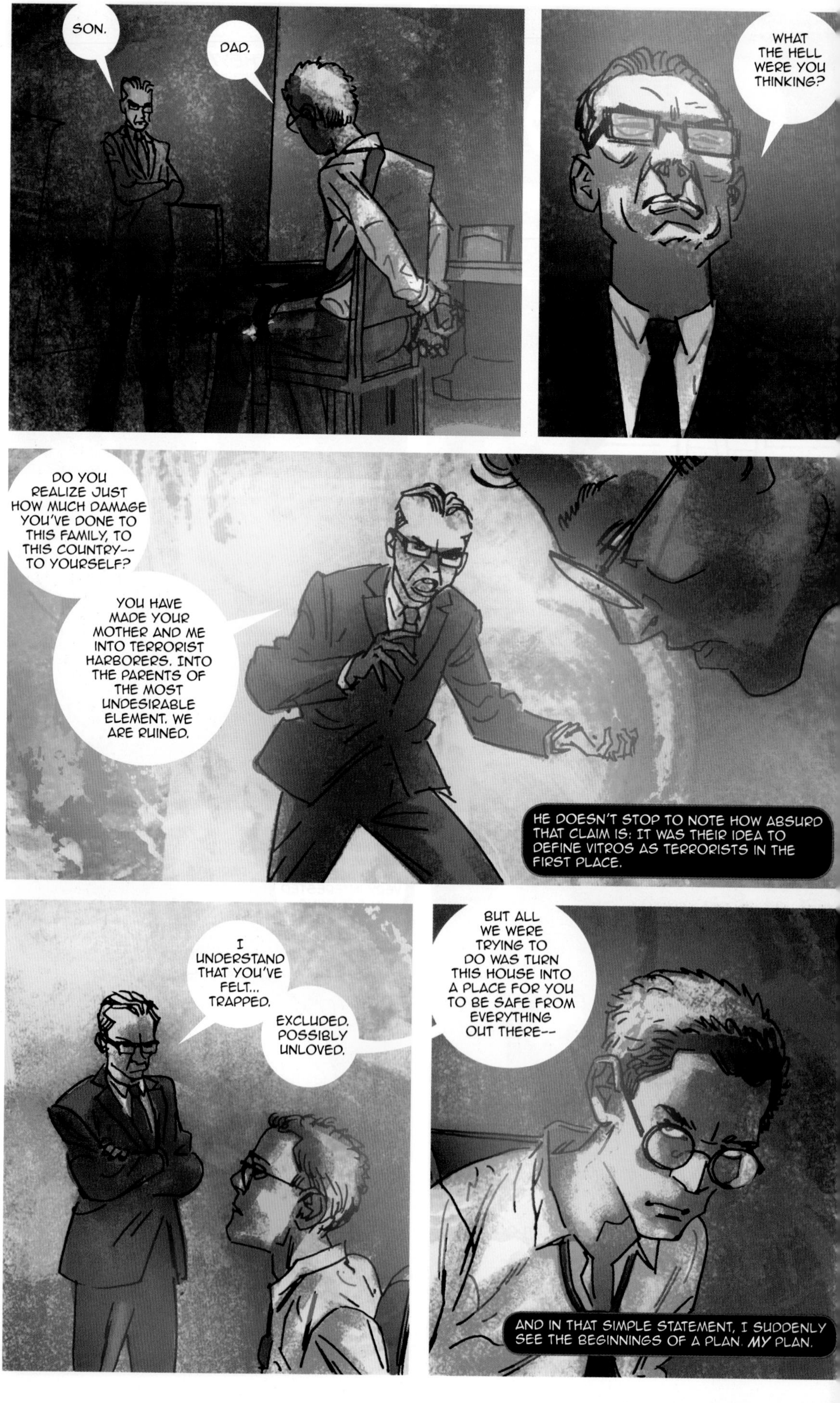
SON.
DAD.
WHAT THE HELL WERE YOU THINKING?
DO YOU REALIZE JUST HOW MUCH DAMAGE YOU'VE DONE TO THIS FAMILY, TO THIS COUNTRY-- TO YOURSELF?
YOU HAVE MADE YOUR MOTHER AND ME INTO TERRORIST HARBORERS. INTO THE PARENTS OF THE MOST UNDESIRABLE ELEMENT. WE ARE RUINED.
HE DOESN'T STOP TO NOTE HOW ABSURD THAT CLAIM IS: IT WAS THEIR IDEA TO DEFINE VITROS AS TERRORISTS IN THE FIRST PLACE.
I UNDERSTAND THAT YOU'VE FELT... TRAPPED.
EXCLUDED. POSSIBLY UNLOVED.
BUT ALL WE WERE TRYING TO DO WAS TURN THIS HOUSE INTO A PLACE FOR YOU TO BE SAFE FROM EVERYTHING OUT THERE--
AND IN THAT SIMPLE STATEMENT, I SUDDENLY SEE THE BEGINNINGS OF A PLAN. *MY* PLAN.

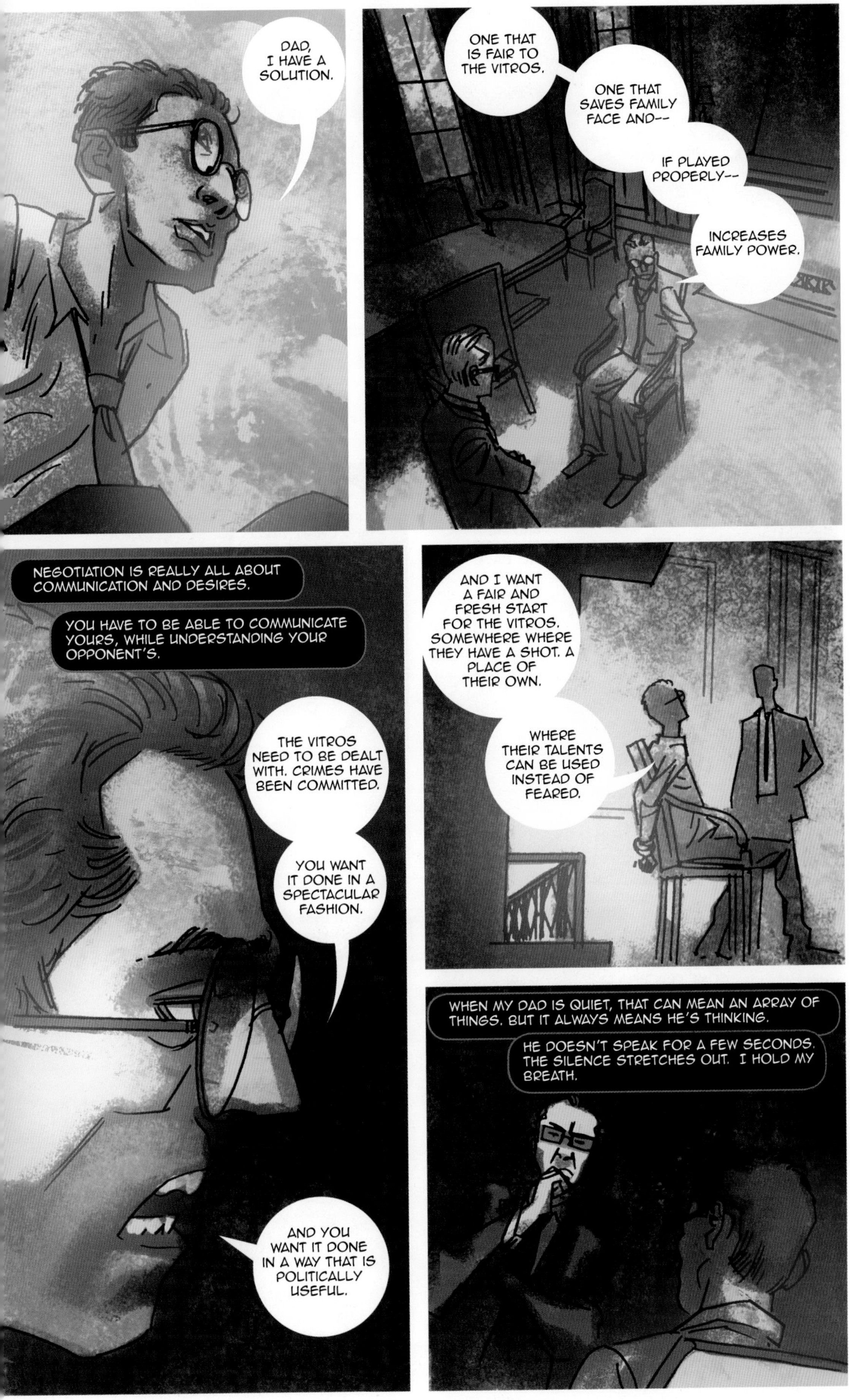
DAD, I HAVE A SOLUTION.
ONE THAT IS FAIR TO THE VITROS.
ONE THAT SAVES FAMILY FACE AND--
IF PLAYED PROPERLY--
INCREASES FAMILY POWER.
NEGOTIATION IS REALLY ALL ABOUT COMMUNICATION AND DESIRES.
YOU HAVE TO BE ABLE TO COMMUNICATE YOURS, WHILE UNDERSTANDING YOUR OPPONENT'S.
THE VITROS NEED TO BE DEALT WITH. CRIMES HAVE BEEN COMMITTED.
YOU WANT IT DONE IN A SPECTACULAR FASHION.
AND YOU WANT IT DONE IN A WAY THAT IS POLITICALLY USEFUL.
AND I WANT A FAIR AND FRESH START FOR THE VITROS. SOMEWHERE WHERE THEY HAVE A SHOT. A PLACE OF THEIR OWN.
WHERE THEIR TALENTS CAN BE USED INSTEAD OF FEARED.
WHEN MY DAD IS QUIET, THAT CAN MEAN AN ARRAY OF THINGS. BUT IT ALWAYS MEANS HE'S THINKING.
HE DOESN'T SPEAK FOR A FEW SECONDS. THE SILENCE STRETCHES OUT. I HOLD MY BREATH.

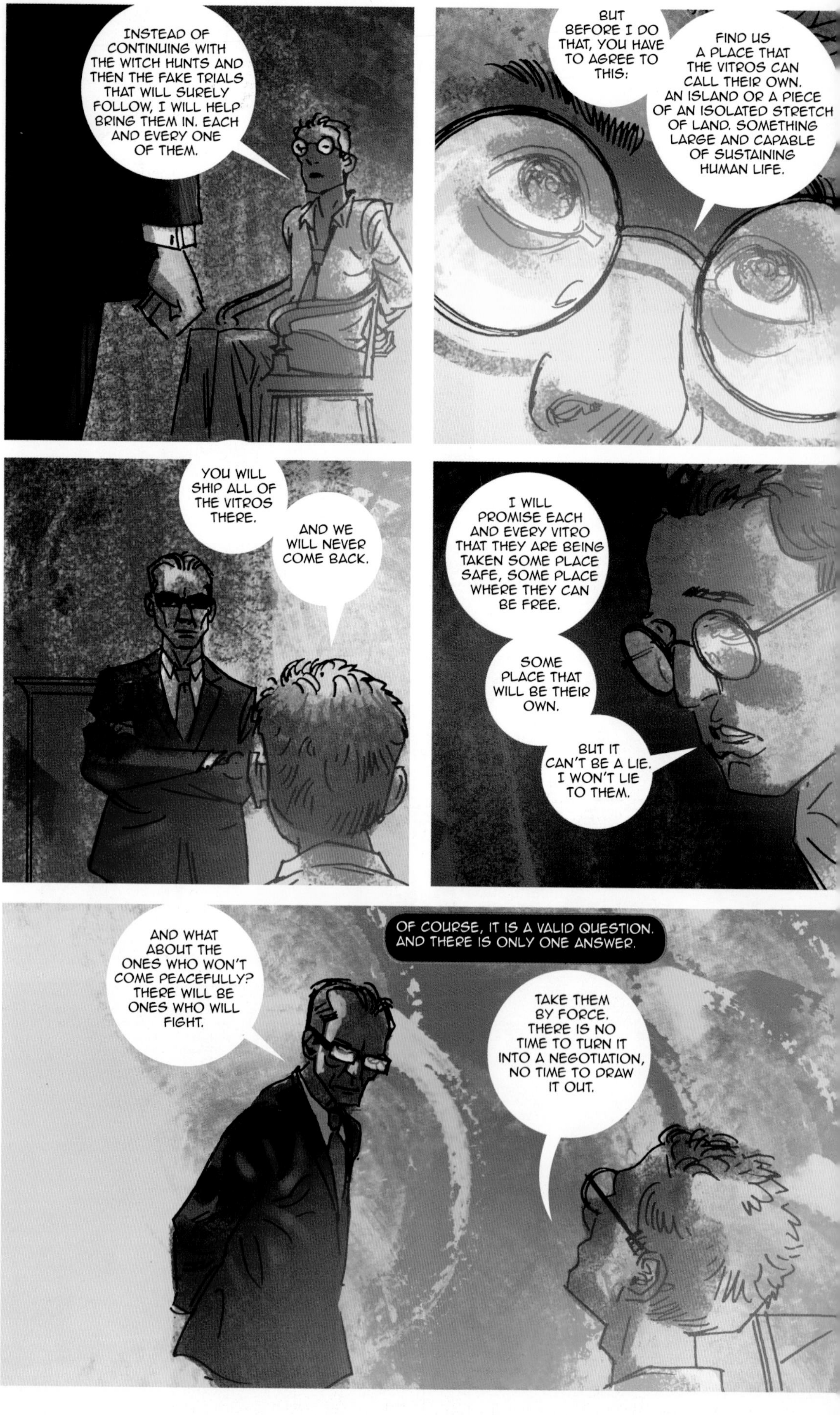

INSTEAD OF CONTINUING WITH THE WITCH HUNTS AND THEN THE FAKE TRIALS THAT WILL SURELY FOLLOW, I WILL HELP BRING THEM IN. EACH AND EVERY ONE OF THEM.
BUT BEFORE I DO THAT, YOU HAVE TO AGREE TO THIS:
FIND US A PLACE THAT THE VITROS CAN CALL THEIR OWN. AN ISLAND OR A PIECE OF AN ISOLATED STRETCH OF LAND. SOMETHING LARGE AND CAPABLE OF SUSTAINING HUMAN LIFE.
YOU WILL SHIP ALL OF THE VITROS THERE.
AND WE WILL NEVER COME BACK.
I WILL PROMISE EACH AND EVERY VITRO THAT THEY ARE BEING TAKEN SOME PLACE SAFE, SOME PLACE WHERE THEY CAN BE FREE.
SOME PLACE THAT WILL BE THEIR OWN.
BUT IT CAN'T BE A LIE. I WON'T LIE TO THEM.
AND WHAT ABOUT THE ONES WHO WON'T COME PEACEFULLY? THERE WILL BE ONES WHO WILL FIGHT.
OF COURSE, IT IS A VALID QUESTION. AND THERE IS ONLY ONE ANSWER.
TAKE THEM BY FORCE. THERE IS NO TIME TO TURN IT INTO A NEGOTIATION, NO TIME TO DRAW IT OUT.

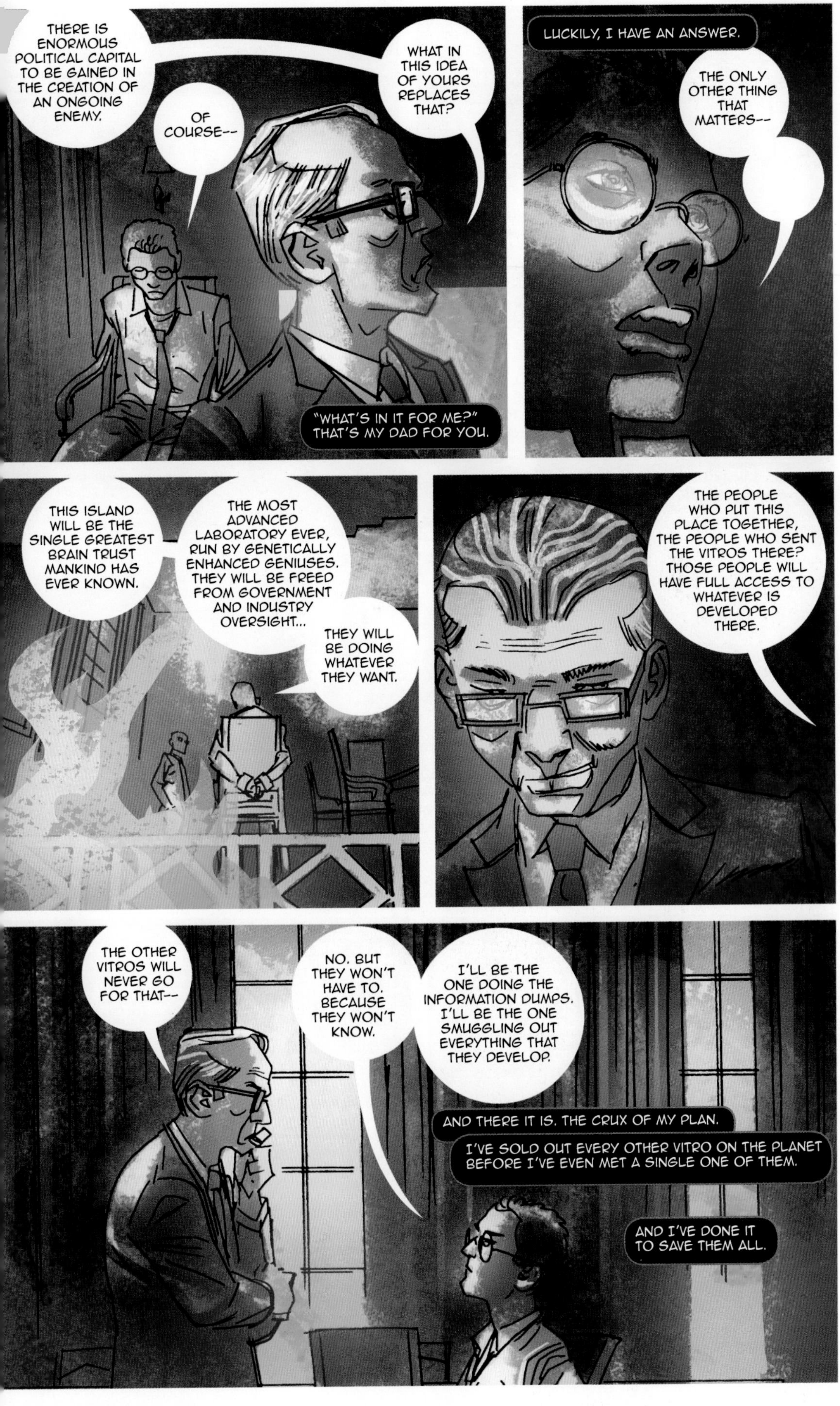

THERE IS ENORMOUS POLITICAL CAPITAL TO BE GAINED IN THE CREATION OF AN ONGOING ENEMY.
OF COURSE--
WHAT IN THIS IDEA OF YOURS REPLACES THAT?
"WHAT'S IN IT FOR ME?" THAT'S MY DAD FOR YOU.
LUCKILY, I HAVE AN ANSWER.
THE ONLY OTHER THING THAT MATTERS--
THIS ISLAND WILL BE THE SINGLE GREATEST BRAIN TRUST MANKIND HAS EVER KNOWN.
THE MOST ADVANCED LABORATORY EVER, RUN BY GENETICALLY ENHANCED GENIUSES. THEY WILL BE FREED FROM GOVERNMENT AND INDUSTRY OVERSIGHT...
THEY WILL BE DOING WHATEVER THEY WANT.
THE PEOPLE WHO PUT THIS PLACE TOGETHER, THE PEOPLE WHO SENT THE VITROS THERE? THOSE PEOPLE WILL HAVE FULL ACCESS TO WHATEVER IS DEVELOPED THERE.
THE OTHER VITROS WILL NEVER GO FOR THAT--
NO. BUT THEY WON'T HAVE TO. BECAUSE THEY WON'T KNOW.
I'LL BE THE ONE DOING THE INFORMATION DUMPS. I'LL BE THE ONE SMUGGLING OUT EVERYTHING THAT THEY DEVELOP.
AND THERE IT IS. THE CRUX OF MY PLAN.
I'VE SOLD OUT EVERY OTHER VITRO ON THE PLANET BEFORE I'VE EVEN MET A SINGLE ONE OF THEM.
AND I'VE DONE IT TO SAVE THEM ALL.

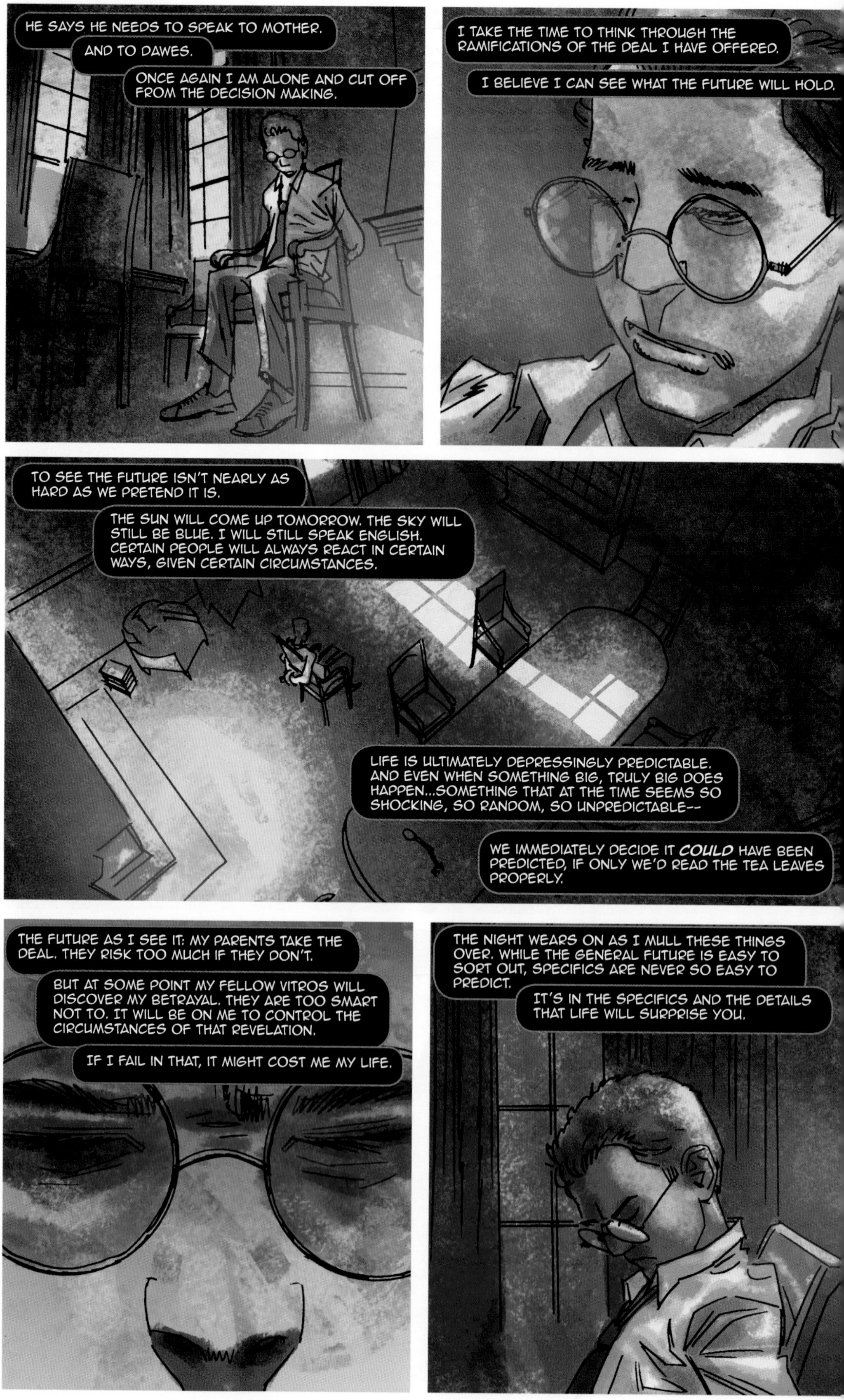
HE SAYS HE NEEDS TO SPEAK TO MOTHER.
AND TO DAWES.
ONCE AGAIN I AM ALONE AND CUT OFF FROM THE DECISION MAKING.
I TAKE THE TIME TO THINK THROUGH THE RAMIFICATIONS OF THE DEAL I HAVE OFFERED.
I BELIEVE I CAN SEE WHAT THE FUTURE WILL HOLD.
TO SEE THE FUTURE ISN'T NEARLY AS HARD AS WE PRETEND IT IS.
THE SUN WILL COME UP TOMORROW. THE SKY WILL STILL BE BLUE. I WILL STILL SPEAK ENGLISH. CERTAIN PEOPLE WILL ALWAYS REACT IN CERTAIN WAYS, GIVEN CERTAIN CIRCUMSTANCES.
LIFE IS ULTIMATELY DEPRESSINGLY PREDICTABLE. AND EVEN WHEN SOMETHING BIG, TRULY BIG DOES HAPPEN...SOMETHING THAT AT THE TIME SEEMS SO SHOCKING, SO RANDOM, SO UNPREDICTABLE--
WE IMMEDIATELY DECIDE IT *COULD* HAVE BEEN PREDICTED, IF ONLY WE'D READ THE TEA LEAVES PROPERLY.
THE FUTURE AS I SEE IT: MY PARENTS TAKE THE DEAL. THEY RISK TOO MUCH IF THEY DON'T.
BUT AT SOME POINT MY FELLOW VITROS WILL DISCOVER MY BETRAYAL. THEY ARE TOO SMART NOT TO. IT WILL BE ON ME TO CONTROL THE CIRCUMSTANCES OF THAT REVELATION.
IF I FAIL IN THAT, IT MIGHT COST ME MY LIFE.
THE NIGHT WEARS ON AS I MULL THESE THINGS OVER. WHILE THE GENERAL FUTURE IS EASY TO SORT OUT, SPECIFICS ARE NEVER SO EASY TO PREDICT.
IT'S IN THE SPECIFICS AND THE DETAILS THAT LIFE WILL SURPRISE YOU.

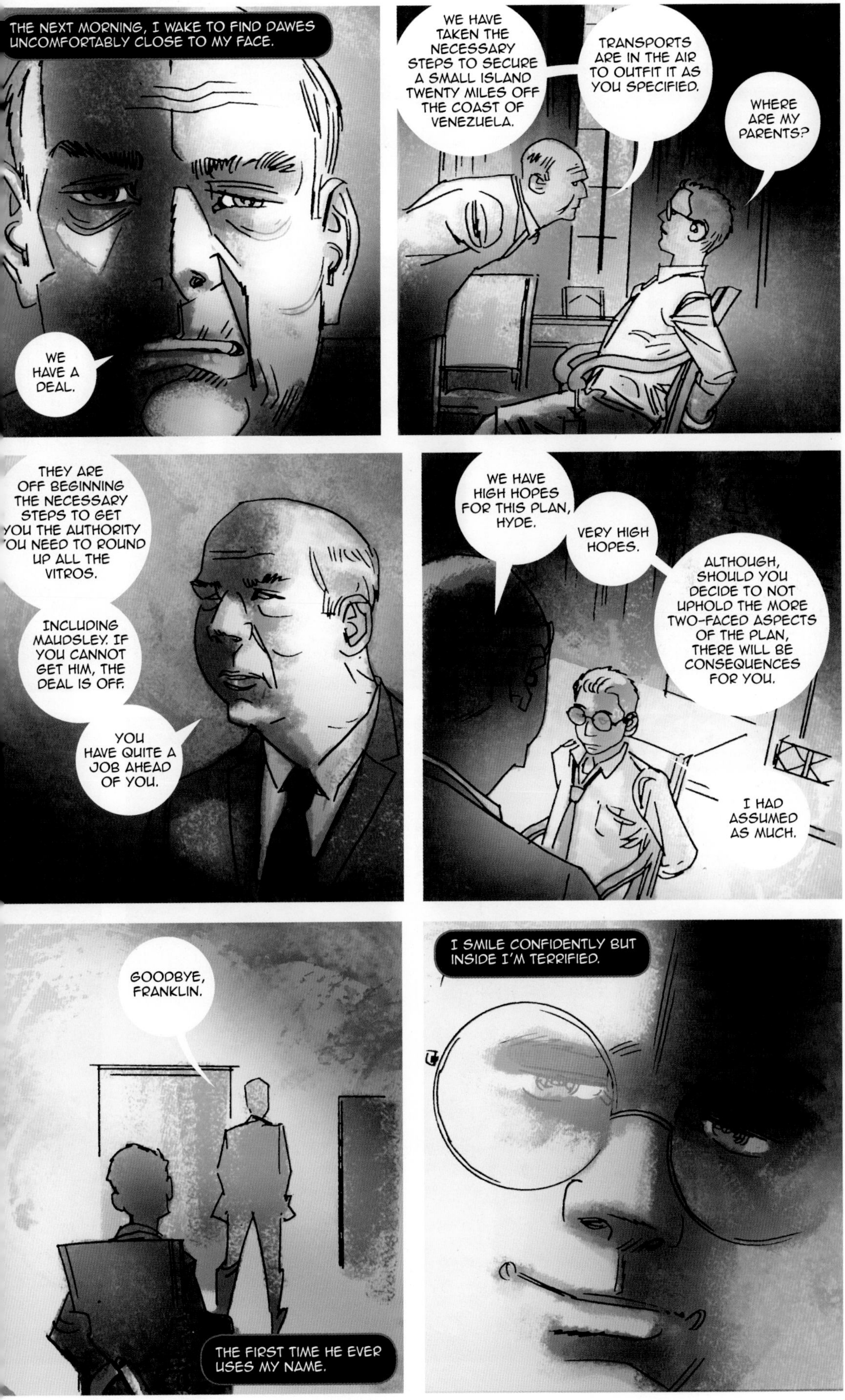
THE NEXT MORNING, I WAKE TO FIND DAWES UNCOMFORTABLY CLOSE TO MY FACE.
WE HAVE A DEAL.
WE HAVE TAKEN THE NECESSARY STEPS TO SECURE A SMALL ISLAND TWENTY MILES OFF THE COAST OF VENEZUELA.
TRANSPORTS ARE IN THE AIR TO OUTFIT IT AS YOU SPECIFIED.
WHERE ARE MY PARENTS?
THEY ARE OFF BEGINNING THE NECESSARY STEPS TO GET YOU THE AUTHORITY YOU NEED TO ROUND UP ALL THE VITROS.
INCLUDING MAUDSLEY. IF YOU CANNOT GET HIM, THE DEAL IS OFF.
YOU HAVE QUITE A JOB AHEAD OF YOU.
WE HAVE HIGH HOPES FOR THIS PLAN, HYDE.
VERY HIGH HOPES.
ALTHOUGH, SHOULD YOU DECIDE TO NOT UPHOLD THE MORE TWO-FACED ASPECTS OF THE PLAN, THERE WILL BE CONSEQUENCES FOR YOU.
I HAD ASSUMED AS MUCH.
GOODBYE, FRANKLIN.
THE FIRST TIME HE EVER USES MY NAME.
I SMILE CONFIDENTLY BUT INSIDE I'M TERRIFIED.

THE BITTERROOT FOREST.

OCTOBER 10, 2025.

MY FIRST ORDER OF BUSINESS IS THE KIDS FROM MARINUS.

I DON'T HOLD OUT HOPE THAT THEY WILL COME PEACEFULLY. WHY WOULD THEY? THEY ARE SCARED, HUNTED.

I BELIEVE THEY ARE INNOCENT. BUT PROVING THAT IS SOMETHING FOR ANOTHER DAY.

I TRY TO LAY THE GROUNDWORK FOR FUTURE COLLABORATION.

I WILL NEED HER TRUST.

I TRAVEL ACROSS THE COUNTRY, ACROSS THE WORLD.

FORTUNATELY, VITROS ARE WELL DOCUMENTED. I DON'T HAVE A PROBLEM FINDING THEM.

AND THEN THERE'S MAUDSLEY.

DEVON MATTHEWS

ROBERT MAUDSLEY

VITRO

PRESENT LOCATION: UNKNOW

A UNIQUE PROBLEM. I GO FOR HIM LAST.

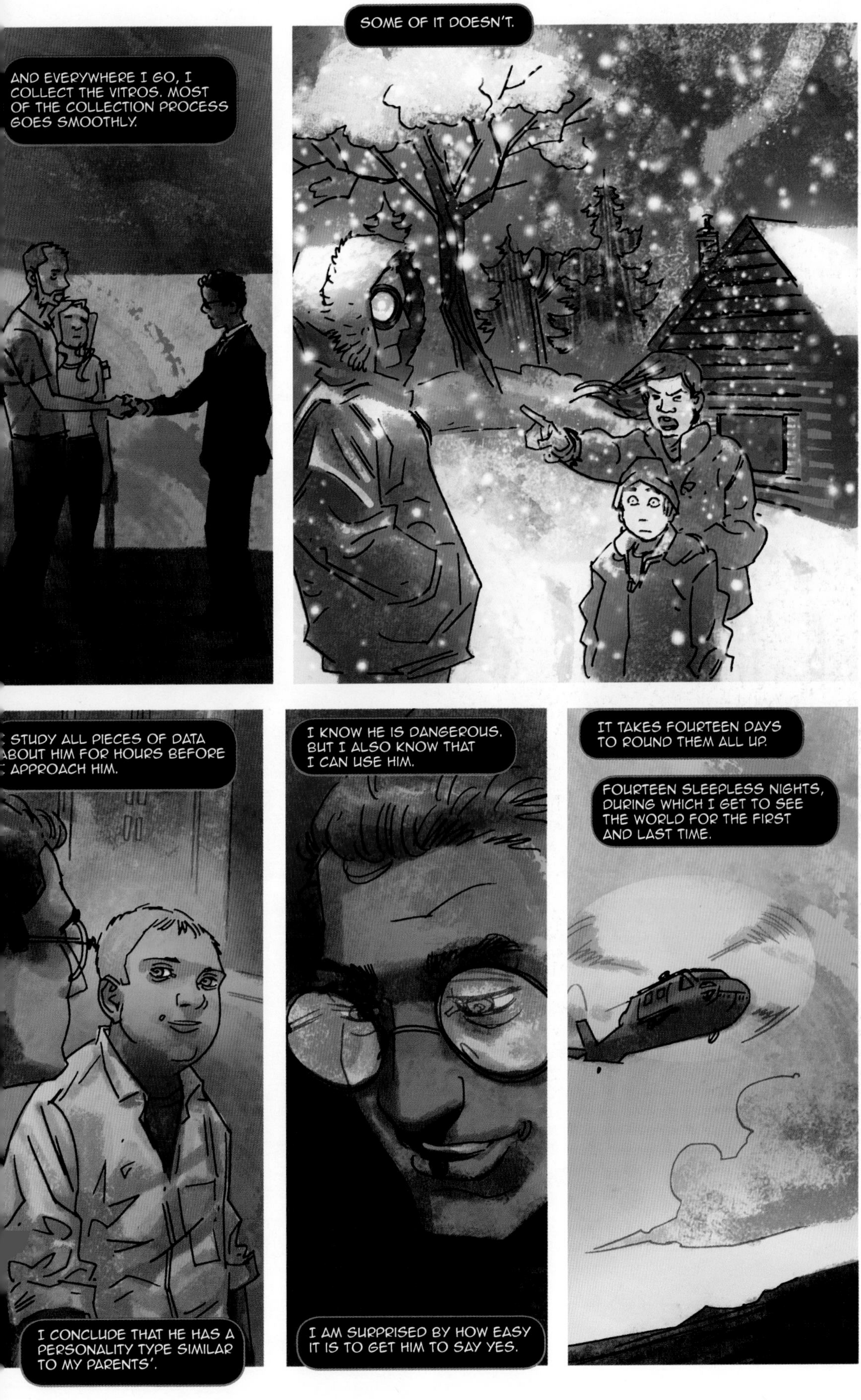
AND EVERYWHERE I GO, I COLLECT THE VITROS. MOST OF THE COLLECTION PROCESS GOES SMOOTHLY.
SOME OF IT DOESN'T.
STUDY ALL PIECES OF DATA ABOUT HIM FOR HOURS BEFORE APPROACH HIM.
I CONCLUDE THAT HE HAS A PERSONALITY TYPE SIMILAR TO MY PARENTS'.
I KNOW HE IS DANGEROUS. BUT I ALSO KNOW THAT I CAN USE HIM.
I AM SURPRISED BY HOW EASY IT IS TO GET HIM TO SAY YES.
IT TAKES FOURTEEN DAYS TO ROUND THEM ALL UP.
FOURTEEN SLEEPLESS NIGHTS, DURING WHICH I GET TO SEE THE WORLD FOR THE FIRST AND LAST TIME.

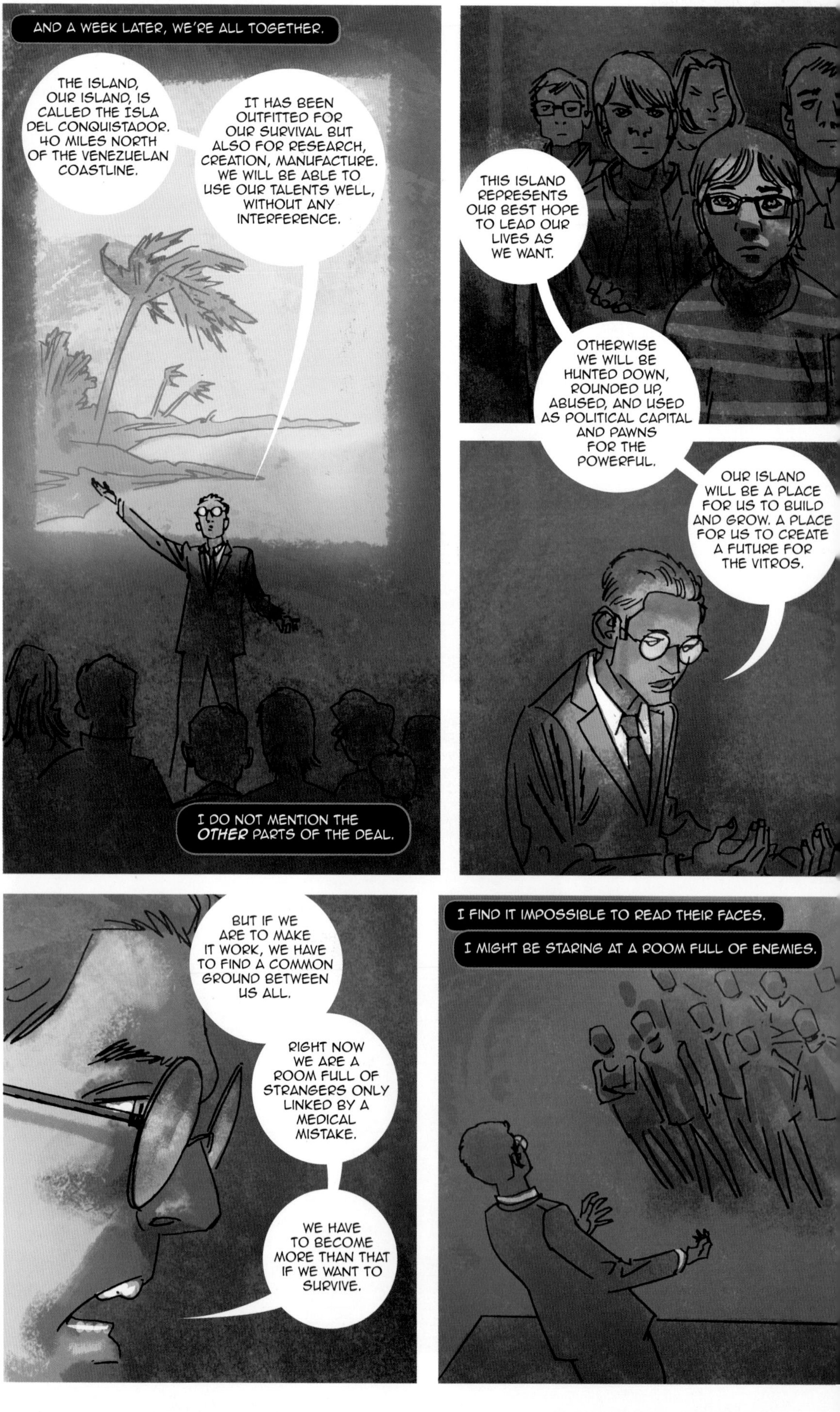
AND A WEEK LATER, WE'RE ALL TOGETHER.
THE ISLAND, OUR ISLAND, IS CALLED THE ISLA DEL CONQUISTADOR. 40 MILES NORTH OF THE VENEZUELAN COASTLINE.
IT HAS BEEN OUTFITTED FOR OUR SURVIVAL BUT ALSO FOR RESEARCH, CREATION, MANUFACTURE. WE WILL BE ABLE TO USE OUR TALENTS WELL, WITHOUT ANY INTERFERENCE.
I DO NOT MENTION THE *OTHER* PARTS OF THE DEAL.
THIS ISLAND REPRESENTS OUR BEST HOPE TO LEAD OUR LIVES AS WE WANT.
OTHERWISE WE WILL BE HUNTED DOWN, ROUNDED UP, ABUSED, AND USED AS POLITICAL CAPITAL AND PAWNS FOR THE POWERFUL.
OUR ISLAND WILL BE A PLACE FOR US TO BUILD AND GROW. A PLACE FOR US TO CREATE A FUTURE FOR THE VITROS.
BUT IF WE ARE TO MAKE IT WORK, WE HAVE TO FIND A COMMON GROUND BETWEEN US ALL.
RIGHT NOW WE ARE A ROOM FULL OF STRANGERS ONLY LINKED BY A MEDICAL MISTAKE.
WE HAVE TO BECOME MORE THAN THAT IF WE WANT TO SURVIVE.
I FIND IT IMPOSSIBLE TO READ THEIR FACES.
I MIGHT BE STARING AT A ROOM FULL OF ENEMIES.

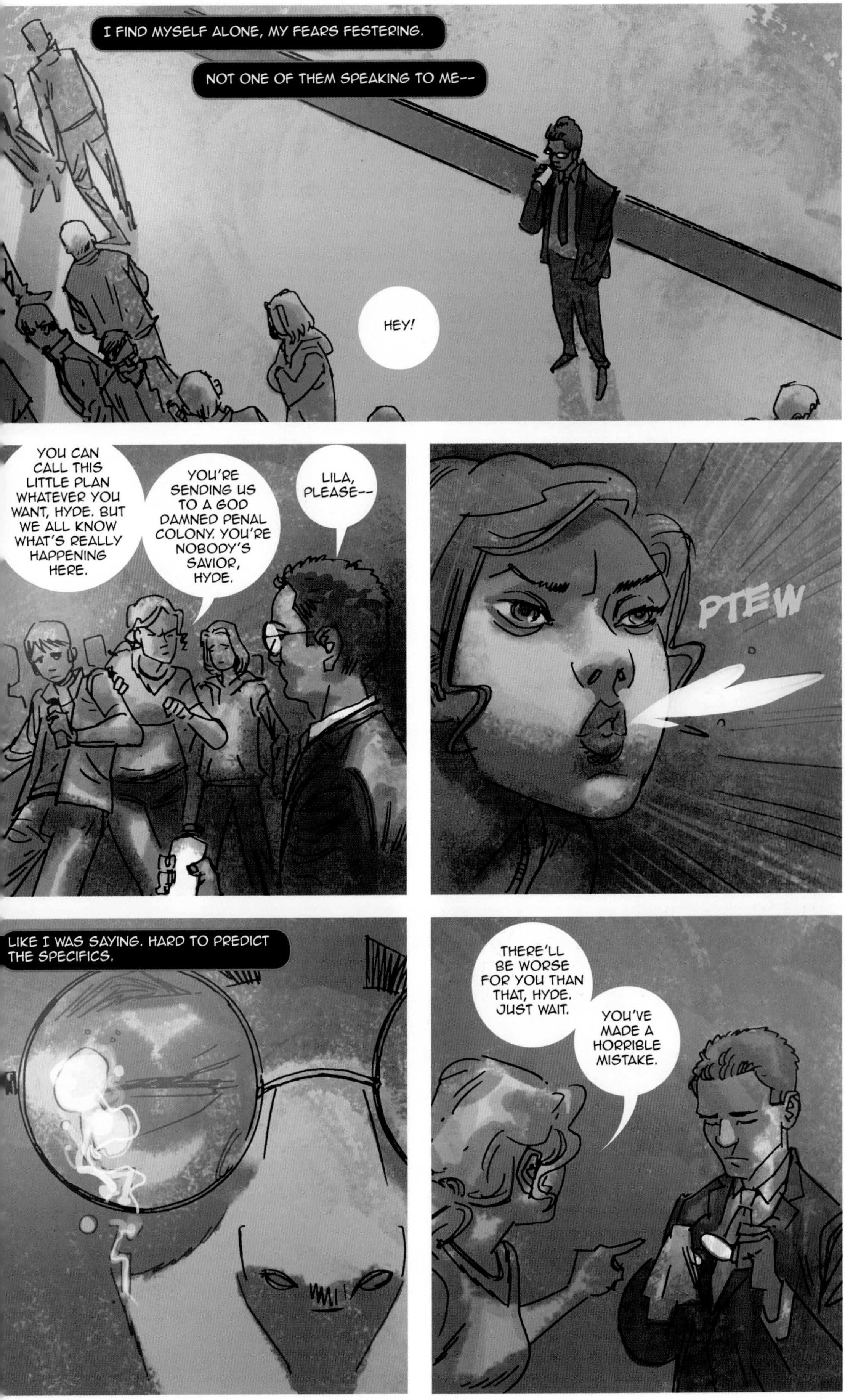

I FIND MYSELF ALONE, MY FEARS FESTERING.
NOT ONE OF THEM SPEAKING TO ME--
HEY!
YOU CAN CALL THIS LITTLE PLAN WHATEVER YOU WANT, HYDE. BUT WE ALL KNOW WHAT'S REALLY HAPPENING HERE.
YOU'RE SENDING US TO A GOD DAMNED PENAL COLONY. YOU'RE NOBODY'S SAVIOR, HYDE.
LILA, PLEASE--
PTEW
LIKE I WAS SAYING. HARD TO PREDICT THE SPECIFICS.
THERE'LL BE WORSE FOR YOU THAN THAT, HYDE. JUST WAIT.
YOU'VE MADE A HORRIBLE MISTAKE.

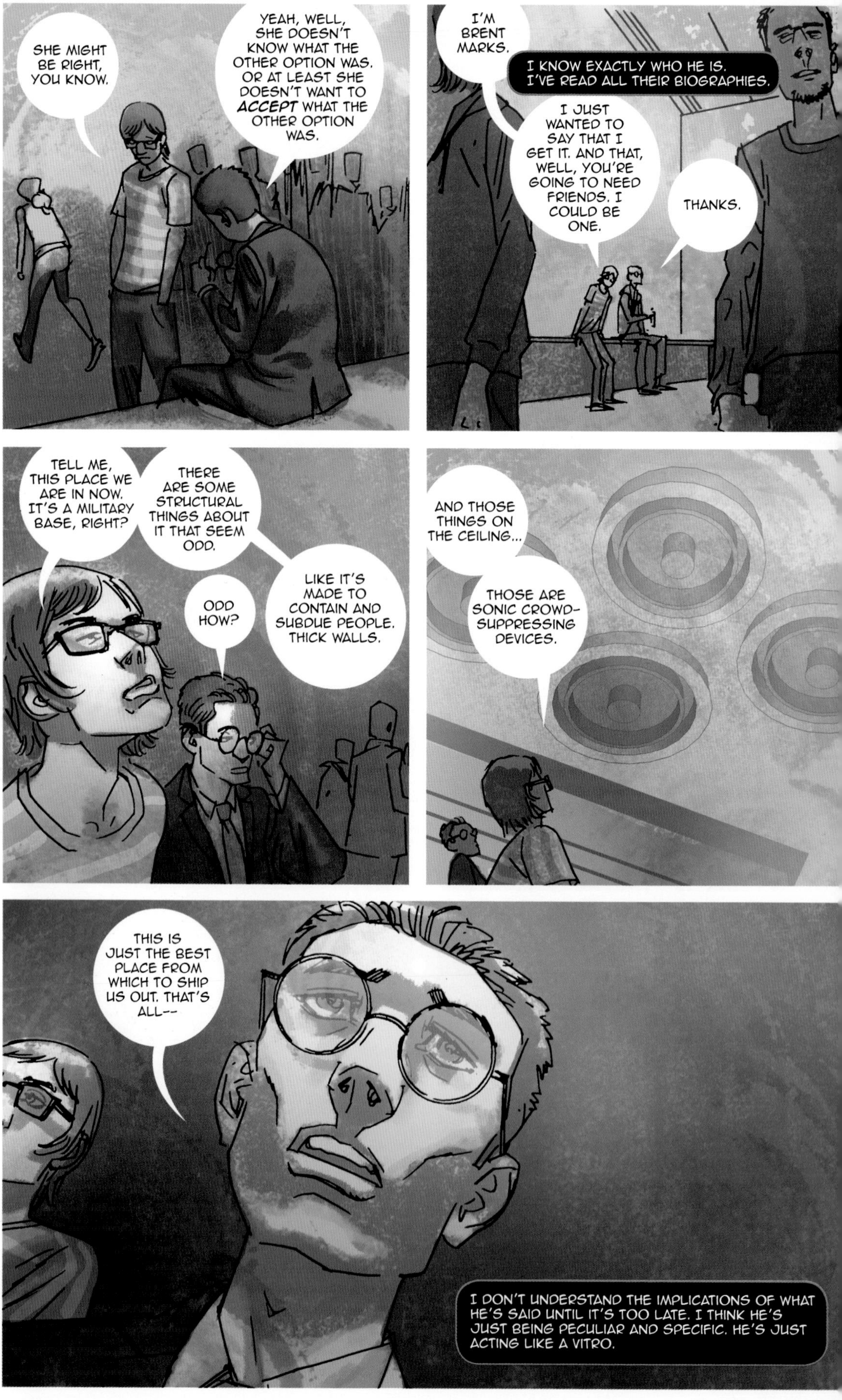
SHE MIGHT BE RIGHT, YOU KNOW.
YEAH, WELL, SHE DOESN'T KNOW WHAT THE OTHER OPTION WAS. OR AT LEAST SHE DOESN'T WANT TO ***ACCEPT*** WHAT THE OTHER OPTION WAS.
I'M BRENT MARKS.
I KNOW EXACTLY WHO HE IS. I'VE READ ALL THEIR BIOGRAPHIES.
I JUST WANTED TO SAY THAT I GET IT. AND THAT, WELL, YOU'RE GOING TO NEED FRIENDS. I COULD BE ONE.
THANKS.
TELL ME, THIS PLACE WE ARE IN NOW. IT'S A MILITARY BASE, RIGHT?
THERE ARE SOME STRUCTURAL THINGS ABOUT IT THAT SEEM ODD.
ODD HOW?
LIKE IT'S MADE TO CONTAIN AND SUBDUE PEOPLE. THICK WALLS.
AND THOSE THINGS ON THE CEILING...
THOSE ARE SONIC CROWD-SUPPRESSING DEVICES.
THIS IS JUST THE BEST PLACE FROM WHICH TO SHIP US OUT. THAT'S ALL--
I DON'T UNDERSTAND THE IMPLICATIONS OF WHAT HE'S SAID UNTIL IT'S TOO LATE. I THINK HE'S JUST BEING PECULIAR AND SPECIFIC. HE'S JUST ACTING LIKE A VITRO.

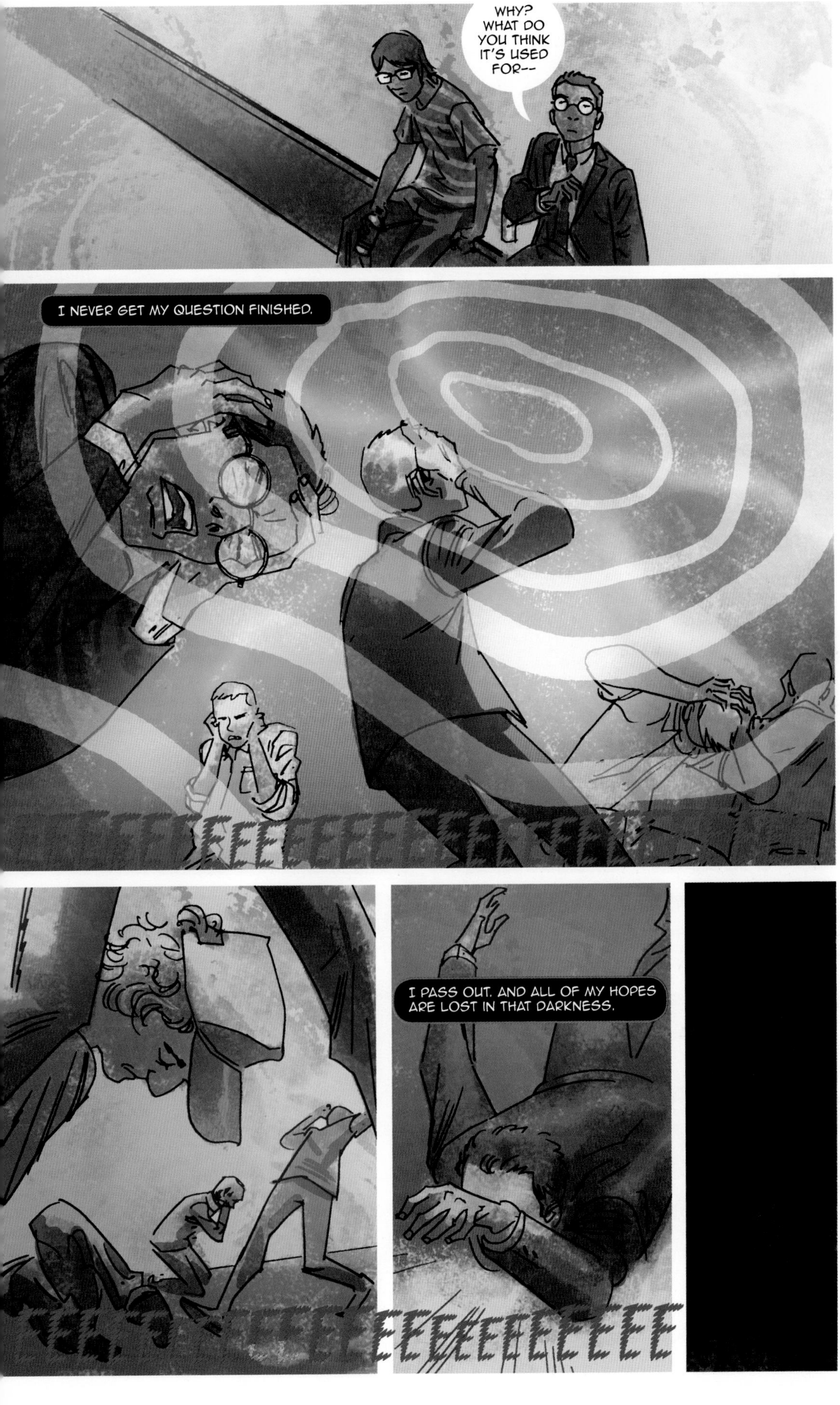
WHY? WHAT DO YOU THINK IT'S USED FOR--
I NEVER GET MY QUESTION FINISHED.
EEEEEEEEEEEEE
I PASS OUT. AND ALL OF MY HOPES ARE LOST IN THAT DARKNESS.
EEEEEEEEEEE

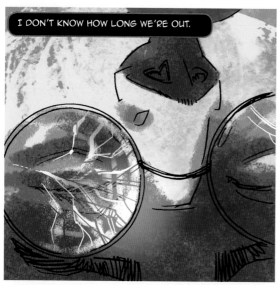

I DON'T KNOW HOW LONG WE'RE OUT.

I DON'T UNDERSTAND WHAT I'M SEEING WHEN I OPEN MY EYES.

WHAT THE HELL IS GOING ON?

YOU DON'T KNOW?

I THOUGHT THIS WAS ALL YOUR PLAN!

NOT THIS... WHATEVER THIS IS. WHERE *ARE* WE?

COME LOOK.

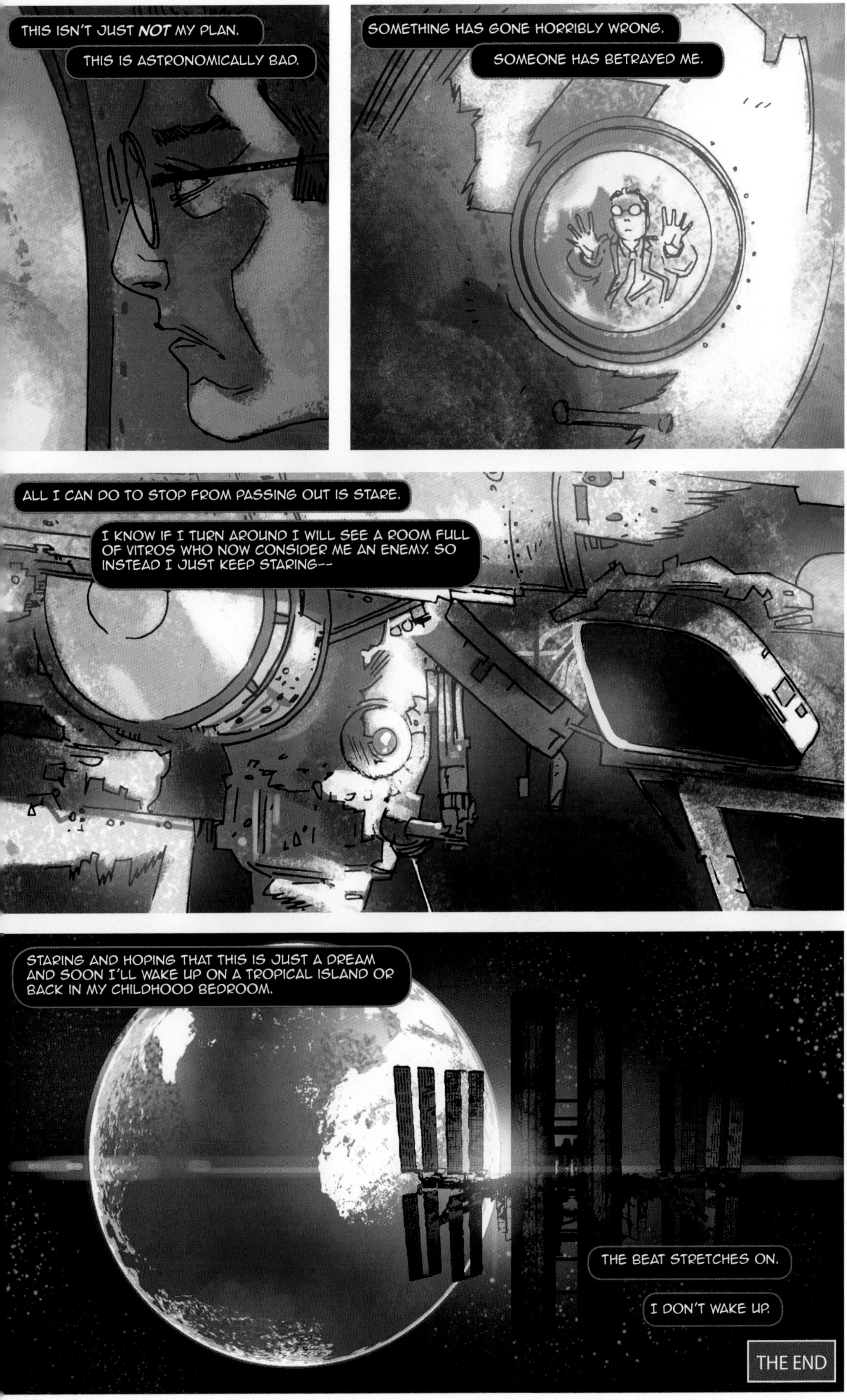
THIS ISN'T JUST *NOT* MY PLAN.
THIS IS ASTRONOMICALLY BAD.
SOMETHING HAS GONE HORRIBLY WRONG.
SOMEONE HAS BETRAYED ME.
ALL I CAN DO TO STOP FROM PASSING OUT IS STARE.
I KNOW IF I TURN AROUND I WILL SEE A ROOM FULL OF VITROS WHO NOW CONSIDER ME AN ENEMY. SO INSTEAD I JUST KEEP STARING--
STARING AND HOPING THAT THIS IS JUST A DREAM AND SOON I'LL WAKE UP ON A TROPICAL ISLAND OR BACK IN MY CHILDHOOD BEDROOM.
THE BEAT STRETCHES ON.
I DON'T WAKE UP.
THE END

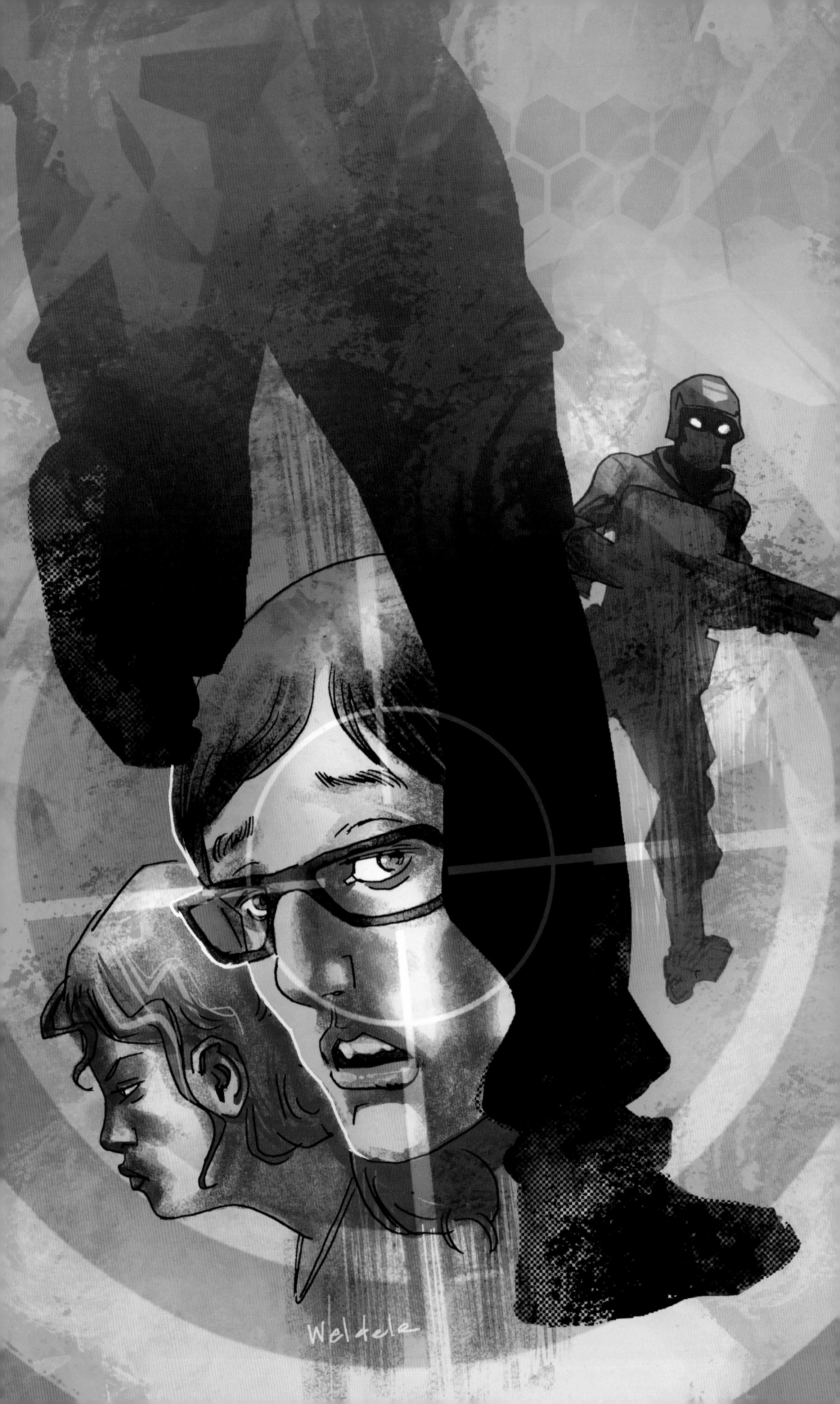
Weltele

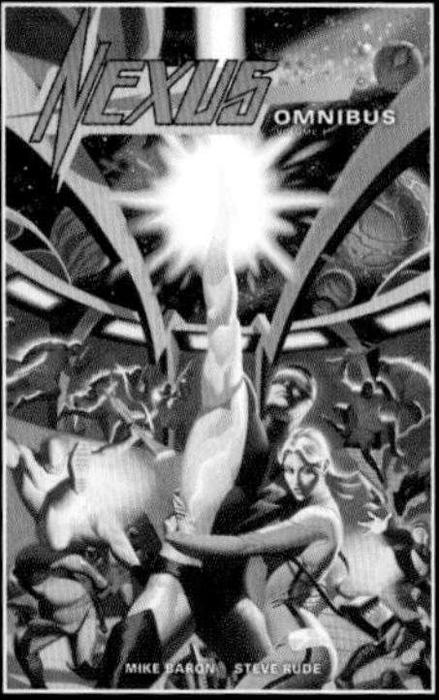
NEXUS
OMNIBUS
MIKE BARON STEVE RUDE

NEXUS OMNIBUS VOLUME 1

Steve Rude and Mike Baron

A multiple Eisner Award–winning series that defined the careers of acclaimed creators Steve Rude and Mike Baron, *Nexus* is a modern classic. In 2841 Nexus, a godlike figure, acts as judge, jury, and executioner for the vile criminals who appear in his dreams. He claims to kill in self-defense, but why? Where do the visions come from, and where did he get his powers?

ISBN 978-1-61655-034-9 | $24.99

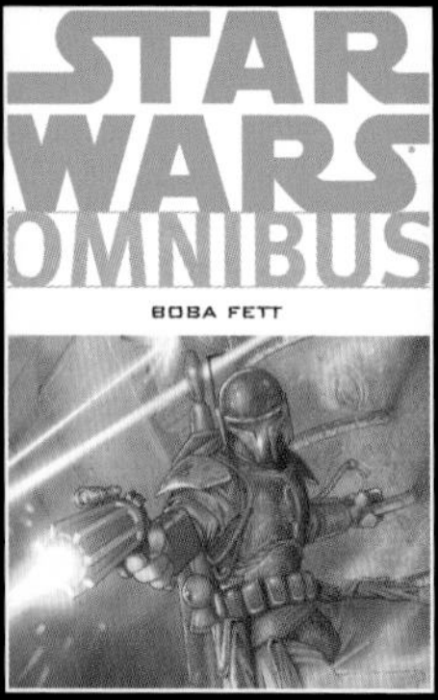
STAR WARS
OMNIBUS
BOBA FETT

STAR WARS OMNIBUS: BOBA FETT

Thomas Andrews, Mike Kennedy, Ron Marz, John Ostrander, Ian Gibson, Cam Kennedy, and Francisco Ruiz Velasco

Boba Fett, the most feared, most respected, and most loved bounty hunter in the galaxy, now has all of his comics stories collected into one massive volume! There's no job too deadly for the man in Mandalorian armor!

ISBN 978-1-59582-418-9 | $24.99

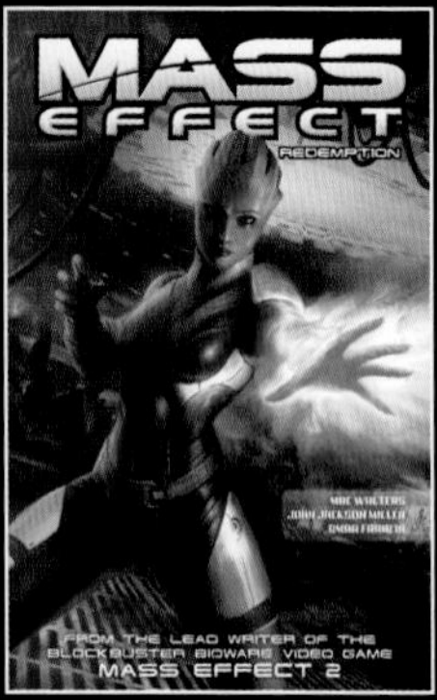
MASS
EFFECT
REDEMPTION
FROM THE LEAD WRITER OF THE BLOCKBUSTER BIOWARE VIDEO GAME MASS EFFECT 2

MASS EFFECT VOLUME 1: REDEMPTION

Mac Walters, John Jackson Miller, and Omar Francia

Collecting the four-issue miniseries, *Mass Effect* Volume 1 features essential developments in the *Mass Effect* gaming saga, plus a special behind-the-scenes section with sketches and more.

ISBN 978-1-59582-481-3 | $16.99

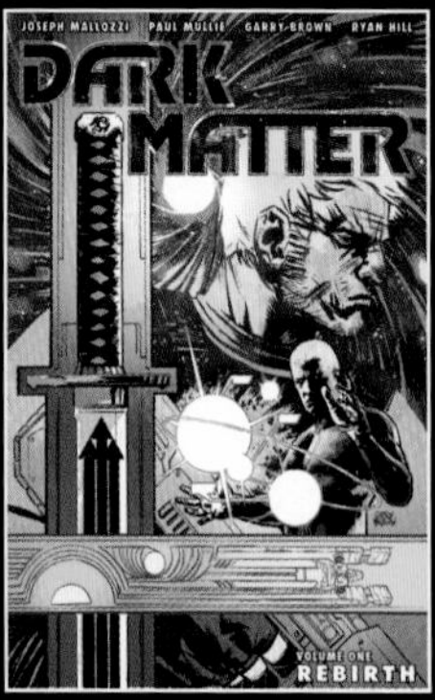
JOSEPH MALLOZZI PAUL MULLIE GARRY BROWN RYAN HILL
DARK
MATTER
VOLUME ONE
REBIRTH

DARK MATTER VOLUME 1: REBIRTH

Joseph Mallozzi, Paul Mullie, and Garry Brown

Sci-fi action from the writers of *Stargate SG-1*! The crew of a derelict spaceship awakens from stasis in the farthest reaches of space. With no recollection of who they are or how they got on board, their only clue is a cargo bay full of weaponry and a destination that is about to become a war zone!

ISBN 978-1-59582-998-6 | $14.99

AVAILABLE AT YOUR LOCAL COMICS SHOP OR BOOKSTORE! • To find a comics shop in your area, call 1-888-266-4226.
For more information or to order direct visit DarkHorse.com or call 1-800-862-0052 Mon.–Fri. 9 AM to 5 PM Pacific Time. Prices and availability subject to change without notice.

MORE SCIENCE FICTION

FROM DARK HORSE BOOKS

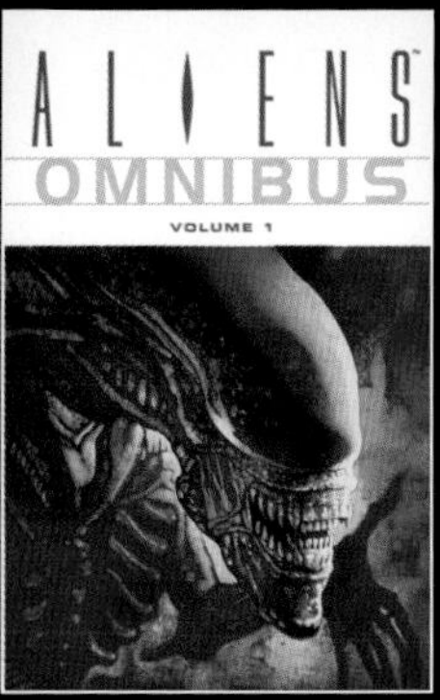
ALIENS
OMNIBUS
VOLUME 1

ALIENS OMNIBUS VOLUME 1

Mark Verheiden, Mark Nelson, Sam Kieth, and Den Beauvais

Dark Horse Comics took the industry by storm with its release of *Aliens*, a comics series that for the first time captured the power of film source material and expanded its universe in a way that fans applauded worldwide. Now, the first three Dark Horse *Aliens* series are collected in a value-priced, quality-format omnibus, featuring nearly four hundred story pages in full color.

ISBN 978-1-59307-727-3 | $24.99

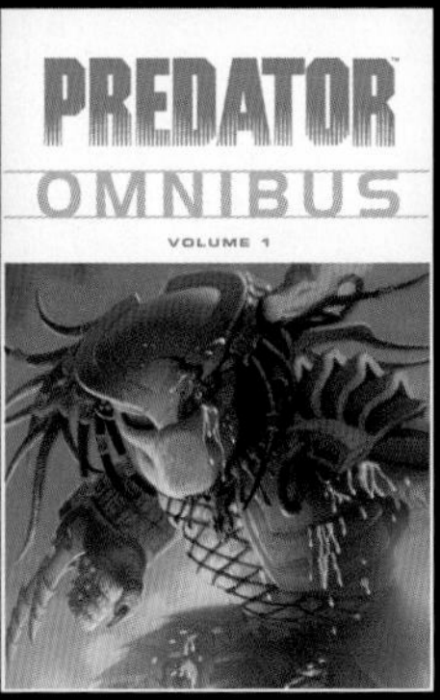
PREDATOR
OMNIBUS
VOLUME 1

PREDATOR OMNIBUS VOLUME 1

Mark Verheiden, Dan Barry, Chris Warner, Ron Randall, and others

Trophy hunters from another world, hiding in plain sight, drawn to heat and conflict. A historical scourge, lethal specters, powerful, savage, merciless. Utilizing their feral instincts and otherworldly technology in the sole pursuit of the most dangerous game . . . Man.

ISBN 978-1-59307-732-7 | $24.99

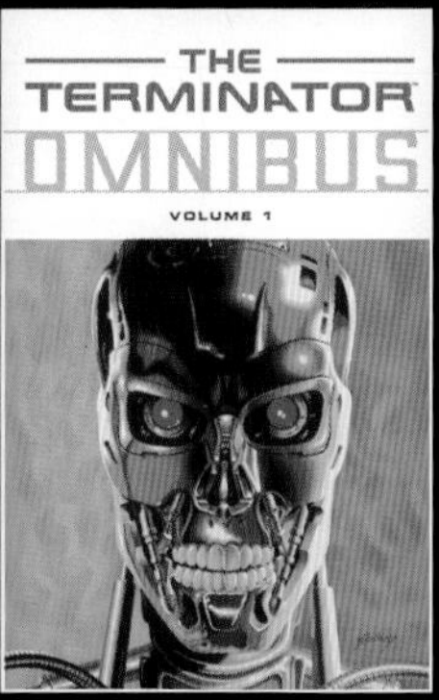
THE
TERMINATOR
OMNIBUS
VOLUME 1

TERMINATOR OMNIBUS VOLUME 1

James Robinson, John Arcudi, Ian Edginton, Chris Warner, and others

Terminators—indestructible killing engines hiding inside shells of flesh and blood. Tireless, fearless, merciless, unencumbered by human emotion, dedicated to the complete eradication of mankind. *The Terminator* is one of the finest examples of bringing top comics talents to the expansion of a premier action/adventure mythos.

ISBN 978-1-59307-916-1 | $24.99

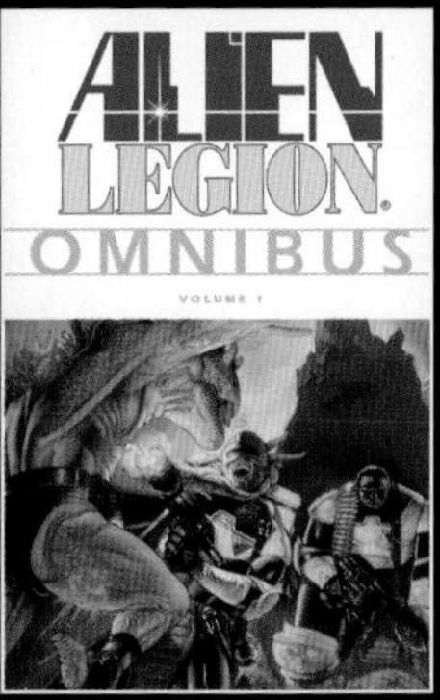
ALIEN
LEGION
OMNIBUS

ALIEN LEGION OMNIBUS VOLUME 1

Alan Zelenetz, Frank Cirocco, Chris Warner, Terry Shoemaker, Terry Austin, and Randy Emberlin

Footsloggers and soldiers of fortune, priests, poets, killers, and cads—they fight for a future Galarchy, for cash, for a cause, for the thrill of adventure. Culled from the forgotten and unwanted of three galaxies, they are trained to be the most elite, and expendable, of fighting forces. *Alien Legion Omnibus* Volume 1 features over three hundred story pages of the groundbreaking series!

ISBN 978-1-59582-394-6 | $24.99

DARK HORSE BOOKS BRINGS YOU

THE BEST IN SCIENCE FICTION!

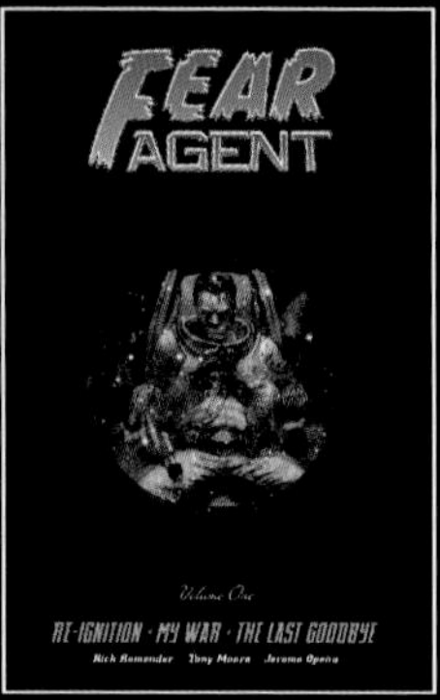
FEAR AGENT
RE-IGNITION · MY WAR · THE LAST GOODBYE

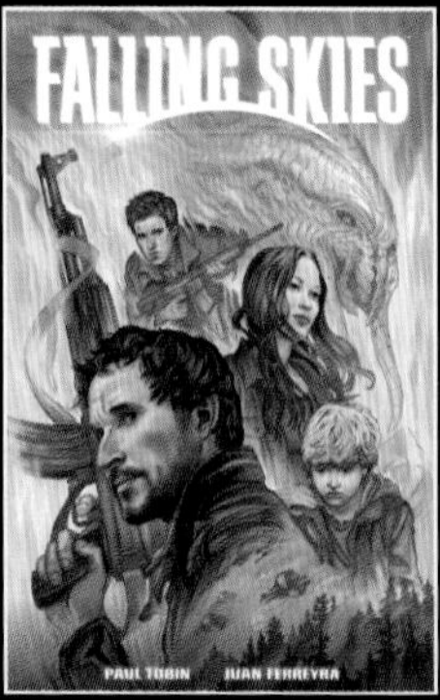
FALLING SKIES
PAUL TOBIN JUAN FERREYRA

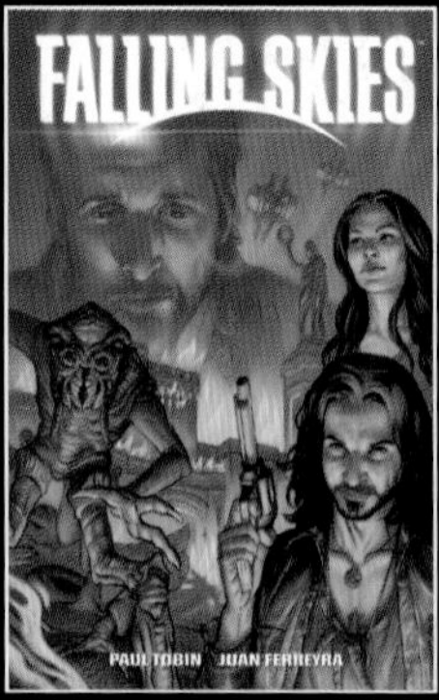
FALLING SKIES
PAUL TOBIN JUAN FERREYRA

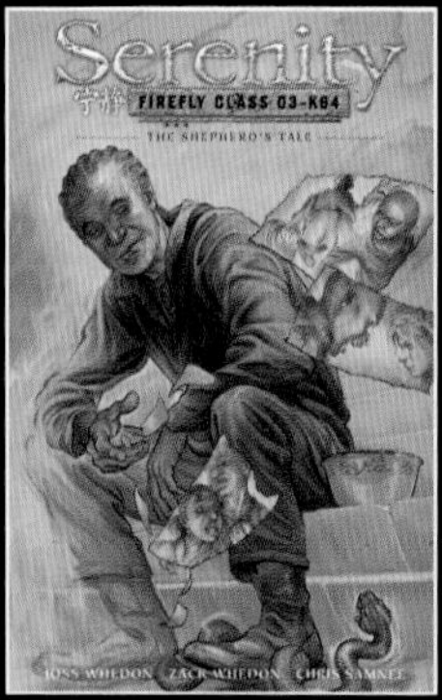
Serenity
FIREFLY CLASS 03-K64
THE SHEPHERD'S TALE
JOSS WHEDON ZACK WHEDON CHRIS SAMNEE

FEAR AGENT LIBRARY EDITION
VOLUME 1 HC

Rick Remender, Tony Moore, Kieron Dwyer, Francesco Francavilla, and Jerome Opeña

When down-and-out alien exterminator Heath Huston stumbles upon an extraterrestrial plot to commit genocide against the human species, he must put down the bottle and resume his role as a peacekeeper . . . as the last fear agent.

ISBN 978-1-61655-005-9 | $49.99

FALLING SKIES

Paul Tobin and Juan Ferreyra

In the heart of Boston, following the devastating events of an alien invasion, history professor Tom Mason and his sons meet up with the second Mass, a militia group determined to wipe out the aliens. But with the militia's supplies running low, Tom must locate an old friend to equip his team in order to ensure the survival of the human race!

VOLUME 1 TPB
ISBN 978-1-59582-737-1 | $9.99

VOLUME 2: THE BATTLE OF FITCHBURG TPB
ISBN 978-1-61655-014-1 | $9.99

SERENITY VOLUME 1: THOSE LEFT BEHIND HC

Joss Whedon, Brett Mathews, Will Conrad, Adam Hughes, and Laura Martin

A previously unknown chapter in the lives of his favorite band of space brigands in this comics prequel of the *Serenity* feature film.

ISBN 978-1-59307-449-4 | $19.99

SERENITY VOLUME 2: BETTER DAYS AND OTHER STORIES HC

Joss Whedon, Patton Oswalt, Zack Whedon, Brett Matthews, Will Conrad, and others

The crew takes on a heist that promises a big payoff. But when someone is taken captive, the gang must put aside their enduring differences and work together, at the risk of losing their cash prize.

ISBN 978-1-59582-739-5 | $14.99

SERENITY VOLUME 3: THE SHEPHERD'S TALE HC

Joss Whedon, Zack Whedon, and Chris Samnee

One of *Serenity*'s greatest mysteries is finally revealed in *The Shepherd's Tale*! Who was Book before meeting Mal and the rest of the *Serenity* crew, how did he become one of their most trusted allies, and how did he find God in a bowl of soup? Answers to these and more questions about Book's past are uncovered in this rollicking, action-packed epic!

ISBN 978-1-59582-561-2 | $14.99

AVAILABLE AT YOUR LOCAL COMICS SHOP OR BOOKSTORE! • To find a comics shop in your area, call 1-888-266-4226.
For more information or to order direct visit DarkHorse.com or call 1-800-862-0052 Mon.–Fri. 9 AM to 5 PM Pacific Time. Prices and availability subject to change without notice.